My First Dictionary

Scott Foresman - Addison Wesley

Editorial Offices: Glenview, Illinois • Menlo Park, California
Sales Office: Reading, Massachusetts

Part of this dictionary is also published under the title
My Second Picture Dictionary.

D'Nealian is the registered trademark of Donald Neal
Thurber.

Illustration and photograph credits appear on page 447.

Library of Congress Cataloging-in-Publication Data

My First Dictionary.—Scott Foresman, 1990
        p. cm.
    Summary: 4000 entries present words used daily by
young children, with definitions and illustrative sentences.

  ISBN 0-673-28509-X
   1. English language—Dictionaries, Juvenile.
[1. English language—Dictionaries.

PE1628.5.M9   1990

423—dc20   90-5074

ISBN 0-673-28509-X

97 98 99 00 01 RRW 10 9

Contents

Introduction

My First Dictionary is a colorful, readable, book of words, meanings, and sentences. It shows the use of more than 4,000 words and includes more than 1,000 illustrations. It is the third in a series of Scott, Foresman picture dictionaries and is designed for children who already have some exposure to books and print and are reading.

The entries in *My First Dictionary* were selected from a list of words that young readers and writers will encounter in their reading. Novels, poems, plays, and books of nonfiction, as well as textbooks in reading, language arts, science, health, math, and social studies, were carefully analyzed to select the list of words included in this dictionary. Names of things that children commonly encounter in their homes and neighborhoods, such as *mall* and *thermometer,* were also included.

At the back of the dictionary is a 12-page section called "Find Out the Facts!" Its colorfully illustrated pages contain useful information on the computer (its parts and use), maps, landforms, the environment, healthy foods, time, measurement, the calendar, holidays, and parts of a letter.

My First Dictionary will help children in the transition to a larger dictionary by familiarizing them with some necessary skills.

- alphabetical order
- guide words
- multiple definitions
- illustrative sentences
- spelling of plurals, adjective forms, etc.

The dictionary is written on the assumption that its users know the alphabet and can alphabetize. Hence, the entries are listed in alphabetical order. Each entry word appears in large, heavy type. Following the entry word, a simple easy-to-read definition is given. For most entries, an example sentence is also given, showing the word in use. Example sentences accompany nearly all of the definitions. Finally, additional forms of the entry word are listed at the end of each entry. These forms (printed in large, heavy type) include noun plurals, verb forms, and adjective forms, such as *smarter* and *smartest.*

Approximately 25 percent of the entries in *My First Dictionary* are illustrated. A variety of original art, photographs, cartoons, and fine art are used. Their purpose is to help children visualize the word being defined. Captions accompany all illustrations. Where necessary, the caption is expanded to include a sentence showing the entry word in use and explaining the illustration itself.

Scott, Foresman and Company has been a leader in producing quality children's dictionaries for more than fifty years. This book was prepared by an experienced team of editors, designers, and illustrators. Throughout its development and production, a panel of primary-school teachers served as product advisers.

Because people use dictionaries throughout their lives, gaining access to the information in dictionaries is an important learning experience. In using *My First Dictionary,* young children take an important step toward acquiring the basic dictionary skills, so that eventually they may move on to more advanced dictionaries.

To insure success, we have suggested on the inside back cover some activities to help your child use this book and learn about words. We hope your child will spend many happy and productive hours with *My First Dictionary.*

The Editors

How to Read an Entry

The entry word is printed in heavy black type so that it is easy to find. It shows you how the word is spelled.

A definition tells you the meaning of the word.

A picture helps show the meaning of the word. Each picture has a caption that is the same as the entry word, or the plural form of the word. Sometimes a sentence goes along with the caption.

A sentence shows how the word is used.

The small raised number tells you that two different entry words with the same spelling have different meanings.

A number is printed before each meaning for a word when more than one meaning is given.

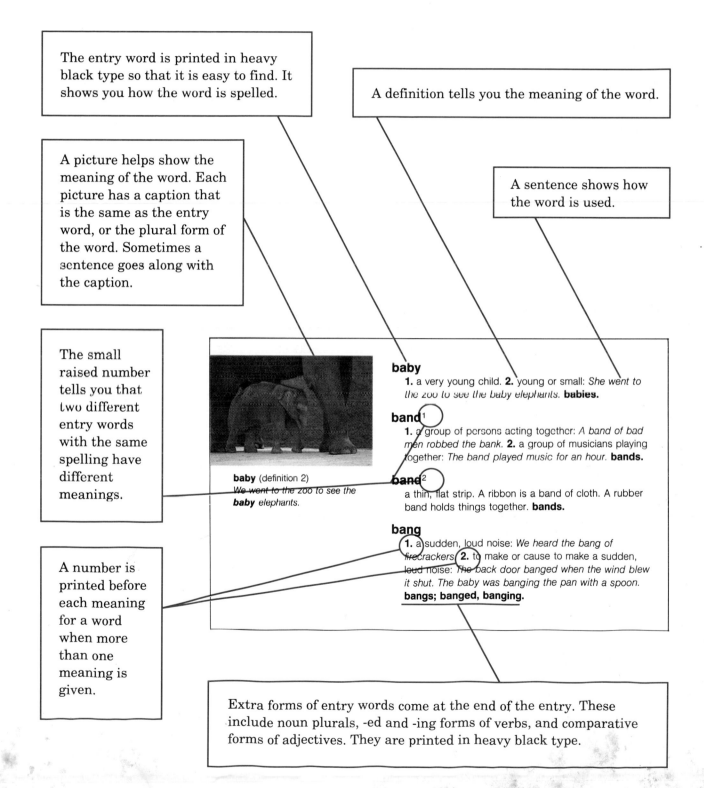

baby
1. a very young child. **2.** young or small: *She went to the zoo to see the baby elephants.* **babies.**

band¹
1. a group of persons acting together: *A band of bad men robbed the bank.* **2.** a group of musicians playing together: *The band played music for an hour.* **bands.**

band²
a thin, flat strip. A ribbon is a band of cloth. A rubber band holds things together. **bands.**

bang
1. a sudden, loud noise: *We heard the bang of firecrackers.* **2.** to make or cause to make a sudden, loud noise: *The back door banged when the wind blew it shut. The baby was banging the pan with a spoon.* **bangs; banged, banging.**

baby (definition 2)
We went to the zoo to see the baby elephants.

Extra forms of entry words come at the end of the entry. These include noun plurals, -ed and -ing forms of verbs, and comparative forms of adjectives. They are printed in heavy black type.

Aa

abbreviation

absent—*Two pupils were* ***absent*** *today.*

a

There's a book for you on the table. Here is a pen. Your birthday comes once a year.

abbreviation

a short form of a word. *St.* is the abbreviation for *Street.* **abbreviations.**

able

having power to do something: *Some animals are able to see well in the dark.* **abler, ablest.**

about

This book is about trains. It is about ten o'clock. About a dozen cars were in the parking lot.

above

The sun is above the trees. Read the line above the picture.

absent

not here; not present: *Two pupils were absent today.*

accident

something bad or unpleasant that happens: *Slipping and falling on the ice was an accident.* **accidents.**

accuse

to say that someone did something bad: *Dad accused us of breaking the window.* **accused, accusing.**

ache

1. a steady pain: *I had a stomach ache after eating too much.* **2.** to have a steady pain: *My muscles ached after doing exercises.* **aches; ached, aching.**

acorns

acorn

the nut of an oak tree. **acorns.**

acrobat

a person trained to swing in the air, and do other acts of skill and strength. **acrobats.**

acrobat

across

The cat walked across the yard. My friend lives across the street.

act

1. something done: *Sharing treats is a kind act.* **2.** to behave: *The girl acted like a baby.* **3.** to pretend to be someone else. People act in movies, on television, in plays, or on the radio. **acts; acted, acting.**

action

1. doing something: *The quick action of the fire-fighters kept the house from burning down.* **2.** the events in a story or play: *We enjoyed the movie because it had a lot of exciting action.* **actions.**

activity

a thing to do: *We enjoyed games, races, and other activities at the picnic.* **activities.**

actor

a person who acts in movies, on television, on the stage, or on the radio. **actors.**

actor

7

add

to put numbers or things together: *Add 5 and 3 to make 8. The cook added two more eggs to the batter.* **added, adding.**

addition

adding a number to another: *The addition of 3 to 5 gives the sum of 8.*

address

1. the place to which mail is sent: *Write the address on the front of the envelope.* **2.** to write on an envelope or package the place to which it is being sent: *Address the letter with a pen.* **addresses; addressed, addressing.**

address (definition 2)
Address the letter with a pen.

adjective

a word that tells more about a person, place, animal, or thing. Adjectives can tell how many, what color something is, what size it is, or what shape it is. "Tom lives in a yellow house." *Yellow* is the adjective that tells what color the house is. "Two bears swim." *Two* is the adjective that tells how many bears swim. "A big lion roars." *Big* is an adjective that tells the size of the lion. **adjectives.**

adjective

admit

to say something is true: *She admitted that I was right.* **admitted, admitting.**

adult

a grown-up person: *Several adults went along with us on our trip to the zoo.* **adults.**

adventure

adventure

an exciting or unusual thing to do: *Riding a raft down the swift river was a great adventure.* **adventures.**

adverb

a word that tells about a verb. An adverb may tell when an action takes place. It may tell where or how an action takes place. "We will run today." *Today* is an adverb. It tells when we will run. **adverbs.**

advertise

to tell people about something you want them to buy. You can advertise in newspapers, magazines, on radio, and on TV. **advertised, advertising.**

advice

a suggestion about what should be done: *The teacher's advice was to read the story again.*

afraid

frightened; feeling fear: *What are you afraid of?*

after

After school we'll go to the park. Wednesday comes after Tuesday. The dog ran after the cat.

afternoon

the part of the day between morning and evening: *On Saturday we played all afternoon.* **afternoons.**

again

once more; another time: *Please say that again.*

against

The two teams played against each other. The rain beat against the house.

age

the amount of time someone or something has lived: *She entered school at the age of five.*

ago

in the past: *I saw him two weeks ago. Long ago people lived in caves.*

adverbs

afraid
*What are you **afraid** of?*

aim (definition 1)

aircraft

aisle

agree

to have the same idea about something: *We all agree that it is a good story.* **agreed, agreeing.**

ahead

Please go ahead of me. Go ahead with your work. She is ahead of everybody in reading.

aim

1. to try to hit something: *He aimed carefully before shooting the arrow.* **2.** the act of aiming at something: *His aim was so bad that he missed the tree.* **aimed, aiming.**

air

what we breathe. Air is all around us. It has no smell, taste, or color. *Fresh air is good for us. Birds fly through the air.*

aircraft

a machine that flies. Airplanes, helicopters, and balloons are aircraft. **aircraft.**

airplane

a machine with wings that flies through the air. Airplanes have engines that make them go. **airplanes.**

airport

a place where airplanes land and take off. **airports.**

aisle

a space between rows of seats: *We walked down the aisle at the movies, looking for empty seats.* **aisles.**

Alabama

one of the fifty states of the United States.

alarm

1. to frighten; make uneasy: *A noise alarmed the deer.* **2.** something that makes a loud noise to warn people: *When the fire alarm went off, we all went outside.* **alarmed, alarming; alarms.**

Alaska

one of the fifty states of the United States.

Alberta

one of the ten provinces of Canada.

alike

like one another: *Twins often look and dress alike.*

alike

alive

living; not dead: *The bird was badly hurt, but it is still alive.*

all

The mice ate all the cheese. All the babies are crying. All of the students go home for lunch.

alley

a narrow street behind buildings in a city or town. Garbage cans are often seen in an alley. **alleys.**

alley

alligator

a large animal with thick skin, a large mouth, and a long tail. Alligators live in warm states, such as Florida. **alligators.**

alligator

allow

to let someone do something; permit: *My parents allowed me to stay up until the TV show was over.* **allowed, allowing.**

almost

I almost missed the bus. It is almost time for lunch.

alone

without other people or things: *He sat alone because he didn't know the other children. One tree stood alone on the hill.*

along

Trees are planted along the street. We took our dog along.

alone—*He sat **alone**.*

11

aloud

loud enough to be heard; not in a whisper: *She read the story aloud so everyone in the class could hear it.*

alphabet

all the letters of a language. The English alphabet is a, b, c, d, e, f, g, h, i, j, k, l, m, n, o, p, q, r, s, t, u, v, w, x, y, z. **alphabets.**

alphabetical

arranged in the order of the alphabet: *The words in the dictionary are listed in alphabetical order.*

already

She ran to the bus stop, but the bus had already gone. He has already read this book.

also

Tom has a dog, but he likes cats also. Sara likes to ride her bike to school, but she also likes to walk.

also—*Tom has a dog, but he likes cats also.*

although

Although it rained all day, we still went on our hike.

always

every time; all the time: *Always ride your bike in the same direction the cars are going.*

am

I am eight years old. I am in the school play.

ambulance

ambulance

a special kind of car or van that takes sick or hurt people to the hospital. **ambulances.**

America

1. the United States of America. **2.** North America. **3.** South America.

American

1. a person born or living in the United States, or in North or South America. **2.** of the United States or its people; from the United States: *The American flag is red, white, and blue.* **Americans.**

among

Divide the fruit among all of us. The house sits among the trees. The United States is among the largest countries in the world.

amount

how much there is or how many there are of something: *The amount of snow that fell yesterday was 2 inches. Five cents is a small amount of money.* **amounts.**

amphibian

an animal that lives both on land and in water. Most baby amphibians live in the water until they grow lungs for living on land. Frogs and toads are amphibians. **amphibians.**

amphibians

amuse

to cause to laugh or smile: *The clown's jokes amused everyone.* **amused, amusing.**

an

Is there an apple in the box? She is an inch taller than I am. She earns two dollars an hour for baby-sitting.

and

Yesterday we went to the beach and to the zoo. The boy asked if 4 and 2 make 6. She washed the dishes and her brother dried them.

angry

feeling or showing that you are upset and not pleased about something: *Dad was angry when he saw the broken car window.* **angrier, angriest.**

annoy—The barking dog **annoyed** the neighbors.

animal

any living thing that can move about. Animals cannot make their own food from sunlight as plants do. People, dogs, birds, fish, snakes, insects, and worms are animals. **animals.**

ankle

the part of the body between the foot and the leg. **ankles.**

annoy

to bother; disturb; make angry: *The barking dog annoyed the neighbors.* **annoyed, annoying.**

another

He asked for another glass of milk. The hat didn't fit, so I chose another.

answer

1. to say or write something when a question is asked: *She answered three questions out of four.* **2.** the words said or written when a question is asked: *I wrote the answers on a sheet of paper.* **3.** to do something when someone calls: *She answered the phone. I answered the door.* **answered, answering; answers.**

ant

a small insect that lives in tunnels in the ground or in wood. Ants live together in large groups. **ants.**

antelope

antelope

an animal that looks like a deer and can run as fast as a deer. **antelope.**

antique

something made long ago: *This steam engine is a real antique.* **antiques.**

antler

a horn that grows on the head of a male deer, elk, or moose. Antlers fall off once a year and grow back again the next year. **antlers.**

antlers

anxious

1. worried because of thoughts or fears of what may happen: *As it grew dark, the boy felt anxious when his dog did not come home.* **2.** wishing very much; eager: *They were anxious to start their vacation.*

any

Choose any game you like. Are there any cookies left?

anybody

The boy yelled down the empty hall, "Is anybody here?"

anymore

now; at present: *He used to jog every morning, but he doesn't anymore.*

anyone

Can anyone go to this movie, or is it just for adults?

anything

She asked if there was anything to eat in the refrigerator. My bike isn't anything like yours.

anytime

You are welcome to visit us anytime.

anyway

She was not invited to the party, but she went anyway.

anywhere

I'll meet you anywhere you say. He could not find his homework anywhere.

apart

1. in pieces or parts: *She took the watch apart to see how it runs.* **2.** away from each other: *Keep the dogs apart or they will fight.*

apartment

a room or group of rooms to live in: *There are ten apartments in that building.* **apartments.**

apart (definition 1)
*She took the watch **apart**.*

15

ape

a large, hairy animal with long arms and no tail. Apes can stand almost straight and walk on two feet. A gorilla is an ape. **apes.**

ape

apiece

for each one; each: *These pencils are ten cents apiece.*

apostrophe

a mark (') of punctuation. An apostrophe shows that a letter has been left out of a word. "She isn't home." An apostrophe takes the place of the letter *o* in the word *not* when you write *isn't.* "We'll meet you at the party." An apostrophe takes the place of the letters *wi* in the word *will* when you write *we'll.* **apostrophes.**

apostrophe

appear

1. to come in sight: *Stars appear in the sky after the sun has gone down.* **2.** to seem; look: *The apple appeared good, but it was rotten inside.* **appeared, appearing.**

apple

a round fruit that grows on a tree. Apples have red, yellow, or green skin. They are eaten either raw or cooked. **apples.**

appliance

a machine that helps make tasks around the house easier. Toasters and refrigerators are appliances. **appliances.**

apricot

a round, orange-colored fruit that grows on a tree. Apricots are smaller than peaches and have a smoother skin. **apricots.**

apricots

apron

April

the fourth month of the year. It has 30 days. It comes after March and before May.

apron

a cloth tied around the waist to protect your clothes: *Wear an apron when you cook.* **aprons.**

aquarium

1. a tank or glass bowl in which living fish or other water animals are kept. **2.** a building where you can see many fish and other water animals. **aquariums.**

are

You are right. We are ready. They are waiting for us.

area

1. the amount of space something covers: *A large area of the earth is covered by water.* **2.** a place: *The playground area is right outside.* **areas.**

aren't

are not: *My friends aren't going to the game with me.*

argue

to fight with words; disagree in an angry way: *Tom argued with his sister about who should wash the dishes.* **argued, arguing.**

argue—*They **argued** about who should wash the dishes.*

Arizona

one of the fifty states of the United States.

Arkansas

one of the fifty states of the United States.

arm

the part of the body between the shoulder and the hand. **arms.**

armadillo

a small animal with a very hard shell. Armadillos are found in such states as Florida and Texas. **armadillos.**

armadillo

army

a large group of soldiers. An army fights to protect its country in a war. **armies.**

around

The top spun around. She planted flowers all around the house. The new children took a walk around the school.

arrange

to put in some kind of order: *The books were arranged in alphabetical order.* **arranged, arranging.**

arrive

to come to a place: *My grandmother arrived a week ago for a visit.* **arrived, arriving.**

arrow

1. a pointed stick that is shot from a bow. **2.** a sign (→) used to show a direction on maps and road signs. **arrows.**

art

paintings, drawings, and statues: *Pupils in second grade are studying art.*

artist

artist

a person who paints pictures. **artists.**

as

Jane ran as fast as she could. Mr. Smith will act as your teacher today. As they were walking, it began to rain.

ashes

ash

a gray powder that is left after something burns: *A little smoke still rose from the ashes.* **ashes.**

ashamed

feeling sorry because one has done something wrong or silly: *I felt ashamed because I had not told the truth.*

ask

1. to try to find out by using questions: *We had to ask the way to the monkey house.* **2.** to invite: *I asked ten people to my party.* **asked, asking.**

asleep

not awake; sleeping: *The cat is asleep.*

asparagus

a tender, green vegetable. Asparagus grows as stalks from the ground.

asparagus

astronaut

a person who has been trained to fly in a spacecraft. While in space, astronauts repair space stations and do experiments. **astronauts.**

astronaut

at

There is someone at the front door. Tom goes to bed at nine o'clock.

ate

Last night he ate dinner late.

athletes

audience

athlete

a person who has trained to be very good at a sport. Baseball players and swimmers are athletes. **athletes.**

attack

to begin fighting against someone or something: *The dog attacked the cat.* **attacked, attacking.**

attention

giving thought or care to someone or something: *Pay attention while she explains this math problem. The boy gives his dog a lot of attention.*

attic

the space in a house just below the roof. An attic is often used for storing things. **attics.**

audience

a group of people that sees or hears something: *The audience liked the circus. The radio station received many phone calls from its audience.* **audiences.**

auditorium

a large room with seats for many people: *The school play was held in the auditorium.* **auditoriums.**

August

the eighth month of the year. It has 31 days. It comes after July and before September.

aunt

your father's sister or your mother's sister, or your uncle's wife. **aunts.**

author

a person who writes books, stories, poems, or plays. **authors.**

auto

a short word meaning automobile. **autos.**

automobile

a machine that people ride in. An automobile has an engine and four wheels. Another word for automobile is car. **automobiles.**

autumn

fall; the season of the year between summer and winter. Autumn is the season when the harvest takes place. **autumns.**

autumn—Leaves lose their green color in **autumn.**

avenue

a street: *We live on Stewart Avenue.* **avenues.**

awake

1. to wake up: *He awoke from a sound sleep.* **2.** not asleep: *She was still awake at midnight.* **awoke, awaking.**

away

Stay away from the street. The dog ran away from the bear. Go away. The neighbors will be away for a week.

awful

very bad; terrible; ugly: *An awful storm came up suddenly. My friend fell down and got an awful bump on her head.*

awful—*An* **awful** *storm woke us up.*

awhile

for a short time: *I usually read awhile before going to bed.*

awoke

He awoke before the sun came up. I awoke them at seven.

ax

a tool with a flat, sharp blade used for chopping wood. **axes.**

axle

a bar that wheels are fastened to. Wagons and cars have axles. **axles.**

axle

Bb

baby (definition 2)
We went to the zoo to see the ***baby*** *elephants.*

baby
1. a very young child. **2.** young or small: *She went to the zoo to see the baby elephants.* **babies.**

baby-sit
to take care of a child while the parents are away for a while. **baby-sat, baby-sitting.**

baby-sitter
a person who takes care of a child while the parents are away for a while. **baby-sitters.**

back
1. the part of the body opposite the chest and stomach: *It's hard to scratch the middle of your back.* **2.** the side of anything opposite the front side: *The back of our neighbor's house has four windows.* **3.** to move or cause to move backward: *He backed away from the snake. She backed the car down the driveway.* **backs; backed, backing.**

backpack
a bag worn on the back by people hiking or going to school. In backpacks you carry things such as clothes, books, and food. **backpacks.**

backpack

backward
in a direction opposite to the front of something: *Be careful not to fall when you walk backward. He dived backward into the pool.*

backyard

the yard behind a house or building. **backyards.**

bacteria

very tiny and simple living things. Bacteria are so small that they can be seen only through a microscope. Some bacteria cause diseases.

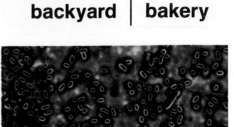

bacteria—These *bacteria* are seen through a microscope.

bad

1. not good; not as it ought to be: *Teasing animals is a bad thing to do.* **2.** sorry: *I feel bad about being late for the parade.* **3.** sick: *I felt bad when I had a cold last week.* **worse, worst.**

badger

a hairy, gray animal that digs holes in the ground to live in. **badgers.**

badger

badly

in a bad manner: *She dances badly.*

bag

something to hold things, made of paper, cloth, plastic, or leather. Bags can be closed at the top. **bags.**

bait

1. anything used to catch fish or other animals: *Worms are good fishing bait.* **2.** to put bait on a hook or in a trap to catch something: *He baited the hook and dropped it in the water.* **baited, baiting.**

bake

to cook in an oven: *The cook bakes bread every morning.* **baked, baking.**

baker

a person who makes or sells bread, pies, and cakes. **bakers.**

bakery

a place where bread and cakes are sold. **bakeries.**

balcony (definition 1)

balance

1. being steady and not falling over: *He lost his balance and fell down.* **2.** to keep or hold something so that it does not fall over: *She balanced the book on her head.* **balanced, balancing.**

balcony

1. a small floor that sticks out from an upper floor of a building. **2.** a floor above the first floor in a theater. **balconies.**

ball¹

1. something round, often a toy used in games: *In football, you throw the ball and kick it.* **2.** a game in which a ball is used: *Let's play ball.* **balls** (for **1.**).

ball²

a large party for dancing: *Cinderella went to the ball.* **balls.**

ball²

balloon

1. a toy made of thin rubber filled with air, or a gas lighter than air. **2.** a large rubber or plastic bag filled with hot air, or a gas lighter than air. Balloons will rise and float in the air, and people can ride in them. **balloons.**

bamboo

a kind of tall grass that grows like a tree. Its hollow stems are used to make furniture and many other things.

bamboo

banana

a curved, yellow fruit that grows in large bunches. Bananas grow in warm countries on a tall plant like a tree. **bananas.**

bananas

band[1]

1. a group of persons acting together: *A band of bad men robbed the bank.* **2.** a group of musicians playing together: *The band played music for an hour.* **bands.**

band[2]

a thin, flat strip. A ribbon is a band of cloth. A rubber band holds things together. **bands.**

bandage

1. a strip of cloth that covers a wound: *The nurse put a bandage on the cut.* **2.** to wrap or cover with a bandage: *The nurse gently bandaged my arm.*
bandages; bandaged, bandaging.

bang

1. a sudden, loud noise: *We heard the bang of firecrackers.* **2.** to make or cause to make a sudden, loud noise: *The back door banged when the wind blew it shut. The baby was banging the pan with a spoon.*
bangs; banged, banging.

bangs

bangs

hair cut short and worn over the forehead.

banjo

a musical instrument with strings. You play it with your fingers. **banjos.**

bank[1]

the ground along a river or lake: *He fished from the river bank.* **banks.**

banjo

bank[2]

a place for keeping money: *Mom and Dad put money in the bank every week. My brother has a bank for nickels and pennies.* **banks.**

barbecue (definition 2)
*We **barbecued** hamburgers.*

barge

bar

1. a long piece of something solid: *They bought three candy bars.* **2.** a long, round piece of wood or metal, used to close an opening: *All the windows were protected by steel bars.* **bars.**

barbecue

1. meat roasted over an open fire: *We ate barbecue last night.* **2.** to roast meat over an open fire: *We barbecued meat for the picnic.* **barbecued, barbecuing.**

barber

a person whose work is cutting people's hair and shaving men's faces. **barbers.**

bare

without covering or clothes: *The sun burned his bare shoulders.* **barer, barest.**

bargain

1. an agreement to trade: *We made a bargain to wash the car for two dollars.* **2.** something for sale or bought for less than it is worth: *This chair is a bargain for five dollars.* **bargains.**

barge

a large boat with a flat bottom. Barges carry things like sand or coal. **barges.**

bark¹

the tough outside covering of the trunk and branches of a tree.

bark²

1. the sharp sound that a dog makes: *She heard two or three loud barks in the middle of the night.* **2.** to make this sound: *The dog growled and then barked loudly over and over.* **barks; barked, barking.**

barley

a cereal grain. Barley is eaten by people and farm animals.

barley

barn

a farm building. It is used to store food for animals. Cows and horses are kept in the barn at night. **barns.**

barrel

1. something large for holding things. Barrels have round, flat tops and bottoms and curved sides. **2.** the amount a barrel can hold: *We picked a barrel of apples.* **barrels.**

base

1. bottom; the part of a thing on which it rests: *The metal base of the floor lamp might scratch the floor.* **2.** a goal in some games: *The runner stopped at third base.* **bases.**

baseball

1. a game played with a bat and ball by two teams of nine players each, on a field with four bases. **2.** the ball used in this game. **baseballs** (for **2.**).

basement

an underground floor of a house or other building. **basements.**

basket

1. something to carry things in, or to store them. Baskets are made of straw, plastic, or strips of wood. **2.** a ring and net, used as a goal in basketball. **baskets.**

basketball

1. a game played with a large, round ball between two teams of five players each. **2.** the ball used in this game. **basketballs** (for **2.**).

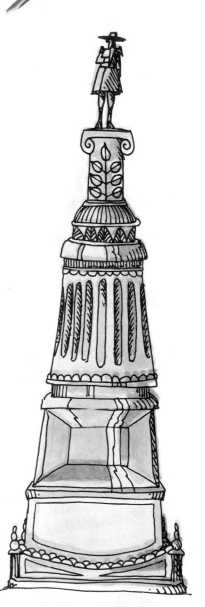

base (definition 1)
*The statue is on a large **base.***

bat¹

1. a thick stick or club, made of wood or aluminum, used to hit the ball in some games. **2.** to hit with a bat: *She batted twice in today's game.* **bats; batted, batting.**

bat²

an animal that looks like a mouse with wings covered by thin skin. Bats fly at night. **bats.**

bats²

bath

a washing of the body: *I took a bath last night.* **baths.**

bathe

to take a bath or give a bath to: *Have you bathed yet? Mother is bathing the baby.* **bathed, bathing.**

bathing suit

clothing worn for swimming. **bathing suits.**

bathroom

a room to take a bath in. **bathrooms.**

bathtub

a large, open tub to take a bath in. **bathtubs.**

batter¹

a liquid mixture of flour, milk, and eggs that becomes solid when cooked. Cakes, cookies, and muffins are made from batter.

batter²

in baseball, a player whose turn it is to bat. **batters.**

battery

something that stores electricity. Flashlights and many toys run off small batteries. Large batteries make cars start. **batteries.**

batteries

be

We will be there in an hour. He tried to be on time. Be good to animals.

beach

land along the edge of a sea, lake, or big river. Beaches are covered with sand or stones. **beaches.**

bead

a small bit of glass, metal, or plastic, with a hole so it can be strung on a thread. **beads.**

beaks

beak

the hard part of the mouth of a bird. Another word for beak is bill. **beaks.**

beam

1. a large, long piece of wood or steel used in building. **2.** a ray of light: *He saw a raccoon in the beam of the flashlight.* **beams.**

bean

1. a smooth, flat seed eaten as a vegetable. Beans grow in pods. **2.** the pod, sometimes also eaten as a vegetable. **beans.**

bean (definitions 1 and 2)

bear

a large animal with thick hair and a very short tail. Many bears sleep through most of the winter. **bears.**

beard

the hair growing on a man's face. **beards.**

beard

beast

any four-footed animal. Lions, bears, cows, and horses are beasts. **beasts.**

29

beat

1. to hit again and again: *The baby beat the toy drum with a stick.* **2.** to do better than: *Our team beat yours.* **3.** to mix by stirring: *Beat three eggs to put in the cake batter.* **beat, beaten, beating.**

beaten

Have you beaten the eggs for the cake?

beautiful

very pretty to see or hear: *After the rain stopped, it became a beautiful, sunny day.*

beauty

something or someone very pretty to see or hear: *We enjoyed the beauty of the sunset.* **beauties.**

beaver

beaver

an animal with soft fur, a wide, flat tail, and large front teeth. Beavers cut down trees with their teeth and build dams in streams. **beavers.**

became

It became dark very early.

because

for the reason that: *Dad called us in because supper was ready.*

become

It is becoming warmer. He has become wiser as he has grown older.

bed

something to sleep or rest on: *When does she go to bed?* **beds.**

bedroom

a room to sleep in. **bedrooms.**

bedtime

time to go to bed: *What's our bedtime tonight?*

bee

an insect that flies and makes honey. Bees sting. Some bees live in groups. **bees.**

beef

the meat from a steer, used for food. Hamburger and steak are beef.

been

This boy has been here for hours. We have been friends for years. Have you been to Canada?

beet

a thick, red root that grows underground. The root and its leaves are eaten as vegetables. **beets.**

beetle

an insect. Its shiny front wings cover its back wings when it is not flying. **beetles.**

before

Wash your hands before you eat. You have been here before. Your turn comes before mine.

beg

to ask for something as a gift: *Some people have to beg for food. The dog begged for a treat.* **begged, begging.**

began

She began to sing.

begin

to start to happen: *The storm began yesterday. The party will begin soon.* **began, begun, beginning.**

beginning

1. the time when something starts: *The beginning of school is usually in September.* **2.** the first part of something: *She liked the beginning of the story.* **beginnings.**

beet

beg
*The dog **begged** for a treat.*

behind

bell

begun
It has begun to rain.

behave
1. to do what is right: *The little boy behaves in school.*
2. to act: *Some people behave badly.* **behaved, behaving.**

behind
Who is behind me? Her class is behind in its work.

being
She is being difficult. Being angry is a waste of time.

believe
1. to think something is true: *We believed the weather report that promised rain.* **2.** to think someone tells the truth: *Did her friends believe her?* **believed, believing.**

bell
a hollow piece of metal shaped like an upside-down cup. It makes a ringing sound when you hit it. **bells.**

belong
1. to be owned by: *Do these gloves belong to you?*
2. to have one's own place: *That chair belongs in the other room.* **belonged, belonging.**

below
In our house, the kitchen is below my parents' room. The temperature is ten degrees below zero.

belt
a strip of cloth or leather worn around your waist. A belt helps to hold up your trousers. **belts.**

bench
a long wooden seat: *We played near a park bench.* **benches.**

bench

bend

1. to make or become crooked; curve: *Try to bend this rod. The branch began to bend as I climbed along it.* **2.** a part that is not straight: *There is a bend in the road here.* **3.** to move the top of your body toward the ground: *Try to bend over and touch your toes.* **bent, bending; bends.**

beneath

below; under; in a lower place: *His coat is beneath that pile of books.*

bent

1. *She bent the fork. I have bent over and touched the floor.* **2.** not straight: *I used a bent pin for a hook.*

berry

a small juicy fruit with many seeds. Strawberries and raspberries are berries. **berries.**

beside

by the side of; near: *His dog sat beside him.*

besides

He didn't want to hurry home; besides, he was having fun. Others came to the picnic besides our family.

beside
*His dog sat **beside** him.*

best

most excellent: *He's a good swimmer, but his brother is the best I've ever seen.*

bet

to say you will give something to someone if that person is right and you are wrong: *He bet that he could beat me to the corner.* **bet, betting.**

better

more than good: *Her plan is good, but I think ours is better. She sang that song well, but she sang this one better.*

between—The rock is **between** two trees.

bib

between

There is a rock between the two trees. We'll be home between two and three o'clock.

beyond

past: *Look beyond the fence for your ball. Don't go beyond the corner.*

bib

a cloth worn under the chin by a baby. **bibs.**

Bible

a holy book. **Bibles.**

bicycle

a thing to ride that has two wheels, one behind the other. You ride it by pushing down on two pedals with your legs and feet. **bicycles.**

big

large in size: *They own a big dog. Is it bigger than ours? It's the biggest dog I've ever seen.* **bigger, biggest.**

big

bike

a short word meaning bicycle: *We rode our bikes to school.* **bikes.**

bill¹

1. a piece of paper that tells how much money you must pay for something you bought: *The waiter brought the bill for our dinner.* **2.** a piece of paper money: *The dollar bill was ripped.* **bills.**

bill¹ (definition 2)

bill²

bill²

the hard part of the mouth of a bird. Another word for bill is beak. **bills.**

bind

1. to fasten; tie together: *She tried to bind the package with string.* **2.** to wrap a wound: *The doctor will bind the cut on your arm.* **bound, binding.**

biography

the story of a person's life written by another person. **biographies.**

birch

a tree with smooth bark and hard wood. **birches.**

bird

an animal that has wings, feathers, and two legs. Most birds can fly. **birds.**

birth

being born: *We heard about the birth of the baby.* **births.**

birthday

the day on which a person was born. **birthdays.**

bit¹

bit¹

a tool for making a hole in something: *As Dad was boring a hole in the wood, the bit snapped in half.* **bits.**

bit²

a small piece: *Would you like a bit of this cake?* **bits.**

bit³

He bit into the candy bar.

bite

1. to cut with the teeth; hurt with the teeth: *Did she bite her tongue? My dog won't bite.* **2.** the amount you bite off: *I only ate a bite of my apple.* **3.** a sore made by biting or stinging: *Mosquito bites itch.* **bit, bitten, biting; bites.**

bitten

She was bitten by the neighbor's dog.

bitter

having a sharp, bad taste. The skin of an orange tastes bitter.

black

1. a very dark color; the opposite of white: *The words in this book are printed in black.* **2.** without light; very dark: *Without a moon the night was black.*

blackberry

a small black or purple fruit. Blackberries grow on bushes. **blackberries.**

blackberries

blackbird

a bird with black feathers. **blackbirds.**

blackbirds

blacksmith

blacksmith

a person who makes things from iron. Blacksmiths also put horseshoes on horses. **blacksmiths.**

blade

the part of a knife or scissors that cuts: *This knife has a very sharp blade.* **blades.**

blame

to think a person or thing is the cause of something bad: *She blamed her brother for the accident.* **blamed, blaming.**

blank

1. an empty space: *Write the correct word in each blank.* **2.** without any writing on it: *This is a blank page.* **blanks.**

blanket

a soft, warm covering for a bed: *We bought a new, wool blanket.* **blankets.**

blaze

1. a bright flame or fire: *You could see the blaze of the forest fire for miles.* **2.** to burn with a bright flame: *The fire blazed up, then died.* **blazes; blazed, blazing.**

bleed—*His nose is* ***bleeding.***

bled

My nose bled for a minute.

bleed

to lose blood: *His nose is bleeding.* **bled, bleeding.**

blew

The wind blew the tree down.

blind

not able to see: *The man with the guide dog is blind.* **blinder, blindest.**

blizzard

a big storm with snow and strong winds. **blizzards.**

blizzard

block

1. a thick piece of wood or plastic: *My little brother plays a lot with blocks.* **2.** to fill so nothing can pass by: *The car with a flat tire was blocking traffic.* **3.** the part of a street between two cross streets: *I walked down the block to my friend's house.* **blocks; blocked, blocking.**

blond

light in color: *His mother's hair is blond.* **blonder, blondest.**

blood

the red liquid that flows from a cut in your skin. Your heart pumps blood to every part of your body. Blood carries oxygen and food.

blond
*His mother's hair is **blond.***

bloom

to have flowers: *Roses bloom every year.* **bloomed, blooming.**

blossom

1. a flower of a plant that produces fruit: *Can you smell the orange blossoms?* **2.** to have flowers: *The plum trees are blossoming.* **blossoms; blossomed, blossoming.**

blow[1]

1. a hard hit: *A blow on his arm made it hurt for days.* **2.** something that suddenly upsets you: *It was a blow for Dad to lose his wallet.* **blows.**

blow[2]

1. to move air quickly: *A strong wind blew all night. She blew all the candles out on her birthday cake.* **2.** to make a sound by blowing air into something: *The factory whistle blows at noon.* **blew, blown, blowing.**

blown

She has blown up the balloon.

blue

1. the color of the clear sky during the day. **2.** having this color: *The water in the lake looks very blue.* **blues; bluer, bluest.**

blue (definition 1)

blueberries

blueberry

a small, blue fruit. Blueberries grow on bushes. **blueberries.**

bluebird

a small, blue bird that sings. **bluebirds.**

blossoms (definition 1)

blue jay

blue jay

a noisy, chattering blue bird. **blue jays.**

bluff

a high, steep bank or cliff. **bluffs.**

board

1. a long, thin, flat piece of wood: *Several boards on the side of the garage need painting.* **2.** to cover with boards: *The windows of the empty house were boarded up.* **boards; boarded, boarding.**

boast

to talk too much about yourself or what you own: *He boasts about his new bike every day.* **boasted, boasting.**

boast—He **boasts** about his new bike every day.

boat

something that carries people and things over the water. A boat can be moved by a motor, sails, or oars. **boats.**

body

all of a person or animal: *Exercise helps keep the body healthy.* **bodies.**

boil¹

1. to get very hot and give off steam: *Has the water boiled yet?* **2.** to cook by boiling: *Boil the egg three minutes.* **boiled, boiling.**

boil²

a red, sore place on the skin. **boils.**

boiler

a tank for holding hot water. **boilers.**

bold

brave; without fear; showing courage: *You must be bold to face a growling dog.* **bolder, boldest.**

bone

one of the hard parts of the body of a person or animal. Bones support the body, and protect inner soft parts. **bones.**

book

sheets of paper inside two covers. The pages in this book have writing and pictures on them. **books.**

bookcase

a piece of furniture with shelves for holding books. **bookcases.**

bookmobile

a truck with shelves of books inside. A bookmobile is a traveling branch of a library. **bookmobiles.**

boot

a heavy covering for the foot and leg: *Wear your boots when it rains.* **boots.**

booth

1. a place where things are sold at a fair or market. **2.** a small closed place: *We ate supper at a booth in the restaurant. Call your mother from that telephone booth.* **booths.**

bore

to make a hole in something by pushing a tool in it or through it: *The drill bored through the wall.* **bored, boring.**

bones—*The scientist is examining fossil **bones**.*

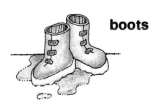

boots

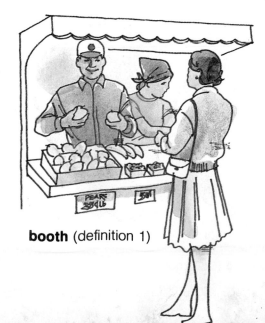

booth (definition 1)

41

boring

not interesting or amusing; dull: *He thought the movie was very boring.*

born

brought into life: *The baby was born yesterday.*

borrow

to get something from a person just for a while: *He has borrowed my book and promised to give it back.*
borrowed, borrowing.

boss

1. a person who hires people or directs them; a person who manages: *She told her boss she would be late today.* **2.** to be the boss of: *He complained that she was bossing him around.* **bosses; bossed, bossing.**

both

Both houses are pink. Both dogs are mine.

bother

to make angry; annoy: *Do not bother me while I work.*
bothered, bothering.

bottle

something used to hold liquids. A bottle can be made of glass or plastic and usually has a cap. **bottles.**

bottom

the lowest part of anything: *There are cookies at the bottom of the jar.* **bottoms.**

bought

She bought a coat. She has bought a pair of shoes.

bounce

1. to spring back after hitting something: *The ball bounced off the wall. She bounced the ball.* **2.** to give back light, heat, or sound; reflect: *The bright sunlight bounced off the surface of the lake.* **bounced, bouncing.**

bounce (definition 1)

bound¹

The doctor bound up the cut.

bound²

to spring lightly: *The deer bounded through the woods.*
bounded, bounding.

bound²—*The deer **bounded** through the woods.*

boundary

a line at the edge of something to show where it ends: *There is a boundary between Mexico and the United States.* **boundaries.**

bow¹ (definition 1)

bow¹

1. to bend your head or body: *He bowed to us.* **2.** a bending of your head or body: *The singer made a deep bow as we clapped.* **bowed, bowing; bows.** (Bow¹ rhymes with <u>how</u>.)

bow²

1. a strip of wood bent by a string. A bow shoots arrows. **2.** a knot with two loops. You make a bow when you tie your shoe. **bows.** (Bow² rhymes with <u>so</u>.)

bow² (definition 2)

bow³

the forward or front part of a ship or boat. **bows.** (Bow³ rhymes with <u>how</u>.)

bow³

bowl

a hollow, deep dish: *He ate a bowl of cereal this morning.* **bowls.**

bowling

bowling

a game in which you roll a heavy ball at wooden pins to knock them down.

box¹

something with four sides, a bottom, and a top. Boxes are made of wood, metal, or paper. We put things in boxes. **boxes.**

box¹

box²

to fight another person with the fists. When you box, you wear heavy gloves and follow special rules. **boxed, boxing.**

boxer

a person who boxes. **boxers.**

boy

a male child. A boy grows up to be a man. **boys.**

Boy Scout

a member of the Boy Scouts of America. This group helps boys grow into healthy, strong young men. **Boy Scouts.**

bracelet

a band or chain worn on the wrist. **bracelets.**

bracelet

braces

metal wires used to straighten crooked teeth: *The dentist put braces on my brother's teeth.*

braid (definition 2)
*Her mother is **braiding** her hair.*

brass—*All of these things are made of **brass**.*

braid

1. a band of hair made by weaving hair together: *She liked to wear her hair in braids.* **2.** to weave hair together: *Every morning Mother braids my hair.* **braids; braided, braiding.**

brain

a part of your body that is inside your head. You use your brain to learn, think, and remember. Your brain also makes it possible for you to talk and move around. **brains.**

brake

anything used to stop something or slow it down. Bicycles and automobiles have brakes. **brakes.**

branch

a part of a tree that grows out from the trunk: *A swing hung from the branch.* **branches.**

brand

a certain kind: *I like this brand of mustard.* **brands.**

brass

a yellow metal. Brass is part copper. It is used to make trumpets, saxophones, candlesticks, and other things.

brave

without fear: *The brave girl pulled her little brother away from the burning garage.* **braver, bravest.**

bread

food made from flour mixed with milk or water and baked.

break

1. to cause to fall to pieces: *The football hit the kitchen window and broke it.* **2.** to fail to keep: *She broke her promise to come over and play.* **3.** a short rest period: *We had a milk break before recess.* **broke, broken, breaking; breaks.**

breakfast

a meal eaten at the beginning of the day: *We ate cereal and fruit for breakfast.* **breakfasts.**

breath

air taken into and sent out of the lungs: *Take a deep breath.* **breaths.**

breathe

to take air into the lungs and then send it out. **breathed, breathing.**

breeze

a light wind: *We enjoyed the breeze today.* **breezes.**

brick

a block of clay that is baked. Bricks are used to build walls and to pave walks. **bricks.**

bride

a woman just married, or just about to be married. **brides.**

bridegroom

a man just married, or just about to be married. Another word for bridegroom is groom. **bridegrooms.**

brick

bridge

bridge

a road built over water. People walk across bridges. Cars and trucks can drive over bridges. **bridges.**

bright

1. shining; giving much light: *The moon is bright tonight.* **2.** clever: *The bright pupil knew the answer.* **brighter, brightest.**

bring

to carry something from another place: *Please bring me a napkin.* **brought, bringing.**

British Columbia

one of the ten provinces of Canada.

broad

wide; a long distance across: *The wagons crossed a broad river.* **broader, broadest.**

broadcast

1. a radio or television program: *Did you watch the TV broadcast about tomorrow's weather?* **2.** to send out a program by radio or television: *The radio station broadcast weather reports every hour.* **broadcasts; broadcast, broadcasting.**

broadcast (definition 1)
Did you see the weather broadcast?

broccoli

a vegetable with green stalks and flower buds.

broke

Who broke this dish?

broken

He has broken a window.

broccoli

47

brook

a small stream of running water. Another word for brook is creek. **brooks.**

broom

a brush with a long handle. A broom is used to sweep the floor. **brooms.**

brother

a boy or man that has the same parents as another person. **brothers.**

brought

He brought raisins in his lunch.

brown

1. a dark color like that of chocolate. **2.** having this color: *Many horses are brown.* **browns; browner, brownest.**

brownie[1]

1. in stories, a good-natured, helpful elf or fairy.
2. Brownie, a young member of the Girl Scouts of America. Brownies are between eight and ten years old. **brownies, Brownies.**

brownie[2]

a small, flat, sweet chocolate cake. **brownies.**

brush[1]

1. a tool made of stiff hairs, plastic, or wire. You use one kind of brush to paint a house and another kind to clean your teeth. **2.** to clean, rub, or paint with a brush: *Brush your teeth.* **brushes; brushed, brushing.**

brush[2]

bushes and small trees growing in the woods: *He heard an animal in the brush outside our tent.*

brush[2]

bubble

a round drop of liquid that is filled with air: *Bubbles rose up when she stirred the soapy water.* **bubbles.**

bucket

something to carry things in. You can carry water or sand in a bucket. Another word for bucket is pail. **buckets.**

buckle

1. something that holds together two loose ends of a belt or strap: *The belt had a silver buckle.* **2.** to fasten together with a buckle: *Buckle your belt.* **buckles; buckled, buckling.**

bud

bud

a small new growing part on a plant. A bud will grow into a flower, leaf, or branch. **buds.**

buffalo

budge

to move just a little bit: *We pushed hard but couldn't budge the door.* **budged, budging.**

buffalo

a large animal with long hair on its head. **buffaloes.**

bug

anything that crawls or flies like an insect. Ants and flies are often called bugs. **bugs.**

buggy

1. something to ride in with four wheels, pulled by a horse: *We rode in a buggy around the park.*
2. something to carry a baby or doll in: *She pushed her doll around the park in a buggy.* **buggies.**

bugle

bugle

a musical instrument like a small trumpet. You play the bugle by blowing into it. **bugles.**

build

to make by putting things together: *It takes many people to build a bridge.* **built, building.**

bulbs (definitions 1 and 2)

bulldozer

bumblebee

building

something that has been built. A building has walls and a roof. Schools, houses, and barns are buildings. **buildings.**

built

They built a sand castle. They have built two castles today.

bulb

1. a hollow glass light that glows when electricity is turned on. **2.** a round bud or stem that you plant in the ground. Onions, tulips, and lilies grow from bulbs. **bulbs.**

bull

a large male farm animal. A male elephant or buffalo is also called a bull. **bulls.**

bulldozer

a heavy machine with a large metal blade in front. Bulldozers are used to clear brush and trees away. They can also level areas where roads or buildings are to be put. **bulldozers.**

bullet

a small piece of metal that is shot from a gun. **bullets.**

bulletin board

a board that you put news, notes, or notices on. **bulletin boards.**

bumblebee

a large bee which makes a loud buzzing sound. **bumblebees.**

bump

1. to hit against something: *I bumped into her when I ran around the corner. She bumped her arm against the door.* **2.** a place that swells up from being hit: *He got a bump on the head when he fell down.* **bumped, bumping; bumps.**

bumpy

rough; causing many bumps: *The plane ride was very bumpy.* **bumpier; bumpiest.**

bun

a small round cake. Buns are often sweet and may have spices or raisins in them. **buns.**

bunch

a group of things that are alike: *He ate a bunch of grapes for lunch. She gathered a bunch of flowers after school.* **bunches.**

bundle

a number of things tied up together or wrapped together: *She carried a bundle of newspapers down to the basement.* **bundles.**

bundle

bunny

a rabbit: *Several bunnies ran across the yard.* **bunnies.**

burn

1. to be on fire or to set on fire: *The campfire burned all night. We burned several logs in the fireplace.* **2.** a sore caused by too much heat: *He got a burn on his arm from the hot iron.* **burned, burning; burns.**

burrow (definition 1)

burrow

1. a hole that an animal digs in the ground. Rabbits live in burrows. **2.** to dig a hole in the ground: *A mole burrowed under the porch.* **burrows; burrowed, burrowing.**

burst

1. to fly apart suddenly: *That balloon burst as I was blowing it up.* **2.** to go into or come out of suddenly: *He burst into the room without knocking.* **burst, bursting.**

bury

1. to put something in the ground: *The children wanted to bury their dead pet.* **2.** to cover up; hide: *It was so cold that she buried her head under the covers.* **buried, burying.**

bus

a large machine with a lot of seats for people to ride in. Buses carry passengers along certain streets or roads. **buses.**

bush

a plant that is smaller than a tree. A bush has branches that start near the ground. Some bushes are grown for their flowers, and some for their fruit. **bushes.**

bushel

bushel

an amount of grain, fruit, or vegetables: *Dad bought a bushel of potatoes and two bushels of apples.* **bushels.**

bushy

spreading out like a bush: *Squirrels have bushy tails.* **bushier, bushiest.**

business

work done to make money: *What business is your father in?* **businesses.**

busy

having a lot to do: *The principal is a busy person. We were busy playing outside.* **busier, busiest.**

busy

but

You may go, but you may not stay late. We wanted to go to the movie, but we couldn't.

butcher

a person who cuts and sells meat. **butchers.**

butt

to hit by pushing or knocking hard with the head: *Goats often butt if they get too close to you.* **butted, butting.**

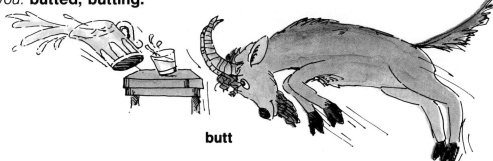

butt

butter

1. a soft yellow food made from cream. **2.** to put butter on: *Please butter my toast for me.* **buttered, buttering.**

butterfly

butterfly

an insect with a small, narrow body. Butterflies have four large, bright-colored wings. **butterflies.**

button

1. a flat, round piece of plastic or metal. Buttons fasten clothes together. A shirt has buttons down the front. **2.** to fasten the buttons of: *It was hard for him to button his shirt.* **3.** a knob you push to make something work: *When she pushed the button, the bell rang.* **buttons; buttoned, buttoning.**

buy

to get something by paying money for it: *Can you buy me a pencil for school?* **bought, buying.**

buzz

1. the humming sound made by flies, mosquitoes, or bees: *The loud buzz of a fly woke me up.* **2.** to make a steady humming sound: *Mosquitoes buzzed outside the screen.* **buzzes; buzzed, buzzing.**

by

Stand by the door. She went by the river road. She travels by bus. Be here by twelve o'clock.

buttons (definition 1)

Cc

caboose

cactus

cab

a car with a driver that you pay to take you somewhere. **cabs.**

cabbage

a vegetable with green or reddish-purple leaves. The leaves are folded into a round head. **cabbages.**

cabin

a small house: *They have a log cabin in the woods.* **cabins.**

cabinet

a piece of furniture with shelves or drawers. A dining room cabinet holds dishes. Televisions are sometimes kept in cabinets. **cabinets.**

caboose

a small railroad car, often the last car of a freight train. Some of the train crew ride in the caboose. **cabooses.**

cactus

a plant with thorns but no leaves. Most cactuses grow in very hot, dry areas of America. Many have brightly colored flowers. **cactuses.**

cafeteria

a place to eat in a school, office building, or factory. You choose your food and carry it to a table. **cafeterias.**

caffeine

a drug found in coffee, tea, and some soft drinks. Caffeine can make your heart beat faster than it should.

cage

a box or place closed in with wires or bars. Birds and wild animals are kept in cages. **cages.**

cage

cake

a baked mixture of flour, sugar, eggs, and other things. **cakes.**

calculator

a machine that is used to find the answers to number problems. When numbers and symbols on a calculator are pressed, answers appear on a screen. **calculators.**

calendar

a chart showing the months, weeks, and days of the year. **calendars.**

calendar

calf[1]

a baby cow, elephant, seal, or whale. **calves.**

calf[2]

the back of the leg below the knee. **calves.**

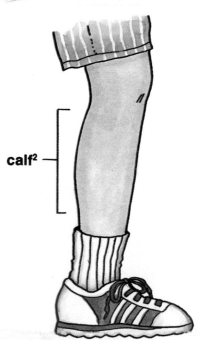

calf[2]

California

one of the fifty states of the United States.

call

1. to speak loudly; shout or cry out: *She called from downstairs.* **2.** to ask to come; command: *Please call your brother to dinner.* **3.** a shout: *I don't think they heard my call.* **4.** to give a name: *We call our dog Brownie.* **5.** to talk to by telephone: *Call me when you get home.* **called, calling; calls.**

calm

quiet; still: *The lake is calm today. She was frightened, but she answered with a calm voice.* **calmer, calmest.**

calves

more than one calf: *We saw several calves in the field with the cows. My calves hurt from hiking.*

came

They came to our house for dinner.

camel

a large animal that can go a long time without water. Camels are used to carry people and things in the desert. **camels.**

camel

camera

a machine for taking pictures or movies. **cameras.**

camp

1. a group of tents or cabins where people live for a while: *I spent a week at summer camp. We set up camp near the river.* **2.** to live outdoors or in a tent for a while: *We camped in the woods for five days.* **camps; camped, camping.**

can¹

She can run fast. Can we go to the circus next week? **could.**

can²

a round, metal thing used to hold other things: *I opened a can of soup. He bought a can of red paint.* **cans.**

Canada

the country north of the United States.

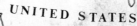

Canadian

1. a person born or living in Canada. **2.** of Canada: *The Canadian flag has a maple leaf on it.* **Canadians.**

canary

a small yellow bird. Canaries sing sweetly and are often kept as pets. **canaries.**

canary

candle

a stick of wax with a kind of string inside it, called a wick. As the wick burns, the candle gives light. **candles.**

candy

a sweet food made of sugar or syrup. It often has chocolate, fruit, or nuts mixed in. **candies.**

cane

a stick used to help a person walk. **canes.**

cannot

He cannot come to the party.

canoe

a small boat that a person moves with a paddle. **canoes.**

canoe

can't

cannot: *I can't go with you tomorrow.*

cantaloupe

a large fruit with a hard, rough outside and a juicy, orange inside. Cantaloupes are melons and grow on vines. **cantaloupes.**

canyon

a narrow valley with high, steep sides. A canyon usually has a stream at the bottom. **canyons.**

canyon

57

cape¹

cap

1. a soft covering for the head: *I can't find my baseball cap.* **2.** anything that covers the top of something. The top of a bottle, tube, or pen is a cap. **caps.**

cape¹

a piece of clothing worn like a coat. A cape covers your arms but has no sleeves. **capes.**

cape²

a piece of land with water almost all around it. **capes.**

capital

1. the city of a nation or state where laws are made. Washington, D.C., is the capital of the United States. Each state has a capital. **2.** A, B, C, D, or any other large letter. Your name starts with a capital. **capitals.**

Capitol

a large building in Washington, D.C. Congress meets in the Capitol to make laws for our country.

Capitol

captain

the leader of a group or team: *She is the captain of the basketball team.* **captains.**

car

a machine that people ride in. A car has an engine and four wheels. Another word for car is automobile. **cars.**

card

a flat piece of stiff paper or plastic. You can take out books with a library card. People buy things with credit cards. You might receive a funny card on your birthday. Some games are played with cards. **cards.**

cardboard

very thick, stiff paper used to make cards and boxes.

cardinals

cardinal

a small, bright red bird with a thick bill. The feathers on a cardinal's head come to a point, called a crest. **cardinals.**

care

1. great thought or attention: *Please take care to do the job right.* **2.** to be in charge of; watch out for: *Will you care for my cat while I am away?* **3.** to like or be interested in: *All he cares about is playing baseball.* **cares; cared, caring.**

careful

1. thinking about what you do; paying attention: *Be careful when you cross the street.* **2.** done with thought and attention; showing care: *She does careful work.*

careless

1. not thinking about what you do; not careful: *She was careless and broke the cup.* **2.** done with little thought or attention; showing little care: *His work was messy and careless.*

carol

a song of joy sung at Christmas. **carols.**

carpenter

a person who builds and repairs things made of wood. **carpenters.**

carpet

a heavy material used to cover floors. **carpets.**

carrot

a long, orange vegetable that grows underground. Carrots are eaten cooked or raw. **carrots.**

carpenter

cart

carry

to take something from one place to another: *We carried the groceries into the house.* **carried, carrying.**

cart

a kind of wagon used for carrying things from place to place. A grocery cart is a metal basket on four wheels. Other carts are wooden and can be pulled by animals. **carts.**

carton

a small cardboard or paper box: *I bought a carton of milk.* **cartons.**

cartoon

1. a short, funny movie made of a series of drawings. **2.** a funny drawing, often found in newspapers or magazines. **cartoons.**

carve (definition 2)

carve

1. to cut into slices or pieces: *I will carve the turkey.* **2.** to make by cutting: *The children carved a jack-o'-lantern.* **carved, carving.**

case¹

an example: *Your poor grade was simply a case of not listening to directions.* **cases.**

case²

1. something that holds or covers something else: *I keep my pencils in this case.* **2.** a large box: *There is a case of canned fruit in the basement.* **cases.**

cash

money in the form of coins and bills: *This store accepts only cash, no checks.*

cashier

cashier

a person in charge of money, often in a bank. **cashiers.**

cast

1. to throw: *Cast your fishing line into the river.* **2.** a hard covering used to shape or support something: *The doctor put a cast on my broken leg.* **3.** all the actors in a play: *The cast came out and bowed at the end of the play.* **cast, casting; casts.**

castle

a large stone building with thick walls and a tower. Long ago, kings and queens lived in castles. **castles.**

cat

a small, furry animal often kept as a pet. Many cats like to chase mice. **cats.**

catch

to take and hold something that is moving: *I caught the ball with one hand.* **caught, catching.**

catcher

a baseball player who stands behind the batter and catches the ball thrown by the pitcher. **catchers.**

caterpillar

an insect that looks something like a furry or colorful worm. Caterpillars turn into moths or butterflies. **caterpillars.**

caterpillar

catsup

a thick, red sauce made from tomatoes and spices: *I like catsup on my hamburger.*

cattle

animals raised for their meat, milk, or skins. Cows, bulls, and steers are cattle.

cauliflower

cave

caught

My uncle caught a fish. I caught the ball. My sister has caught a bad cold.

cauliflower

a vegetable with a solid, white head. The head is broken apart and cooked for eating.

cause

1. something that makes something else happen: *Lightning was the cause of the fire.* **2.** to make something happen: *The fire caused a lot of damage.* **causes; caused, causing.**

cave

a hollow space in the side of a hill or mountain. Caves are usually underground. **caves.**

cavity

a hole or hollow place. Germs that live on the teeth can help cause a cavity. **cavities.**

ceiling

the top of a room; the part opposite the floor. Lights hang from the ceiling. **ceilings.**

celebrate

to do something special in honor of a special person or day: *We celebrated my birthday with a big party.* **celebrated, celebrating.**

celebration

special activities in honor of a special person or day: *We had a birthday celebration.* **celebrations.**

celery

a long greenish-white vegetable. Celery grows in stalks and can be eaten cooked or raw.

cell

a very small unit of living matter. All living things are made up of cells. **cells.**

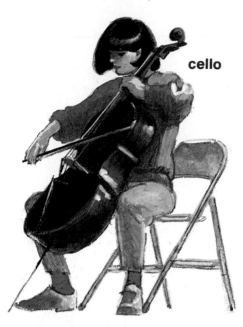

cello

cellar

a space under a building, usually used to store food. **cellars.**

cello

a musical instrument with strings. It is like a violin, but much larger and has a lower sound. **cellos.**

cent

the smallest amount of money in the United States and Canada. One hundred cents make one dollar. Another word for cent is penny. **cents.**

center

1. the middle part of something: *Lou sat in the center of the circle. The vase was in the center of the table.*
2. a place people go for a certain purpose: *We skate at the recreation center.* **centers.**

centimeter

a unit of length about this long: ———. There are 100 centimeters in a meter. **centimeters.**

cereal

a food made from wheat, corn, rice, or other grains. Many people eat cereal with milk for breakfast. **cereals.**

certain

1. very sure: *I am certain I am right.* **2.** some but not all: *Certain plants grow in sandy soil.*

cereal—*Corn, wheat, and rice are plants from which* **cereal** *is made.*

certainly

surely; without a doubt: *I will certainly be there.*

chain

1. a row of metal rings joined together. **2.** to fasten with a chain: *We chained our dog in the yard.* **chains; chained, chaining.**

chair
a seat with a back and four legs and, sometimes, arms. **chairs.**

chalk
a soft, white rock used for writing or drawing. Chalk is often used on a chalkboard.

chalkboard
a smooth, hard surface on which you can write or draw with chalk. **chalkboards.**

challenge
something that tests your skill: *Fractions are a real challenge to me.* **challenges.**

chance
1. a good time to do something: *I had a chance to visit Washington, D.C.* **2.** an event that is possible: *There is a chance that it may snow.* **chances.**

change
1. to make or become different: *We changed the color of our house from white to yellow.* **2.** something different that happens: *Since it rained, we had to make a change in our picnic plans.* **3.** to put different clothes on: *Please change that dirty shirt.* **4.** the money you get back when you pay too much: *I gave the cashier ten dollars and got fifty cents change.* **changed, changing; changes** (for **2.**).

chapter
one of the main parts of a book. **chapters.**

character
a person or animal in a story. **characters.**

charge
1. to ask as a price: *My friend charged me ten dollars for his old computer.* **2.** to buy something now and pay for it later: *Mom charged my new shoes.* **charged, charging.**

change (definition 1)
*We **changed** the color of our house from pink to yellow.*

chart

a list or drawing that shows facts: *This chart shows the amount of snow we had last winter.* **charts.**

chase

to run after to catch: *The cat chased the mouse. The children chased the ball down the hill.* **chased, chasing.**

chat

an easy, friendly talk: *The grandparents had a chat about old timcs.* **chats.**

chatter

1. to talk a lot in a quick, foolish way: *They chattered on about the new neighbors.* **2.** to make a rattling sound: *Cold makes my teeth chatter.* **chattered, chattering.**

chat—*The two friends are having a* **chat.**

cheap

low in price: *Fresh carrots are cheap in the summer.* **cheaper, cheapest.**

check

1. to prove true or right by comparing: *I checked my answers against those at the back of the book.* **2.** to seek information and advice from: *Check the dictionary if you don't know how to spell a word.* **3.** a mark (√) to show that something has been looked at or compared. **4.** a written order for money from a bank. **checked, checking; checks.**

check (definition 4)

checker

the person you pay for the things you buy at a supermarket or store. **checkers.**

checkup

a visit to a doctor in which the doctor checks to see that you are healthy. **checkups.**

checkup

cheek

the part of the face just below the eye: *Her cheeks are red.* **cheeks.**

cheer

1. to call out or yell loudly to show you like something: *Let's cheer for our team.* **2.** good feelings; hope; joy: *My friend's warmth and kindness brought me cheer.* **cheered, cheering.**

cheer (definition 1)

cheerful

full of good feelings; glad; joyful: *She is a smiling, cheerful girl.*

cheese

a solid food made from milk: *I like cheese and crackers.*

cherry

a small, round, red fruit that grows on trees. Cherries have a hard seed, called a pit. **cherries.**

chest

1. the front part of the body between the neck and the stomach. **2.** a large box with a lid: *The pirates buried a chest filled with jewels and coins.* **chests.**

chestnut

a brown nut with a hard shell. Chestnuts grow on trees. **chestnuts.**

chestnut

chew

to crush or grind with the teeth: *Chew your food well before swallowing.* **chewed, chewing.**

chick

a young chicken. **chicks.**

chicken

1. a bird raised for food. Hens and roosters are chickens. **2.** the meat of this bird used for food: *I like fried chicken.* **chickens** (for **1.**).

chief

the head of a group; leader: *Mr. Clark is the chief of police. Red Cloud was an American Indian chief.* **chiefs.**

child

1. a young girl or boy: *That child is only two years old.* **2.** a son or daughter: *My mother is my grandfather's only child.* **children.**

chimney

a tall, hollow column built to carry away smoke from a fireplace or furnace. **chimneys.**

chimpanzee

a hairy animal with long arms and no tail. Chimpanzees are small apes. **chimpanzees.**

chimpanzee

chin

the part of the face below the mouth. **chins.**

chip

1. a small, thin piece of something: *We used chips of wood to start the fire.* **2.** to break a small, thin piece from: *I chipped the cup when I knocked it against the cupboard.* **chips; chipped, chipping.**

chipmunk

a small, striped animal like a squirrel. Chipmunks live underground. **chipmunks.**

chipmunks

chocolate

1. a powder or syrup made from the seeds of a certain tree. It has a rich, sweet taste. **2.** a candy made of chocolate: *They gave us a box of chocolates.* **chocolates** (for **2.**).

choice

1. a picking out from a group; selection: *I had to make a choice as to which book to read.* **2.** the person or thing picked or selected: *He is my choice for president.* **choices.**

choke

to be unable to breathe because something is blocking your throat: *I choked on a piece of meat.* **choked, choking.**

choose

to pick out from a group; select: *Will you help me choose a new hat?* **chose, chosen, choosing.**

chop

to cut by hitting with something sharp: *He used an ax to chop the tree down.* **chopped, chopping.**

chop

chose

We chose to see the movie about robots.

chosen

He was chosen to be the leader.

Christmas

December 25, a day when some people give gifts and go to church. **Christmases.**

chuckle

to laugh softly or quietly: *She chuckled to herself as she read.* **chuckled, chuckling.**

church

a building where some people go to pray. **churches.**

churn

1. a machine used to beat cream into butter. **2.** to beat cream into butter. **churns; churned, churning.**

cider

a sweet drink made from the juice of apples.

circle

1. a round line. A ring is a circle. **2.** something round like a circle: *Sit in a circle on the rug.* **3.** to put a circle around: *Circle the correct answer.* **circles; circled, circling.**

circus

a show that travels from place to place. A circus has clowns, horses, riders, acrobats, and wild animals. **circuses.**

city

a large, important town with many people living in it. Los Angeles and London are cities. **cities.**

clam

a sea animal with a soft body inside a hard shell. A clam's shell has two halves. **clams.**

clap

1. to hit the hands together to make a sound: *We clapped to the music.* **2.** a sudden loud noise: *We heard a clap of thunder.* **clapped, clapping; claps.**

clarinet

a wooden musical instrument that is played by blowing into it and pressing keys. **clarinets.**

churn (definition 2)

clam

clarinet

class

a group of students learning together: *Our class is working on a project.* **classes.**

classify

to arrange in groups or classes: *A librarian classifies books according to what they are about.* **classified, classifying.**

classmate

a member of the same class in school. **classmates.**

classroom

a room in a school in which classes are held. **classrooms.**

claws (definition 1)

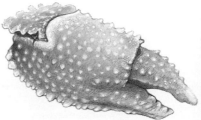

claw (definition 2)

claw

1. one of the sharp, curved nails on the foot of an animal or bird. **2.** the pinching part of a lobster or crab. **claws.**

clay

powdered rock that comes from the earth. Wet clay can be easily shaped. It becomes hard when it dries.

clean

1. not dirty; free from dirt: *Please put on clean clothes.* **2.** to make something free from dirt: *We cleaned the kitchen floor.* **cleaner, cleanest; cleaned, cleaning.**

clear

1. bright; not cloudy or dark: *A clear sky is free of clouds.* **2.** easy to see through: *I poured the milk into a clear glass.* **3.** easy to hear, see, or understand: *Everyone understood her clear directions.* **4.** to make clean and free: *Please clear the table. I cleared my throat.* **clearer, clearest; cleared, clearing.**

clearing

an open space in a forest. **clearings.**

clerk

a person who sells things in a store or shop. **clerks.**

clever

smart; quick at learning and understanding: *My clever friend won a math contest.* **cleverer, cleverest.**

click

1. a short, sharp sound: *I heard a click as the key turned in the lock.* **2.** to make a short, sharp sound: *The key clicked in the lock.* **clicks; clicked, clicking.**

cliff

cliff

a steep, rocky side of a hill. **cliffs.**

climate

the kind of weather a place has. Climate includes how hot, cold, wet, or dry a place is. *The climate in Arizona is hot and dry.* **climates.**

climb

to go up something, usually by using the hands and feet: *We climbed the hill. The children climbed into the bus.* **climbed, climbing.**

cling

to hold tightly; hang on: *The kitten was clinging to the branch of the tree.* **clung, clinging.**

clip¹

to cut or cut off; trim: *The barber clipped the hair around the boy's ears. Mom clipped the bushes in our yard.* **clipped, clipping.**

clip²

to fasten together; hold together: *He clipped the note to the papers.* **clipped, clipping.**

cling

clock

a thing that shows what time it is. Some clocks have hands that point to the hour and the minute. Other clocks show only numbers. **clocks.**

clog

to fill up or block: *Hair and grease clogged the drain.* **clogged, clogging.**

close¹

1. to shut: *Please close the door. Close your eyes.*
2. to finish; end: *The show closes next week.* **closed, closing.** (Close¹ rhymes with rose.)

close²

1. without much space between; near: *The houses were built close together.* **2.** careful; complete: *Pay close attention to me.* **3.** very friendly; feeling deeply about: *Those two are close friends.* **closer, closest.** (Close² rhymes with dose.)

closely

1. without much space between; very near: *The puppy followed closely behind its master.* **2.** carefully; completely: *Watch closely while I do this trick.*

closet

a small room used to store clothes, shoes, or other things. **closets.**

cloth

wool, cotton, silk, or other material. Cloth is used to make clothes, curtains, and other things.

clothes

coverings for the body. Dresses, pants, shirts, sweaters, and jeans are clothes.

closely (definition 1)
*The puppy followed **closely** behind its master.*

clothing

clothes: *People need food, clothing, and a place to live.*

cloud

a white or gray mass floating high in the sky. Clouds are made up of tiny drops of water or ice. **clouds.**

cloudy

full of clouds; not clear: *The sky was dark and cloudy.* **cloudier, cloudiest.**

clown

a person who dresses in funny clothes and tries to make people laugh: *The clown tripped over a bucket and slid into a row of pies.* **clowns.**

club

1. a group of people joined together for some special reason: *My sister belongs to the science club.* **2.** a large stick, thicker at one end than the other. Clubs are used as weapons. **clubs.**

clue

something that helps find an answer to a question or puzzle: *Give me a clue so I can answer the riddle.* **clues.**

clung

The child clung to his mother. Mud had clung to his boots.

coach

1. a person who teaches or trains others: *My swimming coach says I'm doing well.* **2.** to train or teach another: *My cousin coached the baseball team.* **coaches; coached, coaching.**

clouds

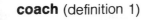

coach (definition 1)

coal

a black rock that gives off heat when it is burned. Coal comes from plants that died millions of years ago.

coast

1. the land along the sea; shore: *We sailed along the coast.* **2.** to slide down a hill on a sled or ride a bike without pedaling: *I coasted down the hill on my bike.* **coasts; coasted, coasting.**

coat

1. a piece of clothing worn over other clothes: *My new winter coat is very warm.* **2.** an animal's hair, fur, or wool: *Collies have a thick coat.* **3.** a thin layer: *This wall needs another coat of paint.* **coats.**

coax

to talk someone into doing something by using soft words and kindness: *I coaxed my sister into helping me clean up.* **coaxed, coaxing.**

cocoa

1. a powder made from the seeds of a certain tree. It tastes like chocolate. **2.** a drink made from cocoa: *We drank hot cocoa after playing in the snow.*

coconut

a large, round fruit with a very hard, brown shell. The inside of a coconut is white and sweet. Coconuts grow on a certain palm tree. **coconuts.**

cocoon

the covering made by caterpillars to live in while they are turning into moths. **cocoons.**

code

letters, numbers, or words used instead of ordinary writing to write a secret message: *The club members wrote each other in code.* **codes.**

coconut

cocoon

coffee

a hot drink made from special seeds. Coffee contains caffeine, a drug that can make the heart beat too fast.

coin

a piece of metal used as money. Pennies, nickels, dimes, and quarters are coins. **coins.**

cold

1. not hot; not as warm as your body: *Snow and ice are cold.* **2.** coldness; being cold: *Come in out of the cold.* **3.** a sickness that makes you cough and sneeze. **colder, coldest; colds** (for **3.**).

collar

1. the part of a coat, dress, or shirt that goes around the neck. **2.** a band that is put around the neck of a dog or other pet. Collars can be made of leather, chain, or plastic. **collars.**

collect

to bring something together; gather together: *Five students in the class collect butterflies. The teacher collected the money for the field trip.* **collected, collecting.**

collection

a group of things that are from many places, but are brought together: *The stamps in his collection are from fifty different countries.* **collections.**

collie

a large dog that makes a good pet. Collies are used to protect sheep and other farm animals. **collies.**

colony

a group of communities in one country that is ruled by another country: *The Pilgrims started a community in an area that became the colony of Massachusetts.* **colonies.**

coins

collection

color

1. red, yellow, blue, or any of them mixed together: *I have eight colors of crayons.* **2.** to give color to something; to put color on something: *She colored the sky blue.* **colors; colored, coloring.**

Colorado

one of the fifty states of the United States.

colt

a young horse, donkey, or zebra. A horse is called a colt until it is four or five years old. **colts.**

colt

column

1. a tall post or pole that holds up a roof or a part of a building. Columns can be made of stone, wood, concrete, or metal. **2.** anything like a column: *Columns of numbers filled the whole page.* **columns.**

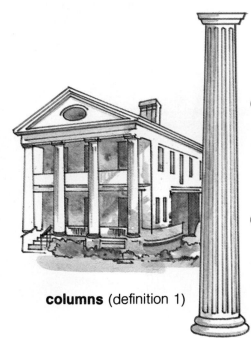

columns (definition 1)

comb

1. a piece of plastic or metal that has teeth. It is used to keep your hair neat. **2.** to fix the hair and make it neat: *Comb your hair every morning before school.* **3.** the thick red part on the top of a rooster's head: *The bright red comb on a rooster makes him easy to see.* **combs; combed, combing.**

come

You can come over anytime. My mom comes home at six o'clock. **came, come, coming.**

comfortable

feeling nice, warm, and snug: *The blanket helped the chilled boy feel comfortable.*

comics

a group of drawings that tell a funny or exciting story.

Hey come here.

comma

comma

a mark (,) of punctuation. A comma is used where you would pause if you were saying a sentence out loud. **commas.**

command

1. an order: *The dog won't move until a command is given.* **2.** to give an order to someone: *The police officer commanded the driver to stop the car.* **commands; commanded, commanding.**

common

often seen or found; usual: *Yellow is a common color for school buses.* **commoner, commonest.**

communicate

to talk about, write about, and listen to facts, news, and ideas. People communicate by radio, TV, telephone, and computer. They also write to one another. **communicated, communicating.**

community

a place where people live, work, and play. Communities are different sizes. Stores, houses, and libraries are all part of a community. **communities.**

company

1. a group of people who work together for some purpose: *The company I work for makes toys.* **2.** a guest or guests: *We are having company for dinner tonight.* **companies** (for **1.**).

compare

to find out or point out how people or things are alike and how they are different: *The boys compared their lunches.* **compared, comparing.**

compass

something that shows directions. A compass has a needle that always points to the north. **compasses.**

compass

complain

to say that something is wrong; find fault: *The children complained about too much homework.* **complained, complaining.**

complete

1. with all the parts; whole: *We have a complete set of pieces for the puzzle.* **2.** to make whole: *They completed the puzzle.* **3.** to get to the end of: *He completed his homework before his favorite TV show came on.* **completed, completing.**

completely

in a complete way; wholly; fully: *She completely finished her dinner so that she could have some dessert.*

compound

two words that are put together to make up one new word. *Outside* and *playground* are two compound words.

computation

a way of using mathematics to figure out a problem. Computation is used when you are adding or subtracting. **computations.**

compute

to figure out the answer to a problem by using mathematics: *He computed the cost of our trip.* **computed, computing.**

computer

a machine that can store and give back information. A computer can do many kinds of work. It can play games and give answers to problems. **computers.**

concert

a show where people play musical instruments or sing. **concerts.**

compound

concrete

cement, sand, small stones, and water mixed together. When concrete dries, it is very hard. It is used to make buildings, sidewalks, roads, dams, and bridges.

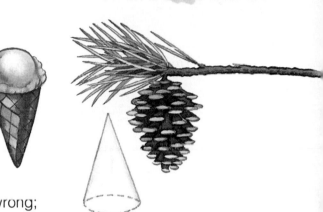

concrete

conduct

the way someone behaves: *The first-grader's conduct during the play was noisy and rude.*

conductor

a person who helps the people who ride trains: *The conductor collects tickets and fares.* **conductors.**

cone

1. something that has a flat, round base and is pointed at the top. **2.** anything shaped like a cone: *The ice cream cone began to melt.* **3.** the part that holds the seeds of trees that have needles. Pines and other evergreens have cones. **cones.**

confess

to tell someone that you have done something wrong; admit: *He confessed that he was the person who threw the paper airplane.* **confessed, confessing.**

cones (definitions 1, 2, and 3)

confuse

1. to mix up: *The directions confused me.* **2.** to not be able to tell apart; mistake one thing for another: *People often confuse this girl with her twin sister.* **confused, confusing.**

connect

to join one thing to another thing; fasten together: *The firefighters connected the hose to the hydrant.* **connected, connecting.**

Connecticut

one of the fifty states of the United States.

connect

constellation

conservation

saving from loss; keeping from being used up or wasted: *The class is interested in the conservation of our forest land.*

consonant

all the letters in the alphabet except a, e, i o, and u. Any letter that is not a consonant is a vowel. **consonants.**

constellation

a group of stars that form a pattern. The Big Dipper is a constellation. **constellations.**

construction

building something; putting something together: *The construction of the bridge took a year.*

consumer

a person who buys and uses food, clothing, or anything that is made or done by someone else. People who buy groceries are consumers. People who get haircuts are also consumers. **consumers.**

contain

to hold inside: *This box contains cereal.* **contained, containing.**

container

a box, can, jar, or anything that can contain or hold something. **containers.**

contented

feeling happy. A contented person is happy with the way things are.

contest

something you enter to win a prize. A contest can be between two people or many people. **contests.**

continent

a very large area of land. There are seven continents on the earth. We live on the continent of North America. **continents.**

continue

1. to keep on going; not stop: *The road continues for miles.* **2.** to go on with something after stopping for a while: *The teacher said that she would continue the story tomorrow.* **continued, continuing.**

contraction

a short form of a word. *Don't* is a contraction for *do not.* **contractions.**

contraction

control

1. to have power over something or someone: *The boy did not lose control of his bike.* **2.** to hold back: *I couldn't control my temper.* **3.** a lever or a switch on a machine. A control can start or stop a machine or move it in different directions. **controlled, controlling; controls.**

controls (definition 3)

cook

1. to make food ready to eat by using heat. Boiling, frying, roasting, and baking are ways to cook. **2.** a person who cooks: *My dad is the cook at our house.* **cooked, cooking; cooks.**

cookie

a small, flat, sweet cake. **cookies.**

cool

1. more cold than hot. On a cool day, a person should wear a sweater or a light jacket, but not a heavy coat. **2.** not excited; calm: *It's hard to keep cool when someone is screaming at you.* **cooler, coolest.**

cool (definition 2)
*She remained **cool** while her friend yelled at her.*

coop

a small cage or pen for chickens, rabbits, or other small animals. **coops.**

coordination

acting or working together in a smooth way: *All athletes have good muscle coordination.*

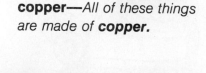

copper—*All of these things are made of* **copper.**

copper

a soft, reddish metal. Copper is used to make pots, pans, pennies, wire, and many other things.

copy

1. to make something like something else: *Copy your spelling list from the chalkboard.* **2.** a thing made to look just like something else: *This copy looks like the famous painting. He made six copies of that page.* **copied, copying; copies.**

coral

a hard red, pink, or white material. Coral is made up of the skeletons of tiny sea animals. It is often used for jewelry.

coral

cord

1. a thick, strong string; a very thin rope. **2.** a pair of wires covered with plastic or rubber. A cord has a plug at one end. It is used to connect an appliance or a lamp to electric current. **cords.**

cork

a light, thick, outer bark of a kind of oak tree. Cork is used to make bottle stoppers and other things. **corks.**

corn

a yellow or white vegetable that grows on a tall, green plant. Farm animals and people eat corn.

corner

1. the place where two lines or two sides meet: *He put his wet boots in the corner.* **2.** the place where two streets meet: *There is a traffic light at the corner.* **corners.**

corral

a pen for horses, cattle, and other animals. **corrals.**

corral

correct

1. without any mistakes; right: *The girl gave the correct answer to the math problem.* **2.** to mark the mistakes in something; remove the mistakes from something: *I corrected the misspelled words in my paper.* **corrected, correcting.**

cost

the amount of money needed to buy something: *The cost of this book is five dollars.* **costs.**

costume

clothes that a person can put on to look like someone else. Costumes are worn in a play. They are also worn just for fun. **costumes.**

cot

a narrow bed. Some cots fold up. **cots.**

costume

cottage

a small house. **cottages.**

cotton

a kind of cloth that people wear in warm weather. Cotton comes from a plant that grows near the ground.

cough

to blow air out from the lungs with a loud noise. *She had a cold and coughed all night.* **coughed, coughing.**

could

She could ski very well. Perhaps I could go with you tomorrow.

couldn't

could not: *He got up early, but he still couldn't make the bus.*

count

1. to name numbers in order: *He can count to one hundred.* **2.** to add up; find the amount of something: *She broke her bank so she could count the pennies.* **3.** to be important: *The teacher said that neatness would count.* **4.** to depend on: *Can I count on you to clean your room after school today?* **counted, counting.**

counter

1. a long table, or some shelves covered with glass. A clerk stands behind a counter to sell things. Food can be prepared and eaten at a counter. **2.** something used for counting: *Use your counters to find the answer to 5 plus 2.* **counters.**

counter (definition 1)

country

1. land outside a city: *There were many farms in the country.* **2.** the land and a group of people with the same leaders. People from the same country usually speak the same language. Our country is the United States. **countries.**

county

a part of a state. A state is made up of a number of counties. Each county has its own officers of government. **counties.**

couple

two things of the same kind that go together; a pair: *She bought a couple of tires for her bike.*

courage

being able to meet danger instead of running away from it: *It takes courage to rescue someone from a burning house.*

course

the direction taken: *After reading the compass, the Cub Scout troop decided to take a course straight north.* **courses.**

court

1. a place where a judge decides questions of law.
2. a place where games such as tennis and basketball are played. **courts.**

court (definition 1)

cousin

the son or daughter of your uncle or aunt. **cousins.**

cover

1. to put something over something else: *He covered his feet with a blanket.* **2.** anything that protects or hides: *I made the cover for my math book from a paper bag.* **covered, covering; covers.**

court (definition 2)

covering

anything that covers: *Hair is covering for the head. Feathers, fur, and fish scales are coverings for different kinds of animals.* **coverings.**

cow

a large farm animal that gives milk. A female elephant or buffalo is also called a cow. **cows.**

coward

a person who is easily scared; one who runs from danger. **cowards.**

cowboy

cowboy

a man who works on a cattle ranch. Cowboys also take part in rodeos. **cowboys.**

85

coyote

crab

crane (definition 1)

cowgirl

a woman who works on a cattle ranch. Cowgirls also take part in rodeos. **cowgirls.**

coyote

a small animal that looks something like a wolf. Coyotes have light yellow fur and bushy tails. They howl at night. **coyotes.**

cozy

warm and comfortable; snug: *The cat lay in a cozy corner near the fireplace.* **cozier, coziest.**

crab

a water animal that has a broad, flat shell. Crabs have eight legs and two claws. Many kinds of crabs are good to eat. **crabs.**

crack

1. a long, narrow break: *The old window had many cracks in it.* **2.** to break without separating into parts: *The baseball didn't make a hole in the window, but it did crack it.* **3.** a sudden, sharp noise like that made by loud thunder. **cracks; cracked, cracking.**

cracker

a thin, crisp biscuit. **crackers.**

cradle

a small bed for a baby. A cradle usually rocks. **cradles.**

crane

1. a machine with a long, swinging arm. A crane is used for lifting and moving heavy things. **2.** a large bird with long legs, neck, and bill. Cranes live near water. **cranes.**

crane (definition 2)

crash

1. a sudden, loud noise: *We heard the crash of thunder.* **2.** to make a loud, sudden noise: *The glass crashed to the floor.* **crashes; crashed, crashing.**

crate

1. a large box made of strips of wood. Crates are used to ship things that might break, such as glass or furniture. **2.** to pack in a crate for shipping: *The mover carefully crated the large mirror.* **crates; crated, crating.**

crawl

to move slowly on hands and knees or with the body close to the ground: *Babies crawl before they begin to walk. Worms, snakes, and lizards crawl.* **crawled, crawling.**

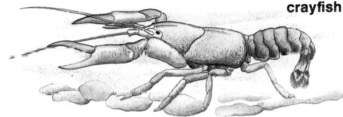

crayfish

crayfish

a water animal that looks like a small lobster. A crayfish has eight legs and two large claws. It lives in lakes and rivers. It eats snails, insects, and small fish. **crayfish.**

crayon

a stick or pencil of colored wax. Crayons are used for drawing and coloring pictures. They come in many colors. **crayons.**

crazy

1. having a sick mind. **2.** foolish: *It was crazy to jump out of such a high tree.* **crazier, craziest.**

creak

to squeak loudly: *The old door creaked when it opened.* **creaked, creaking.**

cream

the oily, yellow part of milk. Butter is made from cream.

creature

any living person or animal: *We fed the lost dog because the poor creature was hungry.* **creatures.**

creek

a small stream of running water. Another word for creek is brook. **creeks.**

creep

to move slowly with the body close to the floor: *I saw the cat creep slowly toward the mouse.* **crept, creeping.**

crept

The tiger crept through the jungle.

crew

crew

a group of people working together: *It takes a crew of ten people to sail that ship. A group of people who make movies is called a film crew.* **crews.**

crib

a small bed with high sides to keep a baby from falling out. **cribs.**

cricket

a black or brown insect that makes a loud noise. Crickets have four wings. They eat plants. The male cricket makes a noise by rubbing its front wings together. **crickets.**

cricket

crisp

hard and thin; easy to break: *Dry toast is crisp. Crackers are crisp.* **crisper, crispest.**

croak

1. a deep, hoarse sound made by a frog or a crow.
2. to make that deep, hoarse sound: *The frog croaked loudly.* **croaks; croaked, croaking.**

crocodile

a large animal with thick skin, four short legs, and a pointed nose. Crocodiles look a lot like alligators. **crocodiles.**

crocodile

crooked

not straight; bent; curved; twisted: *The crooked road was hard to follow.*

crop

plants grown by farmers for food. Corn and wheat are important crops in the United States. **crops.**

cross

1. a straight line with another across it to form a T, an X, or a +. **2.** to mark with an X or draw a line through something: *He crossed out his mistake.* **3.** to move from one side to another: *The children looked both ways before they crossed the street.* **crosses; crossed, crossing.**

crossing

a place where railroad tracks cross a road: *She had to wait a long time at the railroad crossing because of the slow train.* **crossings.**

crosswalk

a place for people to cross the street. The crosswalk is marked with white lines. **crosswalks.**

crosswalk

crow¹

1. the loud cry of a rooster: *The rooster woke us with a loud crow.* **2.** to make this cry: *The rooster crowed and woke us up.* **crows; crowed, crowing.**

crow²

a large, shiny black bird with a loud cry. **crows.**

crow²

crown

crowd

1. a large number of people together: *A crowd waited for the actor.* **2.** to collect or gather in large numbers: *Don't crowd around the campfire.* **crowds; crowded, crowding.**

crown

a head covering for a king or queen. A crown is made out of gold or silver and jewels. **crowns.**

cruel

ready to hurt others: *The cruel man kicked his dog.* **crueler, cruelest.**

crumb

a very small piece of something that has broken off from a larger piece: *The boy carefully ate his piece of cake, but he still left crumbs all over.* **crumbs.**

crunch

1. to bite or chew with a noisy sound: *The rabbit likes to crunch on carrots.* **2.** to make such a sound: *The hard snow crunched under her feet.* **crunched, crunching.**

crunchy

sounding like something being crushed: *The crunchy apple tasted good.* **crunchier, crunchiest.**

crush

1. to squeeze or be squeezed together very hard in order to break: *The box was crushed in the mail.* **2.** to break into very small pieces by grinding, pounding, or pressing: *The stones have to be crushed before they can be used in concrete.* **crushed, crushing.**

crust (definition 1)

crust

1. the hard outside part of bread. **2.** the bottom and top coverings of pies. **crusts.**

cry

1. to weep; sob with tears falling: *The child cried with pain after falling down on the gravel.* **2.** a loud call: *The parents heard the child's cry for help.* **3.** to call loudly: *The man ran after the bus crying, "Stop! Please let me get on!"* **4.** the call of an animal: *The cry of the injured dog made us all feel sorry for it.* **cried, crying; cries.**

cub

a baby bear, fox, lion or other large animal. **cubs.**

cube

a block with six square sides that are all equal in size. **cubes.**

cub scout

a young member of the Boy Scouts of America. Cub scouts are between eight and eleven years old. **cub scouts.**

cucumber

a long, green vegetable that grows on a vine. Cucumbers are eaten in slices and used to make pickles. **cucumbers.**

cub—*This is a bear* **cub.**

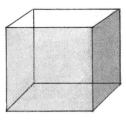

cube

cucumber

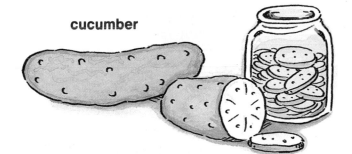

cuddle

1. to hold close in one's arms or lap: *The baby cuddled close to her mom.* **2.** to lie close; curl up: *The baby kittens cuddled together for warmth.* **cuddled, cuddling.**

cup

1. a dish you use to drink from. A cup is usually round and has a handle. **2.** an amount of liquid. You also use a cup to measure sugar and flour in recipes. **cups.**

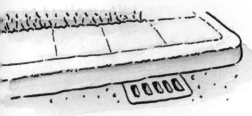

curb

cupboard

a set of shelves that are sometimes closed in by a door. Clothes, dishes, and food can be stored in cupboards. **cupboards.**

cupcake

a small cake about the size and shape of a cup. **cupcakes.**

curb

the raised edge of cement on a sidewalk or street: *The back wheel hit the curb as he parked the car.* **curbs.**

curious

eager to know: *Small children are very curious, and they ask many questions.*

curl (definition 3)
*She wore her hair in **curls.***

curl

1. to twist into rings: *She curled her hair for the party.* **2.** to curve or twist out of shape: *He curled up in the big chair to read.* **3.** a lock of hair that is twisted and curved: *The hat covered the curls on her head.* **curled, curling; curls.**

curly

something that is curved or curling: *He was born with curly hair.* **curlier, curliest.**

current

1. a flow; stream. Running water or moving air makes a current. **2.** a flow of electricity through a wire: *When the current went off, all of his clocks and lights stopped working.* **currents** (for **1.**).

curtain

1. a cloth or other material hung across a window or other space. Curtains are often used to keep out light and to keep a room private. **2.** in a theater, a cloth or screen that hangs between the stage and the audience. **curtains.**

curve

1. a line that has no straight part. A circle is a closed curve. **2.** a bend in the road: *Mountain roads have many curves.* **curves.**

cushion

a soft pillow or pad used to sit, lie, or kneel on. **cushions.**

customer

a person who buys things in a store: *Stores are full of customers during the holidays.* **customers.**

cut

1. to divide something into pieces with something sharp: *Mom cut the orange into two pieces. He cut the paper with scissors.* **2.** an opening made by something sharp: *She covered the cut with a bandage.* **3.** to hurt with something sharp: *She cut her finger on broken glass.* **cut, cutting; cuts.**

cute

pretty; good-looking: *He is a cute baby. The girls thought the new boy was cute. That's a cute sweater.* **cuter, cutest.**

cyclone

a storm with very strong winds; tornado. During a cyclone, the winds move in a circle. **cyclones.**

cymbal

a round brass plate used as a musical instrument. Cymbals are used in pairs. They make a loud, ringing sound when struck against each other. **cymbals.**

cyclone—*This is a picture of a* **cyclone** *taken from outer space.*

cymbal

Dd

daffodil

dam

dad

a father. **dads.**

daffodil

a yellow flower that blooms in the spring. Daffodils grow from bulbs. **daffodils.**

daily

1. done or happening every day: *He reads a daily paper to learn the news.* **2.** every day: *She exercises daily.*

dairy

a place where milk and cream are kept and made into butter and cheese. **dairies.**

daisy

a flower with white, pink, or yellow petals around a yellow center. **daisies.**

dam

a wall built to hold back the water of a creek or river. **dams.**

damp

a little wet: *Use a damp cloth to wipe the table.* **damper, dampest.**

dance

1. to move in rhythm with music: *She dances very well.* **2.** a movement in rhythm with music: *We learned a new dance.* **danced, dancing; dances.**

dandelion

dancer

a person who dances. **dancers.**

dandelion

a weed with bright-yellow flowers. **dandelions.**

danger

1. a chance of harm: *The big waves put the small boat in danger of sinking.* **2.** something that may cause harm: *An icy road is a danger to drivers.* **dangers** (for **2.**).

dangerous

not safe: *Skating on thin ice is dangerous.*

dare

1. to be bold; be bold enough: *Would you dare to walk on stilts?* **2.** to challenge: *I dare you to dive into that pool.* **dared, daring.**

dark

1. without light: *Don't go into that dark cave.* **2.** not light colored: *He wore a dark green shirt.* **3.** darkness: *Come home before dark.* **darker, darkest.**

darkness

being dark: *I couldn't see the black cat in the darkness.*

dash

1. to rush: *We dashed down the street to catch the bus.* **2.** a rush: *We made a dash for the bus.* **dashed, dashing; dashes.**

date[1]

1. the time when something happens or happened: *August 21, 1959, is the date that Hawaii became a state.* **2.** to put a date on: *I dated my letter March 5.* **dates; dated, dating.**

date[2]

the sweet fruit of a kind of palm tree. **dates.**

dates[2]

95

daughter

a female child. A girl or woman is the daughter of her mother and father. **daughters.**

dawn

the beginning of day; the first light in the east: *In summer dawn comes early.* **dawns.**

day

1. the time of light between sunrise and sunset: *Days in summer are longer than days in winter.* **2.** the 24 hours from one midnight to the next: *Few people could stay awake a whole day.* **3.** the hours for work or other activity: *Our school day is from nine to three.* **days.**

daylight

1. the light of day: *Bats do not often fly around in daylight.* **2.** the dawn: *We were up at daylight.*

daytime

the time when it is day and not night: *He works in the nighttime, so he sleeps in the daytime.*

dead

not alive; no longer living: *The plant is dead because no one watered it.*

deaf

not able to hear or to hear well: *Some deaf people can read the lips of others to know what they are saying.* **deafer, deafest.**

deal

1. to carry on business; buy and sell: *That shop deals in clothing and jewelry.* **2.** a bargain: *Mom and Dad got a good deal on a new car.* **dealt, dealing; deals.**

dear

1. much loved: *Her aunt was very dear to her.* **2.** much valued; very respected. *Dear Grandmother is a polite way to begin a letter.* **dearer, dearest.**

dead—*The plant is **dead** because no one watered it.*

December

the twelfth month of the year. It has 31 days. It comes after November and before January.

decide

1. to agree on something: *We decided to stay home.*
2. to make up your mind: *She decided to buy the green skirt.* **decided, deciding.**

deck

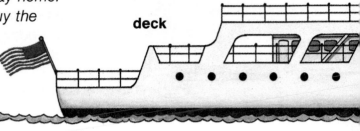

deck

one of the floors of a ship. A deck divides a ship into different levels. **decks.**

deep

1. going a long way down from the top or surface: *The snow was deep in our backyard.* **2.** low: *The man had a deep voice.* **deeper, deepest.**

deer

deer

a very fast animal with hoofs. The male deer has antlers. **deer.**

defense

any thing or act that guards or protects: *Medicine can be a defense against sickness.* **defenses.**

definition

an explaining of what a word means. One definition of ''school'' is ''a place for teaching and learning.'' **definitions.**

Delaware

one of the fifty states of the United States.

delay

1. to put off until a later time: *They decided in May to delay the picnic for a month and have it in June.* **2.** a putting off until a later time: *The delay of the picnic surprised us.* **3.** to make late; keep waiting: *The rain delayed the baseball game for an hour.* **delayed, delaying; delays.**

deliver

delicious

very pleasing or satisfying, usually to the taste or smell: *The cookies were delicious.*

delight

1. a great pleasure; joy: *Our visit was a delight to our grandparents.* **2.** to please very much: *The surprise birthday party delighted my sister.* **delights; delighted, delighting.**

deliver

to carry and give out: *He delivered the invitations on his bicycle.* **delivered, delivering.**

demand

to ask for something that should be yours: *He demanded pay for his work.* **demanded, demanding.**

den

a wild animal's home: *Some bears sleep in their dens all winter.* **dens.**

dent

1. a bent place made in the surface of something by hitting it: *Bumping the garage door put a dent in the fender of the car.* **2.** to damage in this way: *We dented the chair when we moved it.* **dents; dented, denting.**

den

dentist

a doctor who takes care of people's teeth. A dentist fills cavities in teeth and cleans, repairs, straightens, or pulls them. **dentists.**

department

a part of a store, business, or government. The fire department is a part of a city government. **departments.**

depend

1. to be a result of: *The success of his garden will depend on the weather.* **2.** to trust: *You can depend on the alarm clock to wake me.* **depended, depending.**

describe

describe

to tell in words how someone or something looks, feels, or acts: *Please describe the giant in the story.* **described, describing.**

description

a telling in words how someone or something looks, feels, or acts: *They gave a description of the stolen car.* **descriptions.**

desert

a place without water or trees. It is usually hot and sandy. **deserts.**

deserve

to have a right to: *A hard worker deserves good pay.* **deserved, deserving.**

desire

1. a wish: *Her desire was to be a doctor.* **2.** to wish very much for: *Starving people desire food.* **desires; desired, desiring.**

desk

a piece of furniture with a flat or slanting top on which to write or place a book. **desks.**

dessert

food such as pie, cake, ice cream, or fruit served at the end of a meal. **desserts.**

destroy

to wreck; break into pieces; ruin: *The earthquake destroyed the house.* **destroyed, destroying.**

detail

a small part; a part that is not important: *Her letter reported the details of the accident.* **details.**

detective

a police officer or other person whose work is getting information and solving mysteries. **detectives.**

destroy—*This building was destroyed by an earthquake.*

dial (definition 1)

diamond (definition 1)

difference (definition 1)
One **difference** between an ape and a monkey is that monkeys have tails.

develop

to grow; bring or come into being: *Will a leaf develop from this bud? Red spots develop on your skin when you have measles.* **developed, developing.**

dew

the water that comes from the air and collects in small drops on cool surfaces during the night.

dial

1. the front part, or face, of a measuring instrument. It has numbers, letters, or marks and a pointer or pointers. A radio has a dial. **2.** the part of some telephones used to call a number. **3.** to call by using a dial. **dials; dialed, dialing.**

diamond

1. a stone of very great value. **2.** a figure shaped like this: ◇. **diamonds.**

dictionary

a book that tells what words mean. The words are listed in alphabetical order. A dictionary tells the meaning and spelling of a word. **dictionaries.**

did

Did she see them yesterday? Yes, she did. You did not clean your room. I did clean my room.

didn't

did not: *He didn't go to the park with them.*

die

to stop living; become dead: *The plant died because no one watered it.* **died, dying.**

difference

1. not being alike: *One difference between an ape and a monkey is that monkeys have tails.* **2.** what is left after you subtract one number from another: *The difference between 8 and 14 is 6.* **differences.**

different

not alike; not like: *Leaves have different shapes. Basketball is different from baseball.*

difficult

hard to do or understand: *Learning to juggle is difficult for some people. This is a difficult problem.*

dig

1. to use a shovel, hands, or claws to make a hole: *The squirrel dug a hole and buried the nut.* **2.** to get by digging: *We dug clams at the beach.* **dug, digging.**

digit

any of the figures 0, 1, 2, 3, 4, 5, 6, 7, 8, 9. Sometimes 0 is not called a digit. **digits.**

dime

a coin in the United States and Canada worth 10 cents. Ten dimes make one dollar. **dimes.**

dine

to eat dinner: *He dined at a restaurant.* **dined, dining.**

dining room

a room in which dinner and other meals are served. **dining rooms.**

dinner

the main meal of the day: *We eat dinner at six o'clock.* **dinners.**

dinosaur

an animal that lived many millions of years ago. Some dinosaurs were bigger than elephants. Some were smaller than cats. No dinosaurs are alive today. **dinosaurs.**

difficult—*Learning to juggle is **difficult** for some people.*

dinosaurs

dip

1. to put something under water or any liquid and lift it out again quickly: *He dipped his hand in the bath to see if it was warm.* **2.** to drop down: *The eagle flew from its perch and dipped to the ground.* **dipped, dipping.**

direct

1. to manage; guide: *The teacher directed the class play.* **2.** straight; without stop or turn: *The library is up the street in a direct line from the museum.* **directed, directing.**

direction

the way something is moving or pointing. North, south, east, and west are directions. *In what direction does this path lead?* **directions.**

directions

something that tells you what to do, or how to do something: *She listened carefully as the policeman gave her directions to the museum.*

dirt

1. anything that is not clean. Mud and dust are dirt. Dirt soils skin, clothing, houses, or furniture. **2.** earth; soil. Flowers and vegetables are planted in dirt.

dirty

soiled by mud, dust, or anything like them; not clean: *I got dirty planting my garden.* **dirtier, dirtiest.**

disappear

1. to go out of sight: *They disappeared down the stairs to the subway.* **2.** to stop being: *Dinosaurs disappeared from the earth many, many years ago.* **disappeared, disappearing.**

directions—*She asked the officer for* **directions.**

disappoint

1. to not satisfy someone's wish or hope: *The game disappointed her because our team lost.* **2.** to not keep a promise to someone: *He disappointed me by not coming on the day he said he would.* **disappointed, disappointing.**

discover

to find out; see or learn of for the first time: *He discovered tiny insects living under the stone.* **discovered, discovering.**

discover—He **discovered** tiny insects living under the stone.

discuss

to talk over: *The class discussed what they liked best about the movie.* **discussed, discussing.**

disease

a sickness. People, animals, and plants can have diseases. Measles is a disease children sometimes get. **diseases.**

dish

1. anything to serve food in. Plates, platters, bowls, cups, and saucers are all dishes. **2.** a food that is served: *Spaghetti is a popular dish.* **dishes.**

dishonest

not honest: *A person who lies is dishonest.*

distance

the space in between two places: *The distance between the dots is an inch.* **distances.**

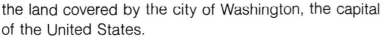

distance—The **distance** between the two dots is one inch.

District of Columbia

the land covered by the city of Washington, the capital of the United States.

disturb

1. to bother someone by talking or by being noisy: *The baby is sleeping; don't disturb her.* **2.** to make uneasy; trouble: *The news of their accident disturbed my mother.* **disturbed, disturbing.**

dive (definition 2)

ditch

a long, narrow hole dug in the ground. A ditch is usually used to carry off water. **ditches.**

dive

1. to jump with the head first into water: *She dived into the pool.* **2.** a jump like this: *He made a perfect dive and won a medal.* **dived, diving; dives.**

divide

1. to break something into equal parts: *Divide the class into four groups.* **2.** to share; give some to each person: *They divided the peanuts.* **divided, dividing.**

division

1. breaking something into equal parts: *The division of the class into teams took time.* **2.** sharing; giving some to each person: *He handled the division of the money.*

dizzy

feeling that you are going to fall or spin around; not steady: *When some people look down from a very high place, they feel dizzy.* **dizzier, dizziest.**

do

Do your arithmetic carefully. We will do the dishes. Do you like rain? What would you do? We do believe you. **does, did, done, doing.**

dock

dock

a concrete or wooden platform built at the edge of the water. Ships load and unload at a dock. **docks.**

doctor

a person who treats diseases and helps keep people healthy. **doctors.**

doe

doe

a female deer, antelope, rabbit, or hare. **does.**

does

He does his work quickly. Does she skate well?

doesn't

does not: *She doesn't own a pet.*

dog

an animal with four legs and fur, often kept as a pet. Dogs are also used to help in hunting, or for guarding property. **dogs.**

doghouse

a small shelter for a dog. **doghouses.**

doll

a toy that looks like a baby, a child, or a grown person. **dolls.**

doll

dollar

an amount of money in the United States and Canada. A dollar is equal to 100 cents. $1.00 means one dollar. A dollar bill is made of paper. **dollars.**

dolphin

a sea animal much like a small whale. **dolphins.**

dolphins

done

She has done her homework. What has he done?

donkey

an animal somewhat like a small horse but with longer ears. **donkeys.**

don't

do not: *Don't be late for dinner. They don't want to come with us.*

door

1. a part that moves to close an opening in a wall, cabinet, car, and the like. **2.** an opening in a wall; doorway. **doors.**

doorbell

a bell you ring as a signal that you want someone to open the door. **doorbells.**

dose

doorway

an opening in a wall where a door is. **doorways.**

dose

a certain amount of medicine taken at one time: *Mom gave me a dose of cough medicine.* **doses.**

dot

1. a tiny, round mark: *Put a dot on your map to show where a city is.* **2.** a small spot: *I wore a green shirt with white dots.* **3.** to mark with a dot: *Dot the letter "i."* **dots; dotted, dotting.**

double

1. twice as much, as large, or as strong: *He got double pay for working on a holiday.* **2.** to make or become twice as much: *The baby puppy doubled in size in only a few months.* **doubled, doubling.**

doubt

1. to not be sure; not believe: *He doubted that the team could win.* **2.** being without belief; feeling uncertain: *His doubts about the team disappeared when they won easily.* **doubted, doubting; doubts.**

doughnut

a small, sweet cake usually made in the shape of a ring. **doughnuts.**

dove

a bird with a thick body and short legs. **doves.**

dove

down[1]

to a lower place; in a lower place: *They ran down the stairs. The dog was down in the basement.*

down[2]

soft feathers: *Baby chickens are covered with down.*

downstairs

1. down the stairs: *They ran downstairs.* **2.** on or to a lower floor: *I live upstairs, and she lives downstairs.*

dozen

12; group of 12: *We needed dozens of cookies for the bake sale. I sold three dozen cookies.* **dozens** or (after a number) **dozen.**

Dr.

Doctor: *Her doctor's name is Dr. J. T. Jones.* **Drs.**

drag

to pull or move along slowly; pull along the ground: *She dragged the big box to the car.* **dragged, dragging.**

dragon

in stories, a huge, fierce animal that was said to look like a lizard with wings, scales, and claws. Dragons are supposed to breathe out fire and smoke. **dragons.**

dragon—*This piece of jewelry is in the shape of a* **dragon.**

dragonfly

a large insect with a long, thin body and two pairs of wings. It flies about rapidly to catch flies, mosquitoes, and other insects. **dragonflies.**

drain

1. to empty; draw water or other liquid from: *The baby drained his bottle.* **2.** a pipe for carrying off water or waste: *The bathtub drain is clogged.* **drained, draining; drains.**

drank

We drank all the lemonade in a few minutes.

draw

1. to make a picture of anything with pen, pencil, or chalk: *Draw a picture of your favorite animal.* **2.** to pull out; pull up; take out: *Each player draws one card from the pile.* **3.** to pull; drag: *The pony can draw the cart.* **drew, drawn, drawing.**

drawer

a box with handles, built to slide in and out of a table, desk, or dresser. **drawers.**

dragonfly

drawn

The pony has drawn the cart before. Has he drawn a card yet? She had drawn a picture of her cat.

dream

1. something thought, felt, or seen during sleep: *He had a scary dream.* **2.** to think, feel, hear, or see during sleep: *I dreamed I won a million dollars.* **dreams; dreamed, dreaming.**

dreary

dull; gloomy: *A cloudy winter day is a dreary day.* **drearier, dreariest.**

dreary—*It was a **dreary** day.*

dress

1. a piece of clothing worn by women and girls. **2.** to put clothes on: *My little brother can dress himself.* **dresses; dressed, dressing.**

dresser

a piece of furniture with drawers for clothes and sometimes a mirror. **dressers.**

dresser

drew

She drew a picture. The pony drew the cart.

drift

1. to be carried along by currents of air or water: *We stopped rowing and the boat drifted.* **2.** to be heaped up by the wind: *The wind drifted the snow.* **3.** snow or sand heaped up by the wind: *After days of snow, big drifts blocked the road.* **drifted, drifting; drifts.**

drill

1. a tool or machine for boring holes. **2.** to bore a hole in something: *I drilled a hole in the wall.* **3.** to teach by having someone do a thing over and over: *The teacher drilled the class in subtraction.* **drills; drilled, drilling.**

drink

1. to swallow anything liquid, such as water or milk: *I drink a glass of milk with every meal.* **2.** a liquid swallowed or to be swallowed: *Lemonade is a good drink on a hot day.* **drank, drunk, drinking; drinks.**

drip

to fall or let fall in drops: *Rain dripped from the roof.* **dripped, dripping.**

drive

1. to make a car, bus, or truck go: *My sister is learning to drive a car.* **2.** to go or carry in a car or bus: *The bus drives us to school.* **drove, driven, driving.**

driven

She has driven us to school every day.

driver

a person who drives an automobile or something like it. **drivers.**

driveway

a road leading from a house or garage to the street. **driveways.**

driveway

droop

to hang down; bend down: *These flowers will soon droop if they are not put in water. The worker's shoulders drooped in the hot sun.* **drooped, drooping.**

drop

1. a small amount of liquid in a round shape. **2.** to fall or let something fall: *He dropped the box on the floor.* **3.** to leave out: *Drop the "e" in "hope" before adding "ing."* **drops; dropped, dropping.**

drove

He drove us to the party.

drop (definition 3)

drug

1. a kind of medicine used to treat sickness.
2. something that can make harmful changes in a person's body. Caffeine is a drug that can make your heart beat faster than it should. **drugs.**

druggist

a person who sells drugs and other medicines in a drugstore. **druggists.**

drugstore

a store that sells drugs, medicines, and other things such as film and magazines. **drugstores.**

drum

a musical instrument that makes a sound when it is beaten. A drum is hollow with a cover stretched tight over each end. **drums.**

drum

drummer

a person who plays a drum. **drummers.**

drunk

The dog has drunk all the water in her bowl.

dry

1. not wet; not damp: *Be sure the paint is dry before you sit down.* **2.** to make or become dry: *Dry your hands on a clean towel.* **3.** having little or no rain: *A desert is a hot, dry place.* **drier, driest; dried, drying.**

dryer

a machine that removes water by heat or air. **dryers.**

duck¹

a wild or tame swimming bird with a flat bill, short neck, and short legs. **ducks.**

ducks¹

duck²

to lower the head or bend the body quickly to keep from being hit or seen: *He ducked and the snowball missed him.* **ducked, ducking.**

dug

We dug a ditch. We have dug a hole for the new tree.

dull

1. not sharp or pointed: *Her dull scissors will not cut the cardboard.* **2.** not interesting; boring: *The book was dull; none of the characters did anything.* **duller, dullest.**

dumb

1. not able to speak: *Even the smartest animals are dumb.* **2.** not smart; silly: *Leaving your coat at the park was a dumb thing to do.* **dumber, dumbest.**

dump

to empty out; throw down: *The boys dumped the trash in the garbage can.* **dumped, dumping.**

during

They talked all during the movie. Call at any time during the morning.

dust

1. fine, dry dirt: *The wind covered the porch with dust.* **2.** to get dust off; brush or wipe dust from: *We dusted all the furniture.* **dusted, dusting.**

dust (definition 1)
*Jackie Robinson slid in a cloud of **dust** and was called out at the plate.*

dusty

covered with dust; filled with dust: *Throw out those dusty old newspapers.* **dustier, dustiest.**

duty

1. the thing that is right to do; what a person ought to do: *It is your duty to obey school rules.* **2.** the thing that someone must do at work: *The duty of the crossing guard is to get children safely across the street.* **duties.**

dwarf

1. a person, animal, or plant that is much smaller than the usual size of its kind. **2.** in fairy tales, an ugly little man with magic powers. **dwarfs.**

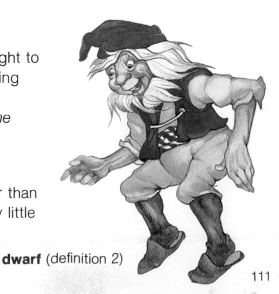

dwarf (definition 2)

E e

each

Each child was invited to the party. Each of them brought a gift. The prizes were fifty cents each.

eager

wanting very much: *The children were eager for the puppet show to begin.*

eagle

eagle

a large bird that can see far and fly far. The eagle is the symbol of the United States. **eagles.**

ear[1]

the part of the body that people and animals use to hear with. **ears.**

ear[2]

the part of certain plants where the grain grows: *We bought six ears of corn at the market.* **ears.**

eardrum

a thin piece of skin inside your ear. It vibrates when sound waves strike it. The sounds are sent to the hearing part of your brain. **eardrums.**

early

1. near the beginning of something: *Early in the school year, the children didn't know each other very well.*
2. before the usual time: *She got up early yesterday morning.* **earlier, earliest.**

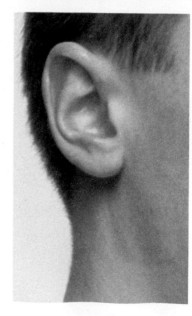
ear[1]

earn

to get money for the work you do: *She earns ten dollars a week for delivering newspapers.* **earned, earning.**

earth

1. the planet we live on. The earth moves around the sun. **2.** the ground: *The earth in the garden was soft enough for planting flowers.*

earth

earthquake

a shaking or sliding of the ground. An earthquake is caused by rocks beneath the earth's surface moving suddenly. Earthquakes can destroy a lot of things. **earthquakes.**

easily

without trying hard: *The boy was strong enough to lift the table easily.*

east

the direction of the sunrise. East is the opposite of west.

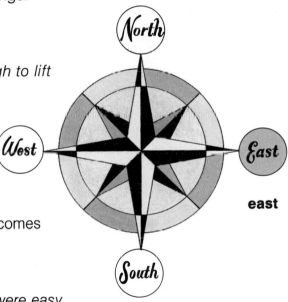

east

Easter

a holiday celebrated by some people. Easter comes once a year on a Sunday in the spring.

easy

not hard to do or understand: *The directions were easy to follow. The question was easy to answer.* **easier, easiest.**

eat

1. to chew and swallow food: *Babies do not eat the same foods as their parents.* **2.** to have a meal: *He went to eat at his friend's house.* **ate, eaten, eating.**

eaten

Have you eaten lunch yet?

echo

a sound that comes back to you so that you hear it again. You hear an echo when a sound bounces back from a hill or a wall. **echoes.**

echo

edge

1. the line or place where something ends: *He parked at the edge of the road.* **2.** the thin side of something that cuts: *The knife has a sharp edge.* **edges.**

education

the facts and skills we learn when we go to school: *We want all children in the United States to get an education.*

effect

something that happens because of something else: *One effect of the heavy snow was the great number of people riding on sleds.* **effects.**

egg

1. something that is laid by female birds, fish, and reptiles. Their young are hatched from eggs. **2.** the inside of an egg, used as food: *She had scrambled eggs for breakfast.* **eggs.**

eggs

eight

one more than seven; 8. Four and four equals eight. **eights.**

eighteen

eight more than ten; 18. **eighteens.**

eighteenth

1. next after the seventeenth; 18th. **2.** one of 18 equal parts. **eighteenths.**

eighth
1. next after the seventh; 8th. **2.** one of 8 equal parts. **eighths.**

eighty
ten more than seventy; 80. **eighties.**

either
Choose either of these toys to give to the baby. Either come in or go out. There are lights on either side of the driveway. If you don't go, she won't go either.

elbow
the part of the arm that bends; the joint in the middle of the arm. **elbows.**

elect
to choose by voting: *Every four years we elect a President.* **elected, electing.**

electric
run by electricity: *He turned on the electric toaster.*

electrician
a person who fixes electric wires, lights, motors, and anything run by electricity. **electricians.**

electricity
a kind of energy that makes light and heat, and that runs motors. Electricity makes light bulbs shine, radios and televisions play, and cars start.

elephant
the largest four-footed animal. Elephants have large ears and long trunks. **elephants.**

elevator
1. a machine that carries people or things up or down in a building. It is like a small room with a door in front. **2.** a very tall building for storing grain. **elevators.**

Either come in or close the door!

either

elevator² (definition 2)

elf

elk

elm

eleven

one more than ten; 11. **elevens.**

eleventh

1. next after the tenth; 11th. **2.** one of 11 equal parts. **elevenths.**

elf

in stories, a tiny make-believe person that is full of mischief. **elves.**

elk

a large deer. **elk.**

elm

a tall shade tree with high, spreading branches. **elms.**

else

What else do you want to eat? Do you expect anyone else? What else could he do?

emergency

a time when you need to do something right away: *In an emergency, dial the operator.* **emergencies.**

empty

1. with nothing inside: *She finished her cereal and left the empty bowl in the sink.* **2.** to pour out or take out all that is in something: *He emptied the trash into the truck.* **3.** to flow out: *The river empties into the ocean.* **emptier, emptiest; emptied, emptying.**

end

1. the last part; part where a thing begins or stops: *A rope has two ends. We read to the end of the story.* **2.** to finish something: *The girls ended their fight when their mother entered the room.* **ends; ended, ending.**

enemy

1. a person or a group of people that is against you or wishes to harm you: *When two countries fight each other, they are enemies.* **2.** anything that will do harm: *Pollution is our enemy.* **enemies.**

energy

1. one's power to work or move or play: *Children have so much energy they can't sit still.* **2.** the power to do work, such as lifting or moving an object. Light, heat, and electricity are different forms of energy.

engine

1. a machine that does work or makes something move. Many engines are run by gas or electricity. **2.** the machine that pulls a railroad train. **engines.**

engineer

1. the person who runs a railroad engine. **2.** a person who plans and builds machines, roads, bridges, and buildings. **engineers.**

engine (definition 2)

English

1. the people of England. **2.** the language of England: *English is spoken in the United States.*

enjoy

to be happy with; take pleasure in: *The children enjoyed their visit to the park.* **enjoyed, enjoying.**

enormous

enormous

very, very large: *The hippopotamus at the zoo was enormous.*

enough

as much or as many as you need: *Are there enough sandwiches for all of us? He has had enough to eat. They have been gone long enough.*

entrance

enter

1. to go into; come into: *People waved to him as he entered the room.* **2.** to join; become a member of something: *She entered the contest to win the prize.* **entered, entering.**

entrance

a place where you go in: *We met at the main entrance of the building.* **entrances.**

entry

a place to enter: *We waited in the entry of the apartment for the package to arrive.* **entries.**

entry word

something written or printed in a book or a list. Each word listed alphabetically in this dictionary is an entry word. **entry words.**

envelope

a folded paper cover. An envelope is used to mail a letter or something else that is flat. **envelopes.**

environment

environment

everything in the world that surrounds a living thing: *Plants grow better in an environment where there is enough light and water.* **environments.**

equal

1. the same in size, number, or amount: *Five pennies are equal to one nickel. The two dogs are equal in size.* **2.** to be the same as something else: *Five plus four equals nine.* **equaled, equaling.**

equator

a line on a map or globe that shows where the middle of the earth is. The equator is between the North Pole and the South Pole. The weather at the equator is the warmest weather in the world.

equator

erase

to rub out; wipe out: *He erased his wrong answer and wrote in the right one.* **erased, erasing.**

eraser

something used to rub out marks made with pencil, ink, or chalk: *The teacher bought a new eraser for the chalkboard.* **erasers.**

escalator

a set of moving stairs. You can go from one floor to another by standing on one step and riding up or down. **escalators.**

escape

1. to get free; get out and away: *The hamster escaped from its cage.* **2.** getting away: *His escape was made at night.* **escaped, escaping; escapes.**

Eskimo

one of the people who live on the northern shores of Alaska and Canada. **Eskimos.**

estimate

1. a guess about how much or how many. An estimate is made from what you already know. *The painter gave an estimate of how much it would cost to paint the house.* **2.** to guess about how much or how many, using what you already know: *She estimated the answer to the addition problem.* **estimates; estimated, estimating.**

Eskimos

evaporate

to change from a liquid into a gas: *Boiling water evaporates quickly.* **evaporated, evaporating.**

eve

the evening or day before some holiday or special day: *We plan to have a party on New Year's Eve.* **eves.**

even (definition 3)

evergreens (definition 2)

even

1. flat; smooth: *The edges of the paper are even.* **2.** at the same level: *The roof is even with the tops of the trees.* **3.** able to be divided by two with none left over: *Two, four, six, and eight are even numbers.*

evening

the part of the day between afternoon and nighttime: *Last evening we stayed up late.* **evenings.**

event

something important that happens: *The visit from the President was an exciting event.* **events.**

ever

Is he ever at home? When will she ever get here?

evergreen

1. having green leaves all year long. Pines are evergreen trees. **2.** a plant that has green leaves all year long. **evergreens.**

every

Every child needs to bring his books to class. Every morning we fix our own breakfast.

everybody

Everybody likes the new principal. Ask everybody to be quiet.

everyone

Everyone got to school on time yesterday. She wanted everyone she knew to come to the party.

everything

She did everything she could to help. He got everything he wanted for his birthday.

everywhere

I looked everywhere for my gloves. Everywhere we went we met people we knew.

exact

without any mistake; no more and no less: *Mom gave the waiter the exact amount for our bill.*

exactly

without any mistake; just the right way: *He followed my directions exactly. He looks exactly like his twin.*

example

1. something that shows what other things should be like: *She is an example of a good student.* **2.** a problem in math: *He wrote the example on the board.* **examples.**

excellent

very, very good; better than others: *An excellent story was printed in this month's magazine.*

except

The store is open every day except Sunday. Except for one question, I had all the answers correct.

exchange

to give something to someone in return for something else: *He exchanged the shoes he bought for a pair in a different size. We exchanged papers so we could check our answers.* **exchanged, exchanging.**

excited

having very strong, happy feelings about something that you like: *We were excited about the circus coming to town.*

excitement

strong, happy feelings about something that you like: *My aunt's having twins caused great excitement in our family.*

exciting

able to cause strong, happy feelings: *It was an exciting game because the score was so close.*

exactly—*The paper dolls look* **exactly** *alike.*

exchange

exclaim

to cry out with strong feelings: *"Oh, no!" she exclaimed as she dropped her ice-cream cone on the sidewalk.* **exclaimed, exclaiming.**

exclamation

something yelled out: *Her exclamation surprised him.* **exclamations.**

excuse

1. to give a reason for: *He excused his mistakes by saying he was tired.* **2.** a reason you give to explain something you said or did: *He had a good excuse for coming home late.* **3.** to forgive: *Please excuse me; I have to go now.* **excused, excusing; excuses.**

exercise

1. moving the body to make it strong, and to improve health: *Exercise helps to build strong muscles.* **2.** to move the body in this way: *If you exercise often, you can work and play longer.* **3.** something that helps develop a skill: *The athlete does exercises every day. After I study, I do the exercises at the end of the chapter.* **exercises** (for **3.**); **exercised, exercising.**

exhibit

1. to show in public: *She exhibited her paintings at the museum.* **2.** something shown in public: *I have an exhibit at the science fair.* **exhibited, exhibiting; exhibits.**

exit

1. a way out: *Our school has eight exits.* **2.** to go out; leave: *Please exit by the doors at the back of the room.* **exits; exited, exiting.**

expect

to think something will probably come or happen: *We expect it to rain tomorrow.* **expected, expecting.**

exercise (definition 2)

ex... ...efinition 2)

expensive

costing a lot of money: *His mother bought him an expensive sweater for his birthday.*

experiment

1. to test or try something out: *The cook experimented with a new recipe.* **2.** a test to find out something: *We do experiments in science class.* **experimented, experimenting; experiments.**

explain

to tell about something so that people are able to understand it: *The teacher explained the instructions to the test. He explained why he couldn't make it to the meeting.* **explained, explaining.**

explore

1. to travel to discover new areas: *Astronauts want to explore outer space.* **2.** to go over a place carefully; examine: *The children explored the new playground.* **explored, exploring.**

expressway

a highway, usually without traffic lights. Expressways are used for traveling long distances at high speed. **expressways.**

extra

more than what is usual, expected, or needed: *We asked for extra milk for our cereal.*

eye

1. the part of the body that people and animals use to see with. **2.** something like an eye: *I put my thread through the eye of the needle.* **eyes.**

human eye   owl's eye   goat's eye   cat's eye

eye (definition 1)

F f

fable

a story that teaches a lesson. Many fables are about animals that talk. **fables.**

face

1. the front part of the head. Your eyes, nose, and mouth are parts of your face. **2.** to have the front toward: *The house faces the street.* **faces; faced, facing.**

fact

a thing that is known to be true: *It is a fact that the Pilgrims came to America in 1620.* **facts.**

factory

a building or group of buildings where people make things. A factory usually has machines in it. **factories.**

fade

1. to lose color or cause to lose color: *My blue jeans faded after they were washed. Sunlight faded the curtains.* **2.** to disappear slowly: *The noise faded away after the jet took off.* **faded, fading.**

fail

1. to not be able to do something; not succeed: *He tried to win the race, but he failed.* **2.** to not do what should be done: *She failed to follow the directions.* **failed, failing.**

fable—*We read the* **fable** *about the fox and the grapes.*

faint

1. not clear or plain; weak: *His faint voice showed how tired he was.* **2.** to suddenly fall down and not be awake. A person who faints is not able to feel or think for a short time. **fainter, faintest; fainted, fainting.**

fair¹

going by the rules; treating everyone the same: *Try to be fair in everything you do.* **fairer, fairest.**

fair²

1. an outdoor show of farm animals and other things: *We enjoyed ourselves at the county fair.* **2.** a sale of some kind: *Our school held a fair to raise money for new library books.* **fairs.**

fairly

in a fair way: *He won the game fairly.*

fairy

in stories, a tiny, make-believe person who can help or harm people. **fairies.**

fall

1. to drop or come down from a higher place: *Leaves fall from the trees.* **2.** dropping from a higher place: *She had a bad fall down the stairs.* **3.** the season of the year between summer and winter. Fall is the season when the harvest takes place. Another word for fall is autumn. **fell, fallen, falling; falls.**

fall (definition 3)
Leaves change color in the fall.

fallen

She has fallen off the swing.

false

not true; not correct; wrong: *What he said is false.*

family

1. a father, mother, and their children. The people who you live with and who take care of you are your family. **2.** all of a person's relatives: *Grandmother invited the family for Thanksgiving dinner.* **families.**

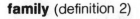

family (definition 2)

famous

very well known; important: *The famous singer was met by a large crowd at the airport.*

fan

1. a machine that blows the air around.
2. a thing, often made of paper, held in the hand and waved to stir the air. **fans.**

fan
(definition 2)

fancy

not plain: *She will wear a fancy dress with ruffles.* **fancier, fanciest.**

far

a long way: *The moon is far from the earth.* **farther, farthest.**

fare

the money that a person pays to ride in a bus, taxi, subway, or the like. **fares.**

fare—*He is paying the bus fare.*

farm

1. the land on which a person grows food and raises animals. **2.** to raise crops or animals to eat or to sell: *My family has farmed for years.* **farms; farmed, farming.**

farmer

a person who raises crops or animals on a farm. **farmers.**

farther

My house is farther from school than your house is.

farthest

In the race my sister ran farthest of all.

fast

taking very little time; quick; swift: *He is a fast runner. Airplanes go fast.* **faster, fastest.**

fasten

to tie, lock, or make hold together: *Please fasten your seat belt before I start the car.* **fastened, fastening.**

fat

weighing more than usual: *That dog is too fat.* **fatter, fattest.**

fat

father

a man who has a child or children. **fathers.**

faucet

something for turning on or off a flow of water from a pipe. **faucets.**

fault

something that is not as it should be or is a cause for blame: *Talking too much is my greatest fault.* **faults.**

favor

a kind act: *He asked me to do him a favor and help him move the heavy box.* **favors.**

favorite

1. liked better than others: *What is your favorite flower?* **2.** a person or thing that you like very much: *Pizza is a favorite with me.* **favorites.**

favorite (definition 1)
*Her **favorite** flower is the rose.*

fawn

a deer that is less than a year old. **fawns.**

fear

1. a feeling that danger or something bad is near: *I have a fear of high places.* **2.** to be afraid of: *We feared the storm that was coming.* **fears; feared, fearing.**

fawn

feast

1. a big meal for some special occasion and for a number of guests: *We had a feast on Thanksgiving Day.* **2.** to eat a big meal; eat well: *We feasted on turkey and pumpkin pie.* **feasts; feasted, feasting.**

feather

feather

one of the light, soft things that cover a bird's body. **feathers.**

February

the second month of the year. It has 28 days, except in every fourth year when it has 29 days. February comes after January and before March.

fed

I fed the dogs. Dad has fed them too.

feed

1. to give food to: *I helped feed the baby.* **2.** to eat: *Cows feed on hay.* **fed, feeding.**

feel (definition 1)
***Feel** this smooth stone.*

feel

1. to touch or to find out by touching: *Feel this smooth stone.* **2.** to be a certain way; have in your mind: *She feels sad. He feels angry.* **felt, feeling.**

feeling

1. the sense of touch. By feeling we know that a stone is hard. **2.** how you feel about something; a state of mind. Joy, fear, and love are feelings. **feelings** (for **2.**).

feet

more than one foot: *I have two feet. Bill is four feet tall.*

fell

She fell on her knees.

fellow

a man or boy: *The old fellow sat on a bench.* **fellows.**

felt

The baby felt the cat's soft fur. Mom felt better today.

female

the kind of person or animal that can give birth, or that can lay eggs. Women and girls are females. A hen is a female chicken. **females.**

fellow

fence

something put around a yard, garden, or field to keep people or animals out or in. A fence also shows where the end of a yard is. Most fences are made of wood, wire, or metal. **fences.**

fern

a kind of plant that has only roots, stems, and leaves, but no flowers or seeds. **ferns.**

fern

ferry

a boat that carries people and things across water. **ferries.**

fever

a body temperature that is higher than normal. When you are sick with a bad cold, a thermometer may show that you have a fever. **fevers.**

ferry

few

not many; a small number: *Few people came to the meeting. Pick the ripe apples and take a few to your grandparents.* **fewer, fewest.**

fiction

a story that is not true: *Our library has many books of fiction.*

field

a piece of land without trees, used to grow crops or for some other special purpose: *The corn field lay behind the barn. The baseball field is only two blocks away.* **fields.**

fierce

dangerous; very great or strong: *A fierce lion roared in the jungle.* **fiercer, fiercest.**

fife

a small musical instrument like a flute, played by blowing. Fifes are used with drums to make music for marching. **fifes.**

fife

fifteen

five more than ten; 15. **fifteens.**

fifteenth

1. next after the 14th; 15th. **2.** one of 15 equal parts. **fifteenths.**

fifth

1. next after the fourth; 5th. **2.** one of five equal parts. **fifths.**

fifty

ten more than forty; 50. **fifties.**

fig

fig

a small, soft, sweet fruit that grows on a tree. Fig trees grow in warm places. **figs.**

fight

1. an angry battle between people; quarrel: *Without rules, the game turned into a fight.* **2.** to take part in a battle or quarrel: *The kids fought over who was going to take the garbage out.* **fights; fought, fighting.**

figure (definition 1)

figure

1. the form or shape of a human body: *In the dark I thought I saw a figure of someone outside the window.* **2.** to use numbers to find out the answer to some problem: *Can you figure out the cost of building a doghouse?* **figures; figured, figuring.**

file¹

1. to put things away in a certain order: *Please file those letters.* **2.** to march or move in a row, one behind another: *The pupils filed out of the auditorium.* **filed, filing.**

file²

1. a tool with many small teeth on it. A file is used to make things smooth. **2.** to smooth or wear away with a file: *My sister uses a nail file to file her nails.* **files; filed, filing.**

file² (definition 1)

fill

to make something so full that there is no more room: *Fill this glass with milk. All the rooms in the hospital were filled.* **filled, filling.**

filling

a thing put in to fill something: *I have fillings in two of my teeth.* **fillings.**

film

1. something used in a camera to take photographs.
2. a movie: *We saw a film about dogs.* **films** (for **2.**).

fin

one of the parts of a fish's body. A fish can swim by moving its fins. **fins.**

fin

final

at the end; coming last: *December 31 is the final day of the year.*

finally

at the end; at last: *Our team finally won a game.*

find

1. to come upon something; look for and get: *He finds friends everywhere. Did you find your hat?* **2.** to learn; discover: *Find the answer to the first problem.* **found, finding.**

fine¹

very good; excellent: *He cooked a fine meal. She was sick last week, but now she feels fine.* **finer, finest.**

fine²

1. money that someone has to pay as punishment for breaking a law: *Mom had to pay a fine for speeding.*
2. to make someone pay money in this way: *The judge fined him for going through a red light.* **fines; fined, fining.**

find (definition 1)
*See, I did **find** my hat!*

131

fir

firefly

finger

1. one of the five end parts of the hand. **2.** to touch or handle with the fingers: *I fingered the keys of the trumpet.* **fingers; fingered, fingering.**

finish

to get to the end of something; complete: *Finish your dinner before you go.* **finished, finishing.**

fir

a tree with evergreen leaves shaped like needles. Fir trees have cones. **firs.**

fire

the flame, heat, and light caused by something burning: *We built a fire to keep warm.* **fires.**

fire engine

a special truck that can pump water to put out fires; a fire truck. **fire engines.**

firefighter

a person whose work is putting out fires. Another word for firefighter is fireman. **firefighters.**

firefly

a small insect that gives off flashes of light when it flies at night. **fireflies.**

firehouse

a building where fire engines are kept. **firehouses.**

fireman

a person whose work is putting out fires. Another word for fireman is firefighter. **firemen.**

fireplace

a place built to hold a fire. **fireplaces.**

fire truck

a special truck that can pump water to put out fires; a fire engine. **fire trucks.**

fireworks

things that make a loud noise or go up high in the air and burst into a shower of stars and sparks.

firm

1. solid; not moving: *We made sure the ground was firm underneath before we put up the tent.* **2.** strong: *My teacher spoke in a firm voice.* **firmer, firmest.**

first

1. coming before all others: *I am in the first row.* **2.** a person, thing, or place that is first: *We were the first to get here.*

first aid

emergency care that someone gives to a hurt or sick person before a doctor sees the person.

fish

1. a group of animals that live in water. Fish are usually covered with scales and have fins for swimming. **2.** fish used for food: *We had fish for supper last night.* **3.** to catch or try to catch fish: *We fished from the boat.* **fish** (for **1.**)**; fished, fishing.**

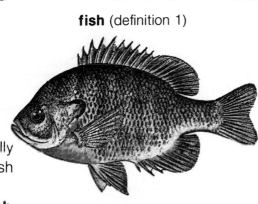

fish (definition 1)

fisherman

a person whose job is catching fish. **fishermen.**

fist

a tightly closed hand: *He held a coin in his fist.* **fists.**

fist

fit¹

1. healthy and strong: *Exercise helps keep us fit.* **2.** to have the right size or shape: *My shoes don't quite fit; they are too small.* **fitter, fittest; fitted, fitting.**

fit²

a sudden, short period of doing or feeling something: *The girls had a fit of laughing.* **fits.**

five

one more than four; 5. **fives.**

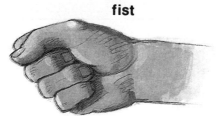

fit¹ (definition 1)
Exercise keeps him fit.

flag

flap

fix
1. to put in good shape again; repair: *Can he fix a watch?* **2.** to make; prepare: *We fixed our own breakfast today.* **3.** to put in order; arrange: *Fix your hair.* **fixed, fixing.**

flag
a piece of colored cloth with stars or other symbols on it. Every country and state has its own flag. **flags.**

flagpole
a pole that a flag flies from. **flagpoles.**

flame
the part of a fire that you can see shoot up into the air: *We could see the flames above the roof of the burning building.* **flames.**

flap
to swing or sway loosely and with some noise; move the wings or arms up and down: *The boat's sails flapped in the wind. The duck flapped its wings before flying away.* **flapped, flapping.**

flash
1. a light or flame that lasts only a short time: *I just saw a flash of lightning.* **2.** to give out such a light or flame: *The light flashed on and off.* **flashes; flashed, flashing.**

flashlight
a small light that can be carried. A flashlight runs on batteries. **flashlights.**

flat
1. smooth and even; level: *The land around the edge of the lake is flat.* **2.** not having enough air inside it: *Mom drove over some broken glass and got a flat tire.* **flatter, flattest.**

flatland
level land. Flatland has no hills or valleys. **flatlands.**

flavor

the special taste a food has: *Chocolate is her favorite flavor.* **flavors.**

flew

The bird flew away. We flew to New York on our vacation.

flight

1. moving through the air with wings: *We watched the flight of the bird.* **2.** a trip in an aircraft: *His flight left at noon.* **flights.**

flip

1. to spin in the air; turn over: *The man flipped a coin.* **2.** a spinning in the air: *I did two flips in a row.* **flipped, flipping; flips.**

flip (definition 2)
*She can do a **flip**.*

float

1. to move slowly on top of the water or in the air. Corks and balloons will float. **2.** a low, flat car that carries something to show in a parade: *The beautiful float was covered with flowers.* **floated, floating; floats.**

float (definition 2)

flock

1. a group of animals of the same kind: *A flock of geese landed near the pond.* **2.** to stay in a group: *The sheep flocked together.* **flocks; flocked, flocking.**

flock (definition 1)

flood

1. a great amount of water over what is usually dry land: *We had a flood in the backyard.* **2.** to cover or fill with water: *Water flooded the streets.* **floods; flooded, flooding.**

floor

1. the part of a room that you walk on: *She picked her pencil up off the floor.* **2.** one of the stories of a building: *We live on the tenth floor.* **floors.**

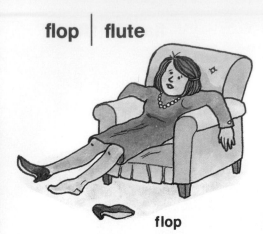

flop

flop

to drop or fall down in a heavy way: *Mother was so tired she flopped into a chair.* **flopped, flopping.**

Florida

one of the fifty states of the United States.

floss

1. a special thread used to clean between the teeth. **2.** to use this special thread: *I flossed my teeth this morning.* **flossed, flossing.**

flour

the fine powder or meal made by grinding wheat or other grain. Flour is used to make bread, cakes, and pies.

flow

1. to run like water; move in a stream: *Most rivers flow toward the ocean.* **2.** a stream; current: *There is a heavy flow of water down this hill every time it rains.* **flowed, flowing.**

flower

a part of a plant or tree that produces the seed. Flowers often have beautiful colors and shapes. **flowers.**

flown

She has flown in an airplane many times.

flu

a disease much like a very bad cold. Flu is caused by a virus.

fluffy

covered with soft, light feathers or hair: *The baby chicks were fluffy.* **fluffier, fluffiest.**

flute

flute

a metal musical instrument that is played by blowing into it and pressing keys. **flutes.**

fly¹

an insect with two wings. **flies.**

fly¹

fly²

1. to move through the air with wings: *Some birds fly south for the winter.* **2.** to float or cause to float in the air: *The boys are flying kites.* **3.** to travel by aircraft: *We flew to Hawaii.* **flew, flown, flying.**

fog

a cloud of fine drops of water that floats in the air just above the ground

fold

1. to bend or turn part of a thing over another part: *Fold the letter before you mail it.* **2.** a mark or line made by doing this: *Cut the paper along the fold.* **folded, folding; folds.**

folk tale

an old story that has been told for many years by many people. **folk tales.**

folk tale—*He told a **folk tale** about Jack and his beanstalk.*

follow

1. to go or come after: *Let's follow him. Tuesday follows Monday.* **2.** to go along: *Follow this path.* **3.** to use; obey; take as a guide: *Follow the directions.* **followed, following.**

fond

liking very much: *He is fond of animals. I am fond of milk.* **fonder, fondest.**

food

anything that living things eat or drink. Food makes them live and grow, and gives them energy. **foods.**

food group

a group of certain kinds of foods. The foods you need to be healthy come from different food groups. Fruits and vegetables are one food group. **food groups.**

fond

football (definition 2)

fool

to joke about or pretend to do something; trick: *I was only fooling. Don't try to fool me.* **fooled, fooling.**

foot

1. the part of the body at the end of the leg; part that a person, animal, or thing stands on. **2.** a unit of length equal to 12 inches. A ruler is one foot long. **feet.**

football

1. a game played on a field by two teams. Each team tries to kick, throw, or carry a ball past the other team's goal. **2.** the ball used in this game. **footballs** (for **2.**).

footstep

the sound of a person's steps: *I heard footsteps on the stairs.* **footsteps.**

for

He gave me a dime for two nickels. Here is a pot for the stew. We talked for a minute.

force

1. power: *The car struck the tree with force.*
2. something that brings about, changes, or stops the motion of something else. A push or a pull against something sitting still is a force. The force of a magnet draws iron or steel toward it. **forces** (for **2.**).

force (definition 2)
*The **force** of a magnet draws iron or steel toward it.*

forehead

the part of the face above the eyes. **foreheads.**

forest

a large area with many tall trees; thick woods: *Many animals live in the forest.* **forests.**

forever

always; all the time: *He's forever asking questions.*

forget

to be unable to remember: *Don't forget to wear your gloves.* **forgot, forgotten, forgetting.**

forehead

forgive

to not have angry feelings toward: *She forgave me for losing her scarf.* **forgave, forgiven, forgiving.**

forgot

I forgot to thank her.

forgotten

She has never forgotten to thank me.

fork

something to eat with, with two or more sharp points. A fork is used to lift solid food from a plate or dish to your mouth. **forks.**

fork

form

1. a shape. Circles and squares are forms. **2.** a kind; sort. Ice is a form of water. **3.** to take shape; become: *Clouds form in the sky.* **forms; formed, forming.**

form (definition 1)
*Squares, triangles, and circles are **forms.***

fort

a strong building that an enemy army cannot get into easily. **forts.**

fort

fortune

1. a great deal of money or property: *The miner made a fortune when he discovered gold.* **2.** luck; what happens or is going to happen: *Good fortune helped us to be the winning team.* **fortunes.**

forty

ten more than thirty; 40. **forties.**

forward

ahead; to the front; near the front: *The cafeteria line moved forward.*

fossil

a part or print of a plant or animal that lived a long time ago. Fossils are found in rock or ice. Fossils of the bones of dinosaurs that lived many millions of years ago have been dug up in North America. **fossils.**

fossil

fountain

fought

The puppies fought over the bones.

found

I found a dime. The cat has found her way home.

fountain

water that rises into the air in a stream: *People stopped to admire the beautiful fountain. The drinking fountain is over there.* **fountains.**

four

one more than three; 4. **fours.**

fourteen

four more than ten; 14. **fourteens.**

fourteenth

1. next after the 13th; 14th. **2.** one of 14 equal parts. **fourteenths.**

fourth

1. next after the third; 4th. **2.** one of four equal parts. **fourths.**

fox

fox

a wild animal that looks something like a dog. A fox has a pointed nose, thick fur, and a bushy tail. **foxes.**

fraction

a part of a whole thing. Each of two halves of something is equal to the fraction 1/2. Two of five equal parts of something is equal to the fraction 2/5. **fractions.**

frame

frame

a thing in which something else is set: *He made a frame for the picture.* **frames.**

frankfurter

a sausage made of beef and pork, or of beef alone. Frankfurters are often called hot dogs. **frankfurters.**

free

1. not under someone else's control or rule: *We live in a free country.* **2.** loose; not shut up or fastened: *A raccoon should be free and not kept in a cage.* **3.** to let loose; let go: *We freed the bear cub.* **4.** not costing any money: *We got free tickets to the play.* **freer, freest** (for **1., 2.**); **freed, freeing.**

freeze

to make or become very cold and hard. Water turns into ice when it freezes. **froze, frozen, freezing.**

freeze—*Water turns into ice when it freezes.*

freight

the things that a train, truck, ship, or aircraft carries.

fresh

1. just made, grown, or gathered; new: *The bread is fresh. Please make a fresh copy.* **2.** not spoiled; pure: *Is this milk fresh? Smell the fresh air.* **fresher, freshest.**

fresh water

water that is not salty.

freight
Boxes, crates, and barrels are freight.

Friday

the day after Thursday; the sixth day of the week. **Fridays.**

fried

1. cooked in hot fat: *We enjoy eating fried chicken.*
2. *He fried the potatoes.*

friend

someone you like and who likes you. **friends.**

friendly

like a friend; kind: *She is a friendly teacher.* **friendlier, friendliest.**

frighten

to scare; make afraid: *The storm frightened the puppy.* **frightened, frightening.**

frog

frosting
The **frosting** on the
cake is pink.

fruit

frog

a small animal that lives part of the time in water and part of the time on land. Young frogs hatch from eggs and are called tadpoles. They live in the water until they grow legs. **frogs.**

from

Steel is made from iron. I start school two weeks from today. She is suffering from a cold.

front

1. the part of anything that faces forward: *The front of our house has six windows.* **2.** the first part; beginning: *Move to the front of the line.* **fronts** (for **1.**).

frost

very small drops of water frozen on the surface of something: *There is frost on the windows today.*

frosting

a flavored, sweet mixture spread on cakes and other foods.

frown

1. wrinkling the forehead to show you are angry or do not like something: *We could see a frown on her face.* **2.** to wrinkle the forehead to show you are angry or do not like something: *She frowned as she asked us not to make so much noise.* **frowns; frowned, frowning.**

froze

·*The pond froze early this year.*

frozen

1. turned into ice; very cold: *The frozen river made travel by boat impossible.* **2.** *The pond has frozen solid. His hands are frozen.*

fruit

the part of a tree, bush, or vine that has seeds in it and is good to eat. Apples, oranges, strawberries, and bananas are fruit. **fruit** or **fruits.**

fry

to cook in hot fat: *Should I fry the potatoes or boil them?* **fried, frying.**

fuel

anything you can burn that gives heat or power. Wood, oil, and gas are different kinds of fuel. **fuels.**

full

not able to hold any more: *His glass is full.* **fuller, fullest.**

fun

a good time; play; joking: *He had fun at the party.*

funny

making you laugh: *All the kids laughed at the clowns' funny faces.* **funnier, funniest.**

funny

fur

the soft, thick hair that covers the skin of many animals.

furnace

something in which to make a very hot fire. Furnaces are used to heat buildings. **furnaces.**

furniture

things needed in a room or house. Beds, chairs, and desks are furniture.

future

the time to come; all the days, months, and years that will come.

fuzzy

covered with loose, light, fluffy hairs. Peaches are fuzzy; pears are not. **fuzzier, fuzziest.**

furniture

Gg

gallon

game

gallon

an amount of liquid. Large amounts of liquid are often measured by the gallon. A gallon is equal to four quarts. **gallons.**

gallop

to run very fast: *The horse galloped down the road.* **galloped, galloping.**

game

something to play or have fun doing: *The children play games at recess.* **games.**

garage

a place where cars are parked or fixed. Mechanics fix cars in garages. *My father parks his car in the garage.* **garages.**

garbage

bits and pieces of uneaten food to be thrown away.

garden

the part of a yard where vegetables or flowers are grown. **gardens.**

gas

1. something that is not solid or liquid. A gas has no special size or shape. Most gases have no color and cannot be seen. The air we breathe is made of several gases. Another kind of gas is put into some stoves to make fire for cooking. **2.** a short word meaning gasoline. **gases** (for **1.**).

gasoline

the liquid that is put into cars and other machines to make them go.

gasp

1. to take in a loud, quick breath of air; try hard to get your breath after running or working very hard: *The girl gasped after running all the way home from school.*
2. to talk while breathing this way: *"Save me!" gasped the drowning man.* **gasped, gasping.**

gas station

a place to buy gasoline and oil. **gas stations.**

gate

a door in a fence or wall. **gates.**

gate

gather

to bring together or come together; collect: *Tom gathered his tools and went to fix his bike. The crowd gathered to hear the governor.* **gathered, gathering.**

gave

She gave her mother a flower.

gaze

to look at for a long time: *We gazed at the sunset.* **gazed, gazing.**

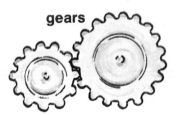

gears

gear

a wheel with teeth that fit into the teeth of another wheel. One wheel makes the other wheel turn. Some machines have gears. **gears.**

geese

more than one goose.

gentle

1. soft and mild; not rough or violent: *The gentle rocking of the boat made us sleepy.* **2.** kindly; friendly: *We have a gentle dog.* **gentler, gentlest.**

geese

145

gentleman

a polite word for a man. **gentlemen.**

gently

in a gentle way; softly: *The rain fell gently. She spoke gently to the baby.*

geography

the study of where people and places can be found on the earth.

geometry

in mathematics, the study of shapes such as triangles and circles.

Georgia

one of the fifty states of the United States.

gerbil

a small animal that looks like a mouse. Many people keep gerbils as pets. **gerbils.**

germ

a very simple form of life, too small to be seen without a microscope. Some germs can make you sick. **germs.**

get

I hope to get a bike for my birthday. It gets hot in the summer. When I get home, I usually have a snack.

ghost

in stories, a white shape that scares people. Ghosts are not real. **ghosts.**

giant

1. in stories, a person of very large size. **2.** huge: *We made a giant sandwich for lunch.* **giants.**

gift

a present; something you get without having to pay for it: *My uncle brought me a gift when I was sick.* **gifts.**

gerbils

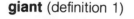
giant (definition 1)

46

giggle

1. to laugh in a silly way: *The children giggled in the corner.* **2.** a silly laugh: *We heard a loud giggle from the back of the room.* **giggled, giggling; giggles.**

gingerbread

a kind of spicy cake or cookie.

gingerbread
*Here's a **gingerbread** man.*

giraffe

a large animal with a very long neck and spots on its skin. Giraffes are the tallest living animals. **giraffes.**

girl

a female child. A girl grows up to be a woman. **girls.**

girl scout

a member of the Girl Scouts of America. This group helps girls grow into healthy, strong young women. **girl scouts.**

give

1. to hand over as a present or gift: *I'll give her my sweater to keep.* **2.** to pay: *I will give you three dollars for the necklace.* **gave, given, giving.**

given

He has given his bike to me.

glad

happy; pleased: *She is glad to be home after a long trip.* **gladder, gladdest.**

glance

1. a quick look: *The teacher gave him an angry glance.* **2.** to look quickly: *I only glanced at her.* **glances; glanced, glancing.**

glare

1. a strong, bright light that hurts the eyes: *The glare of the sunlight made it hard to sit on the beach.* **2.** to look at someone angrily: *He glared at us after we laughed at him.* **glared, glaring.**

giraffe

glare (definition 2)

glass

1. something that you can see through. Glass is hard, but easy to break. Windows are made of glass.
2. something to drink from: *Would you like a glass of water?* **glasses** (for **2.**).

glasses

a pair of glass lenses, often set in a frame. Glasses are worn on the face, in front of your eyes, to help you see better.

gleam

1. a quick flash of light: *We saw the gleam of a flashlight in the dark hall.* **2.** to shine: *The flashlight gleamed in the dark.* **gleams; gleamed, gleaming.**

globe

a round copy of the earth. A globe has a map of the earth drawn on it. *Can you find Canada on the globe?* **globes.**

globe

gloomy

sad: *I felt gloomy for a while after my friend moved away.* **gloomier, gloomiest.**

glossary

a list of hard words with their meanings. Some books have glossaries at the back. **glossaries.**

glove

a covering for the hand, with a place for each finger and for the thumb. Gloves keep your hands warm, and are made of cloth or leather. **gloves.**

glow

1. to shine with a bright, warm color: *See how the fire glows.* **2.** the shine from something that is hot or bright: *There was a glow in the sky from the city lights.* **glowed, glowing; glows.**

glow (definition 2)
Young Lincoln reads by the **glow** *of the fire.*

glue

1. something used to stick things together: *Mom fixed the broken chair with glue.* **2.** to stick together with glue: *We glued the parts of the model plane.* **glued, gluing.**

go

1. to move from one place to another: *We wanted to go to the store yesterday. Are you ready to go?* **2.** to act or work: *The car won't go because the battery is dead.* **3.** to have its place; belong: *This dish goes on the first shelf.* **went, gone, going.**

goal

1. the place that players run to in races and some games. **2.** something you want very much: *His goal was to become a lawyer.* **goals.**

goat

an animal with horns. Goats have hair under their chins. Goats are raised for their milk and their skins. **goats.**

goat

gobble[1]

to eat fast and noisily: *The hungry dog gobbled his dinner.* **gobbled, gobbling.**

gobble[2]

1. the noise a turkey makes. **2.** to make this noise: *We could hear the turkeys gobbling.* **gobbles; gobbled, gobbling.**

goblin

in stories, a mean dwarf. **goblins.**

God

the all-powerful being that many people believe in and worship.

goes

Everywhere I go, my little sister goes.

gold—*This necklace is made of **gold** coins and a **gold** chain.*

gold

a bright yellow metal of very great value. Gold is used to make jewelry and some coins.

golden

1. made of gold: *She wore a golden chain.* **2.** shining like gold; yellow: *Her hair is golden.*

goldfish

a small orange fish. Many people keep goldfish in glass bowls. **goldfish.**

gone

He has gone to a movie.

good

1. right; as it should be; well-done: *He does good work.* **2.** doing what is right: *That's a good dog.* **3.** pleasant: *I hope you have a good time at the ball game.* **better, best.**

good-by

what people say when they are going away. People also use these words when they finish talking on the telephone. **good-bys.**

goods

things for sale in stores.

goose

a large bird with a long neck. A goose looks like a duck but is larger. **geese.**

gopher

a small animal like a rat. Gophers dig holes in the ground. **gophers.**

gorilla

gorilla

a large, hairy animal with long arms and no tail. A gorilla is the biggest and strongest of the apes. **gorillas.**

gopher

got

It got chilly last night. He got a sweater.

gotten

She has gotten many presents this year. Has Mom gotten up yet?

government

a group of people that rule or manage a country, a state, a county, or a city. **governments.**

governor

a person that people elect to be head of a state of the United States. **governors.**

grab

to take suddenly: *The dog grabbed the bone and ran.* **grabbed, grabbing.**

grade

1. a year of study in school: *He is in second grade.* **2.** a number or letter that shows how well you have done: *Did you get a good grade on the test?* **3.** to give a grade to: *We graded each other's papers.* **grades; graded, grading.**

grain

1. the seed of wheat, oats, rice, and corn. **2.** one of the tiny bits that make up sand, salt, or sugar. **grains.**

gram

a unit of weight. A paper clip weighs about one gram. **grams.**

grammar

the rules about the forms and uses of words in sentences. We study grammar to help us read and write well.

grain—corn; rice; wheat

grand

large and wonderful to look at: *The king and queen lived in a very grand palace.* **grander, grandest.**

grandchild
a child of one's son or daughter. **grandchildren.**

granddaughter
a daughter of one's son or daughter. **granddaughters.**

grandfather
the father of your mother or father. **grandfathers.**

grandma
another word for grandmother. **grandmas.**

grandmother
the mother of your mother or father. **grandmothers.**

grandpa
another word for grandfather. **grandpas.**

grandparent
a parent of your mother or father; grandfather or grandmother. **grandparents.**

grandson
a son of one's son or daughter. **grandsons.**

grape
a small, round fruit that grows on a vine. Grapes are red, purple, or green. **grapes.**

grapefruit
a yellow fruit that looks like a large orange, but is not as sweet. Grapefruit grow on trees. **grapefruit.**

graph
a line or drawing showing information. A graph can show how your height has changed over the last four years. **graphs.**

grass
a plant with thin leaves like blades. Grass is green and grows in fields, parks, and yards. Horses, cows, and sheep eat grass.

Number of Books Read by Each Child					
	1	2	3	4	5	6
Kim						
Lynn						
Carlos						
Pat						
Sara						

graph—*A bar* **graph** *shows the number of books each child has read.*

grasshopper

an insect with wings and strong legs for jumping. **grasshoppers.**

grate

a frame of iron bars to hold a fire: *Put the logs on the grate in the fireplace.* **grates.**

gravy

a sauce for meat and vegetables. Gravy is made from the juice that comes out of meat when it is cooked.

grasshopper

gray

1. a color made by mixing black and white. **2.** having this color: *We saw the gray clouds in the sky.* **grays; grayer, grayest.**

graze¹

to eat grass: *Sheep were grazing in the meadow.* **grazed, grazing.**

graze²

to scrape or touch in passing: *Dad grazed the garage door with the car.* **grazed, grazing.**

graze¹

grease

thick fat or oil: *We saved the grease after cooking the bacon.*

greedy—*The **greedy** boy is taking almost all the candy.*

great

1. very big or large: *A great cloud of smoke rose over the fire.* **2.** very good or important: *This painting was done by a great artist.* **greater, greatest.**

greedy

wanting more than your share: *Help yourself to some candy, but don't be greedy.* **greedier, greediest.**

green

1. the color of most growing plants. **2.** having this color: *She wore a green sweater.* **greens; greener, greenest.**

greet

to say hello to someone: *She came to the door to greet us.* **greeted, greeting.**

greeting

1. something you say or do when you meet someone. "Hello" is a greeting. **2.** a word or phrase you use to begin a letter. "Dear Ann" is a greeting. **greetings.**

grew

The grass grew very fast from all the rain.

grid

a group of squares formed by two sets of lines. Sometimes map-makers use a grid to help people find places on a map. **grids.**

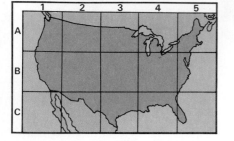

grid

grin

1. to smile with the teeth showing: *She grinned and said, "Hello."* **2.** a wide smile that shows the teeth: *He had a friendly grin on his face.* **grinned, grinning; grins.**

grind

to crush or cut into small pieces or powder: *The machine grinds the coffee beans into a fine powder.* **ground, grinding.**

groan

1. a sound made in the throat when you are unhappy or in pain: *They heard groans from the injured player.* **2.** to make this sound: *He groaned with pain when he hurt his knee.* **groans; groaned, groaning.**

grocery

a store that sells food. **groceries.**

groom

a man just married or about to be married. Another word for groom is bridegroom. **grooms.**

ground¹

the soil or dirt on the surface of the earth: *The ground was hard and rocky.*

ground²

He ground three pounds of meat to make hamburgers.

groundhog

a small animal with a bushy tail. Another word for groundhog is woodchuck. **groundhogs.**

groundwater

water that has flowed underground. Groundwater supplies springs and wells.

groundhog

group

1. a number of persons or things together: *We saw a group of children laughing.* **2.** to gather a number of persons or things together: *I grouped the pictures of all the cats into one column.* **groups; grouped, grouping.**

grove

a group of trees: *There are many orange groves in Florida.* **groves.**

grove

grow

to get bigger: *A cactus will grow in sand. She wants to be a doctor when she grows up.* **grew, grown, growing.**

growl

to make a deep, angry sound in the throat: *The dog growled at the squirrels.* **growled, growling.**

grown

Our sunflowers have grown very tall.

grown-up

a person who has finished growing; an adult: *A grown-up coaches the soccer team.* **grown-ups.**

gruff

rough and unfriendly: *The old man spoke in a gruff voice.* **gruffer, gruffest.**

grumble

to complain; find fault: *She grumbled about the weather all day.* **grumbled, grumbling.**

grumpy

having a bad temper: *My brother is grumpy when he gets up in the morning.* **grumpier, grumpiest.**

grunt

1. a deep, hoarse sound that a pig makes, or a sound like it: *I lifted the heavy box with a grunt.* **2.** to make this sound: *He grunted as he lifted the heavy box.* **grunts; grunted, grunting.**

guard

1. to take care of; keep safe: *The dog guards the house at night.* **2.** a person who takes care of something: *The crossing guard helped them cross the street.* **guarded, guarding; guards.**

guard (definition 2)

guess

1. to try to give the answer to something when you are not sure: *She tried to guess before she looked up the answer. I guess it will rain tomorrow.* **2.** an idea you have when you are not sure of something: *My guess is that the tree is ten feet high.* **guessed, guessing; guesses.**

guide (definition 2)

guest

a person who is visiting someone else's house: *She was our guest for dinner.* **guests.**

guide

1. to show the way or lead someone: *The compass will guide us back to camp.* **2.** a person who leads you or shows the way: *We hired a guide to show us the cave.* **guided, guiding; guides.**

guide word

a word put at the top of a page as a guide. Guide words tell what the first and last words on the page are. The guide words for this page are guide word and gymnasium. **guide words.**

guinea pig

a small, fat animal with short ears and a short tail or no tail. People often keep guinea pigs as pets. **guinea pigs.**

guinea pig

guitar

a musical instrument with six strings. You play a guitar with your fingers. **guitars.**

gull

a bird that lives near lakes and oceans. A gull has long wings and a strong beak. **gulls.**

gum[1]

something sweet that you chew but don't swallow: *We are not allowed to chew gum in school.*

gum[2]

the soft, pink part that the teeth grow out of. **gums.**

guitar

gull

guppy

a small, brightly colored fish. Guppies are found in many aquariums. **guppies.**

gush

to rush out suddenly; pour out: *Oil gushed from the well.* **gushed, gushing.**

gym

a short word meaning gymnasium. **gyms.**

gymnasium

a room or building in which people exercise and play games. **gymnasiums.**

gush

Hh

habitat—*This is a desert* **habitat***.*

habit

something you do over and over again, sometimes without thinking: *Brushing your teeth often is a good habit. Biting your nails is a bad habit.* **habits.**

habitat

the place where a plant or an animal lives. The jungle is the habitat of monkeys. **habitats.**

had

I had a pet cat. We had to leave early for school. You had plenty of time.

hadn't

had not: *She hadn't seen him in a long time.*

hail

1. small, round pieces of ice that come down like rain; frozen rain: *The noise of hail on the roof awoke us.*
2. to fall in frozen drops: *Sometimes it hails during a summer storm.* **hailed, hailing.**

hair

thin pieces that look like threads that grow from the skin of people and some animals. Hair may be straight, curly, or wavy. **hair** or **hairs.**

half

one of two equal parts: *He ate half of an apple for lunch. He had the other half after school. Both halves tasted good.* **halves.**

halfway

one half of the distance or amount: *She walked me halfway home. I'm halfway done with my homework.*

hall

1. a long, narrow space that leads to other rooms in a building: *The hall leads to the auditorium.* **2.** a large room for meetings and parties: *We rented a hall for our family holiday party.* **halls.**

Halloween

the evening of October 31, when children dress up in costumes and ask for treats at other people's houses. **Halloweens.**

ham

meat from the upper part of a pig's hind leg. **hams.**

ham

hamburger

ground beef. Hamburgers are cooked in a round, flat shape. **hamburgers.**

hammer

1. a tool you use to hit nails with. A hammer has a long handle with a heavy piece of metal at one end. **2.** to hit with a hammer: *She hammered a nail into the wall to hold up a picture.* **hammers; hammered, hammering.**

hammer (definition 1)

hamster

an animal that looks something like a mouse, but larger. Some people keep hamsters as pets. **hamsters.**

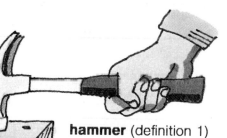

hamster

hand

1. the part of the body at the end of the arm. Each hand has four fingers and a thumb. **2.** something like a hand: *The hands of a watch tell what time it is.* **3.** to give something with the hand; pass: *Please hand me the salt.* **hands; handed, handing.**

handful

as much or as many as the hand can hold: *He reached into the jar for a handful of raisins.* **handfuls.**

handkerchief

a square piece of soft cloth used to wipe your nose, face, and hands: *We use a handkerchief when we sneeze.* **handkerchiefs.**

handle

1. the part of a thing you hold on to. Pans, suitcases, and rakes have handles. **2.** to touch, feel, or use with the hand: *He handled the puppy very gently when he picked it up.* **handles; handled, handling.**

hand signal

the motions that bike riders and car drivers use to tell others they are turning or stopping: *She used a hand signal to show that she was making a left turn.* **hand signals.**

hand signal

handsome

good-looking; pleasant to look at. We usually say that a man is handsome, but that a woman is pretty or beautiful. **handsomer, handsomest.**

handwriting

writing done by hand, with a pen or a pencil: *She used her neatest handwriting when she wrote to her aunt.*

handy

1. easy to reach or use: *She kept the dish towels handy near the sink.* **2.** good at using your hands: *He was handy in the kitchen; he could cook and bake very well.* **handier, handiest.**

hang

1. to be held from above on a hook, branch, or the like: *Hang up your coat and hat. Monkeys hang by their tails.* **2.** the way of using or doing something: *Riding a bike is easy after you get the hang of it.* **hung, hanging.**

hanger

a thing that something hangs on: *I bought more clothes hangers for my closet.* **hangers.**

Hanukkah

a holiday celebrated by some people once a year. Hanukkah usually comes in December and lasts for eight days. *At Hanukkah we give each other presents and light Hanukkah candles.*

Hanukkah—*The boy is lighting eight candles at* **Hanukkah.**

happen

to take place: *What happened at the game yesterday?* **happened, happening.**

happily

in a happy way; with pleasure and joy: *The children played happily in the swimming pool.*

happiness

a being happy; joy: *We wished the bride and groom much happiness.*

happy

feeling as you do when you are having a good time; glad; pleased: *He is happy that you came to visit.* **happier, happiest.**

harbor

an area of quiet water where ships are safe: *The boat headed for the harbor when the storm began.* **harbors.**

harbor

hard

1. solid; not soft; not moving when someone touches it: *The turtle has a hard shell.* **2.** taking a lot of work or energy; difficult: *Cleaning out the garage is a hard job; it is not easy.* **harder, hardest.**

hardly

only just; not quite: *We had hardly finished eating when the telephone rang.*

hare

hare

an animal very much like a large rabbit. A hare has long ears, a short tail, and long hind legs. **hares.**

harm

1. something that hurts you or causes pain: *He fell down but no harm came to him.* **2.** to hurt: *She petted the kitten gently so she wouldn't harm it.* **harmed, harming.**

harmful

dangerous; causing harm: *Smoking is harmful to your health.*

harvest

1. the ripe crops that are picked after the growing season is over: *The corn harvest was poor after the hot, dry summer.* **2.** to gather the crops: *We harvested the apples in late fall.* **harvests; harvested, harvesting.**

harvest (definition 2)

has

The teacher has my paper. He has to go to sleep. She has been on vacation.

hasn't

has not: *He hasn't started his drawing yet.*

hat

a kind of clothing you wear on your head: *She wore a hat outside in the cold.* **hats.**

hatch

to come out from an egg or eggs: *Two chickens hatched today.* **hatched, hatching.**

hatch

hate

to not like someone or something at all: *Cats and dogs often hate each other. He hated to go to the barber.* **hated, hating.**

haul

to pull or drag something heavy: *The truck hauled her car out of the ditch.* **hauled, hauling.**

have

I have a nickel in my pocket. We have to go now. We always have breakfast in the kitchen. They have asked for their mail.

haven't

have not: *We haven't eaten yet. They haven't any money.*

Hawaii

one of the fifty states of the United States.

hawk

a bird with a strong beak and large claws. Hawks eat birds and other small animals. **hawks.**

hawk

hay

grass and other plants that are cut and dried. Hay is used as food for cattle and horses.

haystack

a large pile of hay stored outside. **haystacks.**

haystack

he

He is my friend. My dog is so old he can't see.

head

1. the top part of the human body, or the front part of most animal bodies. The head is where the eyes, ears, nose, mouth, and brain are. **2.** the top or front part of something: *We put the pillow at the head of the bed. She went to the head of the line.* **heads.**

headache

a pain in the head: *He had a headache and a sore throat.* **headaches.**

heading

heading

something written or printed at the top of a page, or at the beginning of a chapter or a letter. An address and date at the top of a letter is a heading. **headings.**

health

being well, not sick: *Food, sleep, and exercise are important to your health.*

healthy

having good health: *We got plenty of exercise because we wanted to stay healthy.* **healthier, healthiest.**

heap

a pile of many things: *There was a heap of dirty clothes next to the washing machine.* **heaps.**

heap

hear

1. to take in sounds through the ear: *She could hear her watch ticking.* **2.** to get news about something: *Did you hear that the circus is coming to town?* **heard, hearing.**

heard

I heard the noise. The siren could be heard a mile away.

hearing

the power to take in sounds through the ears. Hearing is one of the five senses, along with sight, smell, taste, and touch. *The doctor tested my hearing.*

heart

1. the part of the body inside your chest that pumps blood to the rest of your body. **2.** the part of a person that has feelings: *She knew in her heart that she had done a good job.* **3.** a figure shaped like this: ♥: *The valentine was covered with hearts.* **hearts.**

heat

1. being hot; great warmth: *We enjoy the heat of a fire on a cold day.* **2.** to make something warm or hot: *She heated the soup on the stove.* **3.** a kind of energy that flows from something hot to something colder. The heat of the sun warms up the water in a swimming pool. **heated, heating.**

heavy

hard to lift or carry; weighing a lot: *The piano was very heavy.* **heavier, heaviest.**

he'd

1. he had: *He'd never been to the city before.* **2.** he would: *He'd like to go with us.*

hedge

a thick row of bushes that makes a fence. **hedges.**

hedge

heel

1. the back part of your foot, below the ankle. **2.** the part of a stocking or shoe that covers your heel. **3.** the back part of a shoe or boot that is under your heel. **heels.**

heel (definition 1)

heel (definition 2)

height

how tall a person is; how high something is: *The school nurse measured my height. We measured the height of the door to see if the sofa would fit through it.* **heights.**

held

He held the kitten gently. The swing is held by strong ropes.

helicopter

a machine that flies without wings. A helicopter has large, turning blades that keep it in the air and make it go. **helicopters.**

helicopter

he'll

he will: *He'll come to our house soon.*

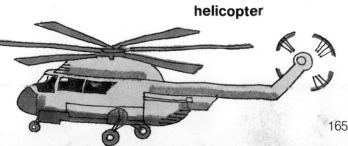

hello

what people say when they greet someone. We usually say ''hello'' when we answer the telephone. **hellos.**

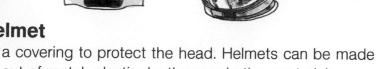

helmets—a football **helmet;**
a military **helmet;**
a biking **helmet;**
an astronaut's **helmet.**

helmet

a covering to protect the head. Helmets can be made out of metal, plastic, leather, and other materials. **helmets.**

help

1. to do something useful for someone: *He helped me with my homework.* **2.** the act of helping someone: *She needed some help in the kitchen.* **3.** to make better: *The medicine helped my cold.* **helped, helping.**

helper

a person or thing that helps others: *The teacher's helper graded the papers.* **helpers.**

helpful

giving help; useful: *A sewing machine is helpful for fixing torn clothes.*

helping

the amount of food served to one person at one time: *She had two helpings of spaghetti.* Another word for helping is serving. **helpings.**

hen

helpless

not able to help or look after yourself: *A baby is helpless.*

hen

a female chicken or other female bird. Hens lay eggs. **hens.**

her

We have her book. We want her to come.

herd

1. a group of animals keeping or feeding together: *We saw a herd of cows when we went driving in the country.* **2.** to form a number of people or animals into a group: *The farmer herded the cows over to the barn. We herded into the cafeteria for lunch.* **herds; herded, herding.**

herd (definition 1)

here

at this place; to this place: *We will stop here. Bring the children here for their lessons.*

hers

This book is hers. His coat is blue; hers is red.

herself

She hurt herself when she fell. She did it by herself.

he's

1. he is: *He's a big boy.* **2.** he has: *He's gone for the day.*

hey

a shout made to get someone's attention: *''Hey, there!''*

hey

hi

a call you use to greet someone; hello: *He said ''hi'' as he passed her in the hall.*

hibernate

to spend all winter sleeping or resting, the way some animals do. Woodchucks are animals that hibernate. **hibernated, hibernating.**

hid

The dog hid his bone. She hid the presents where the children wouldn't find them.

hidden

1. kept out of sight; secret: *The story is about hidden treasure.* **2.** *The boy had hidden behind a big old tree.*

hide¹

1. to put or keep out of sight: *Hide the package where no one else can find it.* **2.** to keep secret: *She tried to hide her fear.* **hid, hidden, hiding.**

hide²

an animal's skin. Leather is made from hide. **hides.**

high

up above the ground: *We walked up the high hill. The airplane flew high in the sky.* **higher, highest.**

highway

a main road: *We took the highway when we visited our grandparents.* **highways.**

hike

1. to take a long walk: *We hiked five miles.* **2.** a long walk: *The campers went on a hike.* **hiked, hiking; hikes.**

hill

a high piece of ground, not as big or as high as a mountain. Hills are usually rounder than mountains. **hills.**

him

Take him home. We want him to come.

himself

He cut himself. He bought the toy for himself.

hind

back; rear: *The dog stood up on his hind legs.*

hinge

something that a door, gate, or lid moves back and forth on: *We oiled the squeaking hinges.* **hinges.**

hint

a clue that helps you know or figure out something: *The teacher gave us a hint on how to solve the puzzle.* **hints.**

hill

hind—*The dog stood up on his **hind** legs.*

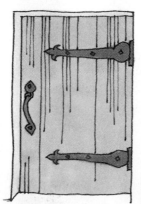

hinges

168

hip

the part of the body where the leg joins the body. **hips.**

hippopotamus

a very large animal with thick skin and no hair. Hippopotamuses live near rivers. **hippopotamuses.**

hire

to pay for the use of something; pay someone to do work: *Our neighbor hired me to mow the lawn.* **hired, hiring.**

his

His bicycle is lost. My car is red; his is tan.

history

the story of what has happened in the past to a person or a nation: *We study the history of the United States in school.*

hit

to move the hand, or something held in the hand, against something or someone with force: *I hit the ball with the bat.* **hit, hitting.**

hive

a house or box for bees to live in. **hives.**

hoarse

sounding rough and deep: *A bad cold and a sore throat made his voice hoarse.* **hoarser, hoarsest.**

hobby

something people like to do in their spare time: *My mother's hobby is sewing; mine is collecting stamps.* **hobbies.**

hockey

a game played by two teams on ice or on a field. The players use curved sticks to hit a ball or a hard piece of rubber, called a puck, into the other team's goal.

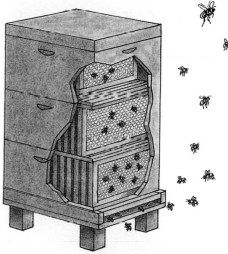

hippopotamus

hive—Part of the **hive** has been cut away to show how the bees live inside it.

hockey

hoe

hoe

a tool used to loosen soil or cut small weeds. A hoe has a thin blade and a long handle. **hoes.**

hog

a pig raised for food. **hogs.**

hold

1. to pick up and keep something in your hands or arms: *Will you hold my hat? His mother held his watch while he swam.* **2.** to keep something in a certain place or position; support: *Magnets hold the maps on the walls. The walls in the room hold up the ceiling.* **3.** to have space inside for something; contain: *That pitcher holds a lot of water.* **held, holding.**

hole

an open or empty space in something: *There is a big hole in this stocking. Rabbits dig holes in the ground.* **holes.**

holiday

a day when you do not work or go to school; a day for having fun or celebrating: *The Fourth of July is a holiday for people in the United States.* **holidays.**

hollow

1. with nothing inside; empty. A tube or a pipe is hollow. **2.** to take out the inside parts of something: *We hollowed out a pumpkin on Halloween.* **hollowed, hollowing.**

holly

holly

an evergreen bush or tree with shiny leaves and red berries.

holy

coming from God, or belonging to God, or set aside for God: *He read to us from the Holy Bible. The minister spoke to us about living a holy life.* **holier, holiest.**

home

1. the place where a person or a family lives: *Her home is on Elm Street.* **2.** the town or country where you were born or brought up: *Indiana is her home.* **homes.**

homework

a lesson to be studied or worked on outside of class: *After dinner, we did our homework for school.*

honest

telling the truth; not lying or stealing: *Parents teach their children to be honest.*

honesty

being honest and fair; doing and saying what is right and true: *The man who owns the bank is known for his honesty.*

honey

a thick, sweet, yellow liquid that is good to eat. Bees make honey out of the drops of juice they collect from flowers.

honk

1. a sound like the cry of a wild goose: *The honk of an automobile horn woke her up.* **2.** to make this sound: *We honked the horn to let them know we were here.* **honks; honked, honking.**

hood

1. a soft cloth covering for the head and neck: *My raincoat has a hood.* **2.** the metal covering over an automobile engine: *Dad checked under the hood to see why the car wasn't starting.* **hoods.**

hoof

the hard part of the foot of some animals. Horses, cattle, sheep, and pigs have hoofs. **hoofs.**

hood (definition 1)

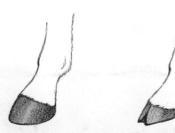

hoofs—*a horse's **hoof**; a cow's **hoof***

hook (definition 1)

hook (definition 2)

hook

1. a curved piece of metal, wood, or plastic to hang things on: *Hang your hat on the hook in the hall.* **2.** a bent piece of wire for catching fish. **hooks.**

hop

1. to jump on one foot: *He hopped on his left foot and then on his right.* **2.** a jump or a leap: *Take two hops forward and one hop back.* **hopped, hopping; hops.**

hope

1. a feeling that what you want to happen will happen: *Her words gave me hope that we could really be friends.* **2.** to wish for something and expect it to happen: *I hope I win the race next week.* **hopes; hoped, hoping.**

hopeful

feeling or showing hope; expecting to get what one wants: *We were hopeful that it wouldn't rain.*

hopeless

feeling no hope: *It was hopeless to look for my ring after I lost it in the snow.*

horn (definition 1)
*This goat has long **horns.***

horn

1. something hard that grows on the heads of some animals. Horns are usually curved and pointed. Cattle and goats have horns. **2.** a musical instrument that you blow into. **3.** something that makes a signal of danger: *He honked his horn to warn that he was coming.* **horns.**

hornet

a large insect that can sting. **hornets.**

hornet

horse

horse

a large animal with four legs, hoofs, and a mane. Horses pull loads and carry riders. Horses can run very fast. **horses.**

hose

a long hollow tube for carrying a liquid or a gas. Hoses are used to water lawns and to fill tires with air. **hoses.**

hospital

a place where sick people are cared for. Doctors and nurses work in hospitals. **hospitals.**

hot

1. not cold; much warmer than your body: *Fire is hot.*
2. having a sharp, burning taste: *These peppers are too hot for her to eat.* **hotter, hottest.**

hot dog

a sausage made of ground beef, or of beef and pork. Hot dogs are also called frankfurters. **hot dogs.**

hotel

a building where people can rent a room to sleep in. People who are traveling away from home often stay at a hotel. **hotels.**

hound

a kind of dog that uses the sense of smell to hunt. A hound has large, drooping ears and short hair. **hounds.**

hound

hour

a unit of time. There are 60 minutes in one hour. Twenty-four hours make one day. **hours.**

house

a building where people live: *She moved into a new house last month.* **houses.**

how

Tell me how it happened. How long will it take? How much does it weigh?

however

He was late for lunch; however, there was plenty of food left.

howl

1. to give a long, loud, sad cry: *Wolves and coyotes often howl at night.* **2.** a long, loud, sad cry: *We heard the howl of the wolf.* **howled, howling; howls.**

hug

1. to put your arms around something or someone and hold tight: *The little boy hugged his teddy bear.* **2.** a tight squeeze with the arms: *I like a hug when I am sad.* **hugged, hugging; hugs.**

huge

very large in size or amount: *An elephant is a huge animal. He won a huge sum of money in the contest.*

huge

hum

1. to make a steady sound like the noise of a bee: *The vacuum cleaner hums when we turn it on.* **2.** to sing with closed lips, not saying any words: *We hum along with the songs on the radio.* **hummed, humming.**

human

like a person; like people: *Men, women, and children are human beings. We treat our pet as though he were human.*

hummingbird

a very small, brightly colored bird with a long bill. A hummingbird moves its wings so fast they make a humming sound. **hummingbirds.**

hundred

the number after 99; ten more than 90; 100. *There are a hundred cents in a dollar.* **hundreds.**

hung

She hung the picture on the wall. He hung up his coat.

hunger

pains in the stomach caused by having nothing to eat: *When I ate, my hunger went away.*

hummingbird

hungrily

in a hungry way: *They ate hungrily after their long walk.*

hungry

feeling a need to eat: *She didn't eat breakfast and was hungry all morning.* **hungrier, hungriest.**

hunt

1. to kill wild birds or animals for food or for sport: *They went to the woods to hunt deer.* **2.** to look for something; try to find: *Mother helped us hunt for our missing book.* **hunted, hunting.**

hurricane

a fierce storm with strong winds and very heavy rain. **hurricanes.**

hunt (definition 2)
*The boy had to **hunt** for his lost book.*

hurry

1. to go very quickly; rush: *He hurried to get to work on time.* **2.** being eager to have something or do something quickly: *She was in a hurry to meet her friends.* **hurried, hurrying.**

hurt

1. to cause or feel pain: *The stone in my shoe hurt my foot. My hand hurts.* **2.** to do harm to something: *He hurt her feelings when he didn't invite her to the party.* **hurt, hurting.**

husband

a man who has a wife; a married man. **husbands.**

hut

a small wooden cabin or house: *The kids built a hut out of old boards and pieces of carpet.* **huts.**

hydrant

a large water pipe that sticks up from the ground. A hydrant has places where firefighters can connect hoses. **hydrants.**

hydrant

175

I i

I

I like dogs. I am going to get one.

ice

frozen water; water made solid by cold: *The pond turns to ice in winter. I put some ice in my glass of water.*

ice cream

a sweet, frozen food made of milk and sugar. Ice cream comes in many different flavors.

ice skate

ice skate

a shoe with a piece of metal on the bottom for skating on ice. **ice skates.**

ice-skate

to skate on ice; use ice skates: *We ice-skated as soon as the pond froze over.* **ice-skated, ice-skating.**

icicle

a hanging pointed stick of ice. An icicle forms when water freezes as it drips. **icicles.**

icy

1. covered with ice; slippery: *The car skidded on the icy street.* **2.** very cold: *You have icy hands.* **icier, iciest.**

Idaho

one of the fifty states of the United States.

icicles

idea

a thought or plan: *It was my idea to go to the zoo.*
ideas.

if

*We'll have a picnic if it doesn't rain. I wonder if it will
be a sunny day.*

igloo

a house made of hard blocks of snow. Some Eskimos
used to live in igloos in the winter. **igloos.**

igloo

ignore

to pay no attention to: *If he teases you, just ignore him
and he'll stop.* **ignored, ignoring.**

iguana

iguana

a large lizard that lives in Mexico and other warm
places. **iguanas.**

ill

sick; not well: *She is not here today because she is ill.*
worse, worst.

I'll

I will: *I'll help you do that.*

Illinois

one of the fifty states of the United States.

I'm

I am: *I'm going to the zoo today. I'm seven years old.*

imagination

the power to make pictures or ideas in the mind: *This
exciting story was written by someone with a good
imagination.*

imagination

imagine

to make a picture or idea of something in your mind: *I
can imagine myself living in outer space.* **imagined,
imagining.**

imitate

imitate

to copy someone else's way of dressing, talking, or moving; try to be like: *The little boy tried to imitate his older brother.* **imitated, imitating.**

important

1. having great meaning or value: *It is important that you learn to read well.* **2.** having power or being famous: *The President is a very important person in the United States.*

impossible

not able to happen; not possible: *It is impossible for a horse to fly.*

improve

to make or become better: *If I study the spelling words, I'm sure my spelling will improve.* **improved, improving.**

in

It rained in the morning. I am leaving in an hour.

inch

a unit of length about this long: There are 12 inches in one foot. **inches.**

inch

income

the money that a person earns. Your yearly income is all the money you earn in a year.

indeed

You are indeed welcome. I was very pleased indeed.

independence

freedom to make one's own decisions: *The American colonies won independence from Great Britain.*

Independence Day

July fourth, a holiday we celebrate in the United States. It honors the day our country became free from Great Britain.

Independence Day—*They enjoyed the **Independence Day** parade.*

index

a list of people, places, and things mentioned in a book. An index gives the page numbers where each of these can be found. It is arranged in alphabetical order at the end of the book. **indexes.**

Indian

a person from any of the groups of people who first lived in America. Indians lived here long before the coming of white people from Europe. **Indians.**

Indiana

one of the fifty states of the United States.

indoor

done or used in a house or building: *We play indoor tennis in the gymnasium.*

indoors

in or into a house or building: *Let's go indoors now.*

information

facts that are known about something; news: *She looked in the library for information about foreign countries.*

ink

a liquid used for writing or printing. These words are printed in black ink.

inn

a place where people can get food and a room to sleep in. **inns.**

insect

a small animal with six legs and a body that has three parts. Most insects have four wings. Flies, bees, butterflies, and mosquitoes are insects. **insects.**

inside

We stayed inside during the rain. There is a cricket inside this box. The inside of my coat is soft.

Chief Joseph ·National Portrait Gallery
United States Postage 6¢

Indian

insect

insist

to demand or say firmly: *He insisted on paying for our lunch.* **insisted, insisting.**

instant

1. a very short time: *She was gone in an instant.*
2. made up ahead of time, and needing no cooking, mixing, or things added to it: *We had instant pudding for dessert.*

instead

in place of something: *I don't like beets, so I ate carrots instead.*

instrument

1. something that helps you do or make another thing: *A telescope is an instrument that makes the stars look bigger.* **2.** something that makes music: *He can play the piano and two other instruments.* **instruments.**

instrument (definition 2)
The tuba is a brass instrument.

interest

1. a feeling of wanting to know about or share in: *The teacher has an interest in art.* **2.** to hold the attention of: *That kind of music does not interest me.* **interests; interested, interesting.**

interesting

holding one's attention: *The book was so interesting that I did not want to stop reading.*

into

The cows walked into the barn. Heat turns ice into water. They ran into the room.

introduce

1. to tell people each other's names when they don't know each other: *I introduced my mom to my new friend Pat.* **2.** to bring in for the first time: *She introduced a new idea at the meeting.* **introduced, introducing.**

introduce (definition 1)
*He **introduced** his mother to his friend.*

introduction

the beginning of a speech, a piece of music, or a book: *In his introduction, the speaker told us what his speech would be about.* **introductions.**

invent

to make or think of something new: *Thomas A. Edison invented the light bulb.* **invented, inventing.**

invention

a new thing that someone makes or thinks of: *The light bulb was a wonderful invention.* **inventions.**

inventor

a person who makes or thinks of new things: *Thomas A. Edison was a great American inventor.* **inventors.**

invisible

not able to be seen: *Germs are invisible.*

invitation

asking someone to come somewhere or do something: *I got an invitation to my friend's birthday party.* **invitations.**

invite

to ask someone to come somewhere or do something: *She invited me to her birthday party.* **invited, inviting.**

Iowa

one of the fifty states of the United States.

inventor—*Thomas A. Edison was the **inventor** of the light bulb.*

iron (definition 2)

iron

1. a very common and useful metal. Iron is made into steel to make tools, machines, and many other things. **2.** something used to make clothes smooth and neat. An iron has a flat bottom, which becomes hot, and a handle. **3.** to use a heated iron on: *My sister ironed my shirt.* **irons** (for **2.**); **ironed, ironing.**

island

is

Is he coming to your party? It is hot outside. She is going now. The house is on the next block.

island

land with water all around it. Islands are found in oceans, lakes, or rivers. The state of Hawaii is made up of a group of islands. **islands.**

isn't

is not: *She isn't home right now.*

it

It is a nice day today. Your cap is where you left it. It is my turn now.

itch

to have a feeling on your skin that makes you want to scratch: *My back itches.* **itched, itching.**

it'll

it will: *It'll probably snow tonight.*

its

The cat licked its paw. The tree lost its leaves.

it's

it is: *It's a beautiful day today. It's not going to rain.*

itself

The bird is washing itself in a puddle.

I've

I have: *I've got a new bicycle. I've never been here before.*

itself—*The dog saw **itself** in the mirror.*

J j

jacket

1. a short coat: *I wore my new jacket to go skating.*
2. a covering for the outside of something: *My dictionary has a book jacket to protect the cover.* **jackets.**

jack-o'-lantern

a pumpkin that has been hollowed out and carved to look like a face: *We burned a candle in our Halloween jack-o'-lantern.* **jack-o'-lanterns.**

jack-o'-lanterns

jacks

a game played with a small ball and little pieces of metal. As the ball is bounced, the pieces are picked up one at a time, then two at a time, then three at a time, and so on.

jail

a place where people are put when they break the law. A person in jail is locked in. **jails.**

jam¹

1. to press or squeeze something tightly together: *He jammed all his clothes into one drawer.* **2.** to be stuck or caught so that it cannot work: *The window is jammed; I can't open it.* **3.** a crowded group of things that cannot move freely: *The traffic jam made us three hours late.* **jammed, jamming; jams.**

jam²

a sweet fruit mixture. Jam is put on bread and toast.

jacks—*The children are playing* **jacks.**

janitor

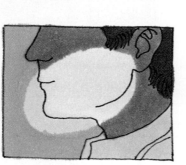

jaws

jeep

janitor

a person who takes care of a building: *He asked the janitor to fix our leaky faucet.* **janitors.**

January

the first month of the year. It has 31 days. It comes after the previous December and before February.

jar¹

a short, wide bottle used to hold things. Many jars are made of glass. Cookies are often kept in a large jar. **jars.**

jar²

to shake or rattle: *Please don't jar the desk while I am writing.* **jarred, jarring.**

jaw

the lower part of the face. Your teeth grow from the gums in your upper and lower jaw. **jaws.**

jealous

unhappy because someone has something that you want to have: *Seeing his friend's new bike made him jealous.*

jeans

pants made of strong cotton cloth. Jeans are often blue, but can be black, white, or other colors.

jeep

a small car often used where roads are rough. Jeeps were first used by the United States Army. **jeeps.**

jelly

a sweet food made from fruit juice and sugar. Jelly is spread on bread and toast.

jerk

to pull suddenly: *She jerked her hand out of the hot water.* **jerked, jerking.**

jet

1. a stream of gas, steam, or liquid forced from a small hole: *A jet of water shot up from the hose.* **2.** a kind of airplane. The engines of a jet do not have propellers. Hot gases that shoot from the back of the engines push the airplane forward. **jets.**

jewel

a valuable stone. Diamonds are jewels. **jewels.**

jewelry

rings, bracelets, necklaces, and such things. Jewelry is often made of silver or gold and, sometimes, jewels.

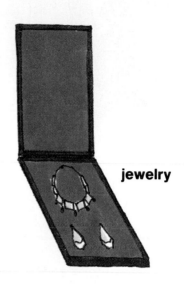

jewelry

job

1. the work that a person has to do: *It is my job to take out the garbage.* **2.** the work a person does for pay: *My mom has a job in a bank.* **jobs.**

jog

to run slowly and steadily: *My parents jog three miles every morning.* **jogged, jogging.**

jogger

a person who runs slowly and steadily for exercise. **joggers.**

join

1. to put together or fasten: *We joined hands in a circle.* **2.** to become a member of: *He joined the Boy Scouts.* **joined, joining.**

joint

the place in the body where two bones are joined. Your knee is a joint in your leg. **joints.**

join (definition 1)
*They **joined** hands.*

joke

a short, funny story you tell to make people laugh: *She told a joke about a talking dog.* **jokes.**

jolly

jolly

happy; cheerful; full of fun: *The jolly group sang and laughed all evening.* **jollier, jolliest.**

journey

a trip; traveling from one place to another: *He took a journey around the world.* **journeys.**

joy

a feeling of great happiness; gladness: *Her new puppy filled the little girl with joy.*

judge

1. a person who decides questions of right and wrong under the law. A judge can fine someone or send someone to jail. **2.** a person who decides who or what wins a contest: *She was one of the judges at the art show.* **3.** to decide who or what wins a contest: *She judged the art show last summer.* **judges; judged, judging.**

judge (definition 2)
*She was a **judge** at the art show.*

juggle

to throw things into the air, catch them, and keep them moving without letting them fall to the ground: *The clown juggled five balls and two sticks.* **juggled, juggling.**

juice

the liquid part of fruits and vegetables: *I drink a glass of orange juice every morning.* **juices.**

July

the seventh month of the year. It has 31 days. It comes after June and before August.

jump

to throw yourself up into the air, or across something: *He jumped over the puddle.* **jumped, jumping.**

jump rope

a piece of rope with handles at both ends. You hold each end, swing the jump rope over your head, jumping over it as it sweeps the ground. **jump ropes.**

June

the sixth month of the year. It has 30 days. It comes after May and before July.

jungle

jungle

a kind of forest, with thick bushes, vines, and many trees. Jungles have many kinds of animals living in them. Jungles are found in hot countries. **jungles.**

junk

old, worn-out things that nobody wants anymore; trash: *Let's throw out all the junk in the garage.*

just

We just got home from our trip. This coat is just my size. I just missed the bus. He is just four days old.

Kk

kangaroo

an animal in Australia with small front legs and very strong back legs. Kangaroos move very fast by jumping. A female kangaroo carries her baby in a pouch in the front of her stomach. **kangaroos.**

Kansas

one of the fifty states of the United States.

keep

1. to have for a long time or forever: *She told me to keep the ring. Please keep his secret.* **2.** to stay or cause to stay in good condition: *Eat the right food to keep healthy.* **kept, keeping.**

Kentucky

one of the fifty states of the United States.

kept

She kept my secret. He has kept all their letters.

kettle

a metal pot for boiling liquids or cooking fruit and vegetables. **kettles.**

kangaroos

kettle

key

1. a small piece of metal for opening and closing a lock. **2.** a list that explains the abbreviations or symbols that are used on a map or graph. **3.** very important: *There are five key words in today's lesson.* **keys.**

kick

1. to hit something with your foot: *He kicked the ball to me.* **2.** a hard hit with a foot: *She gave the door a kick to close it.* **kicked, kicking; kicks.**

kickball

a game something like baseball. The ball is rolled instead of thrown, and kicked instead of hit.

kid

1. a young goat. **2.** a child: *The kids are coming over to my house to play.* **kids.**

kill

to cause to die: *A fire killed the trees.* **killed, killing.**

kilogram

a unit of weight equal to 1000 grams. This book weighs about one kilogram. **kilograms.**

kilometer

a unit of great length equal to 1000 meters. A kilometer is a little more than half a mile. Distances between cities are sometimes measured in kilometers. **kilometers.**

kimono

a long, loose coat that men and women wear in Japan. **kimonos.**

kid (definition 1)

kid (definition 2)

kimono

kind¹

friendly; nice; doing good rather than harm: *A kind woman opened the heavy door for me.* **kinder, kindest.**

kind²

a group of things that are alike in some way; sort: *Dogs are a kind of animal. I like all kinds of fruit.* **kinds.**

kindergarten

a school for very young children. Kindergarten is the year of school before first grade. **kindergartens.**

kindly

1. kind; friendly: *Their kindly smiles made me feel happy.* **2.** in a kind or friendly way: *We thanked him kindly for his help.* **kindlier, kindliest.**

king

a man who rules a country. Many countries do not have kings. **kings.**

kingdom

a country that is ruled by a king or queen. **kingdoms.**

kiss

1. to touch with the lips as a sign of love: *Mom always kisses me when I come home.* **2.** a touch with the lips as a sign of love: *I gave Grandmother a kiss.* **kissed, kissing; kisses.**

kit

a package of all the parts that someone puts together to make something: *He bought a model airplane kit.* **kits.**

king

kitchen

a room where food is cooked and stored. **kitchens.**

kite

a light wooden frame that is covered with paper, cloth, or plastic. Kites are flown in the air on the end of a long string. **kites.**

kites

kitten

a young cat. **kittens.**

knee

the part of your leg that bends; the joint between your thigh and your lower leg. **knees.**

kneel

to go down on your knees: *They often kneel and pray.* **knelt, kneeling.**

knelt

I knelt to tie my little sister's shoelaces. He had knelt on the ground to pull weeds.

knew

I knew the answer.

knife

a flat piece of metal with a handle, used to cut or spread something. You use a knife to spread butter. A sharper knife can cut wood. **knives.**

knight

a soldier who rode a horse and fought for a king long ago. Knights often wore metal suits, called armor. **knights.**

knight

knit

to make clothing by hooking yarn together, using long needles: *Grandma knitted me a scarf.* **knitted, knitting.**

knives

more than one knife.

knob

the round handle on a drawer or door. **knobs.**

knock

1. to hit or bump into something: *He knocked on their door. You knocked my glasses off.* **2.** a hit or bump: *They didn't hear his knock at the door.* **knocked, knocking; knocks.**

knots

knot

a place where rope or cloth has been tied together: *His shoelaces were tied in knots.* **knots.**

know

1. to have the facts about something or someone; have the information in the mind: *I know how to swim. I know the answer to that question.* **2.** to have met and spoken to; be friendly with: *I know him, but I don't know his sister.* **knew, known, knowing.**

known

I have known her for a long time.

koala

a small gray animal that looks something like a bear. It has no tail. Koalas live in Australia. **koalas.**

koala

Ll

label

1. a piece of paper or cloth that is sewed or glued onto something. A label tells what something is, who it belongs to, or who made it. **2.** to put or write a label on something: *The teacher asked them to label one group of pictures with the word "plants."* **labels; labeled, labeling.**

laboratory

a room or building where scientists work and do experiments. **laboratories.**

lace

1. very thin threads that are woven together to make a pattern: *She sewed lace around the collar.* **2.** a cord, string, or leather strip for pulling and holding something together: *These shoes need new laces.* **3.** to pull or hold together with laces: *Lace your ice skates tightly to support your ankles.* **laces** (for **2.**); **laced, lacing.**

lace (definition 1)

ladder

a set of steps, called rungs, fastened between two long pieces of wood, metal, or rope. Ladders are used for climbing up and down. **ladders.**

lady

a polite word for a woman. **ladies.**

ladybug

a small, red beetle with black spots. Ladybugs eat some harmful insects. **ladybugs.**

ladybug

laid

He laid down the heavy bundle. The chickens have laid fewer eggs this morning than yesterday.

lain

She has lain down to take a nap.

lake

water with land all around it. A lake is larger than a pond. It usually has fresh water in it. **lakes.**

lamb

1. a young sheep. **2.** the meat from a lamb: *My mom serves mint jelly with roast lamb.* **lambs** (for **1.**).

lamb (definition 1)

lame

not able to walk very well; having a hurt leg or foot: *He was lame and had to walk with a cane.* **lamer, lamest.**

lamp

a thing that gives light. Some lamps use oil to give off light. Most lamps use electricity. **lamps.**

land

1. the solid part of the earth's surface: *After many weeks at sea, the sailors saw dry land.* **2.** ground; soil: *The farmer planted wheat on his land.* **3.** to come down from the air; come to rest: *The airplane landed in a field.* **lands** (for **2.**); **landed, landing.**

lane

a narrow road or street. **lanes.**

language

words that people write or speak: *People in different countries sometimes speak and write different languages.* **languages.**

lantern

a light that can be carried. A lantern has sides that are made out of glass or paper. Light shines through the sides. **lanterns.**

lantern

lap

the upper legs of a person who is sitting down: *The baby sat on her mom's lap.* **laps.**

large

big; of great size, amount, or number: *The United States is a large country. Large crowds come to see the team play.* **larger, largest.**

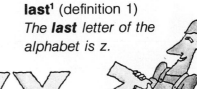

last[1] (definition 1)
*The **last** letter of the alphabet is z.*

last[1]

1. coming after all others: *The last letter in the alphabet is Z.* **2.** just past: *I saw him last night.*

last[2]

to go on; keep on: *How long do you think the snow will last?* **lasted, lasting.**

latch

something that keeps a door, gate, or window closed. A latch is made of a piece of metal or wood that moves and fits into an opening. Latches usually do not need keys. **latches.**

latch

late

1. after the usual time that something happens: *He had a late breakfast because he got up late.* **2.** near the end of: *The movie came on late that night.* **later, latest.**

lately

a little while ago; not long ago: *I made two visits to the dentist lately.*

laugh

1. to make sounds that show you are happy: *We all laughed at the clown's tricks.* **2.** sounds made when a person laughs: *The tiny girl had a loud laugh.* **laughed, laughing; laughs.**

laughter

the sounds of laughing: *When the boy told the joke, laughter filled the room.*

laugh (definition 2)

launch

lawn—*He is mowing the **lawn.***

lazy

launch

to send out into the air with force: *The rocket was launched into space.* **launched, launching.**

launching pad

the place from which a rocket or spacecraft is sent into the air. **launching pads.**

laundry

1. a room or building where clothes are washed and ironed: *He stopped by the laundry to pick up his shirts.* **2.** clothes that are washed or need to be washed: *Mom asked us to put our dirty laundry in the basket.* **laundries** (for **1.**).

lavender

a light purple color. **lavenders.**

lavender

law

a rule made by the government of a country or state for all the people who live there. Laws are rules that everyone must follow. **laws.**

lawn

a piece of land near a house or building, that is covered with grass. A lawn is usually cut often. **lawns.**

lay[1]

1. to put something down: *Please lay the book on the table.* **2.** to produce an egg or eggs: *Birds, fish, and snakes lay eggs.* **laid, laying.**

lay[2]

At about nine o'clock she lay down and fell asleep.

lazy

not willing to work or to move fast: *The lazy cat lay on the porch all day.* **lazier, laziest.**

lead¹

1. to show the way by going along with someone or by being in front of someone: *The teacher led the children across the street.* **2.** to be a way to get somewhere: *This road leads to the lake.* **3.** to be first; to be ahead: *Our team was leading when the bell rang.* **led, leading.** (Lead¹ rhymes with seed.)

lead²

1. a heavy gray metal. Lead is used to make pipe. **2.** the gray material in the middle of a pencil that you write with. (Lead² rhymes with bed.)

leader

a person who shows the way; a person who goes first: *He was the leader on our hike.* **leaders.**

leader

leaf

one of the thin, flat, green parts of a tree or plant. **leaves.**

leak

1. a hole or crack that should not be there. A leak lets something in or out. **2.** to let something in or out: *My feet are wet because my boots leak.* **leaks; leaked, leaking.**

leaky

having a leak or leaks; leaking: *The drip of the leaky faucet kept me awake all night.* **leakier, leakiest.**

lean¹

1. to bend; stand in a slanting position: *The small trees lean over in the wind.* **2.** to put against something: *The boy leaned his bike against the garage door.* **leaned, leaning.**

lean²

thin; not fat: *The lean and hungry lost dog ate the meat quickly.* **leaner, leanest.**

lean¹ (definition 2)
*He **leaned** his bike against the garage door.*

197

leap (definition 1)
*He crossed the ditch in one **leap.***

left[1]—*The arrow points to the **left.***

leap

1. a jump: *He crossed the ditch in one leap.* **2.** to jump: *The boy leaped as high as he could.* **leaps; leaped, leaping.**

learn

to find out about something; come to know: *We learned that a desert is a hot, dry, sandy place.* **learned, learning.**

least

1. less than any other: *He is the least friendly of the puppies.* **2.** the smallest thing: *The least you can do is say you're sorry.*

leather

the skin of an animal that has been treated in a special way. Leather is used to make shoes, gloves, jackets, saddles, and the like.

leave

1. to go away: *They are going to leave the room.* **2.** to go without taking something: *Don't leave your roller skates in the hall.* **left, leaving.**

leaves

more than one leaf.

led

She led her younger brother across the street. We were led through the cave by a guide.

left[1]

toward the direction of the first word on this line; the opposite of right. Words are read from left to right. *Turn left at the next light.*

left[2]

She left at noon. She had left the book at home.

leg

1. the part of the body between the hip and the foot. People and animals stand and move around on their legs. **2.** anything that is shaped or used like a leg: *Most chairs have four legs.* **legs.**

lemon

a sour, yellow fruit. Lemons grow on trees. **lemons.**

lemonade

a drink made of lemon juice, sugar, and water.

lend

to let someone have something or use something for a time, until you get it back: *Will you lend me your bike for an hour?* **lent, lending.**

lemons

length

1. how long something is; the distance from one end to the other: *The length of the rug is ten feet and the width is eight feet.* **2.** how long something lasts in time: *The length of the movie was two hours.* **lengths.**

lens

a special, curved piece of glass or plastic. Lenses are used in glasses for eyes, cameras, and microscopes. **lenses.**

lenses

lent

She lent the boy her book. I have lent her my pencil.

leopard

a large animal like a cat that has yellow fur with black spots. Leopards can grow to be up to eight feet long. **leopards.**

less

We are eating less meat these days. The book report is less important than the test. My brother weighs ten pounds less than I weigh.

leopard

lesson

something that you learn; something that you are taught: *We had a spelling lesson today. My sister takes piano lessons.* **lessons.**

let

to not stop someone or something from doing something; allow; permit: *I let her ride my bike. She let the door slam.* **let, letting.**

let's

let us: *Let's plan the party together.*

letter

1. a part of the alphabet; a mark or sign that stands for any one of the sounds that make up words. There are 26 letters in the alphabet. **2.** a written message: *I wrote a letter to Grandmother yesterday.* **letters.**

lettuce

a vegetable with crisp green leaves. Lettuce is used in salads.

lettuce

level

1. flat and even; having the same height everywhere: *The floor is not level; it slants down.* **2.** how high something is; height: *The level of the water in the pitcher rose as he poured more water in.* **levels.**

lever

a bar used for lifting a weight on one end by pushing down on the other end. **levers.**

lever—*He used a **lever** to move the rock.*

librarian

a person who directs or helps to manage a library. **librarians.**

library

a room or building where many books are kept. You can borrow books from most libraries. **libraries.**

lick

to move the tongue over something: *She licked all the stamps. The cat licked its fur.* **licked, licking.**

lid

a cover that can be taken off something: *He lifted the lid to see what was cooking in the pot.* **lids.**

lid—*He lifted the **lid** to see what was cooking in the pot.*

lie[1]

1. something said that is not true: *He told a lie about the broken window.* **2.** to say something that is not true: *He lied about his grade.* **lies; lied, lying.**

lie[2]

1. to have your body in a flat position: *I have a headache and I want to lie down.* **2.** to be flat: *The book was lying on the table.* **lay, lain, lying.**

lie[2] (definition 1)

life

1. being alive; living, breathing, and growing. People, animals, and plants have life. Rocks do not have life. **2.** the time a person, an animal, or a plant is alive. A dandelion has a very short life. **lives** (for **2.**).

lifeguard

lifeguard

a person who works at a beach or a swimming pool. A lifeguard helps a swimmer who gets into trouble in the water. **lifeguards.**

lift

to raise something up higher; pick up: *He lifted the heavy box and put it on the table.* **lifted, lifting.**

light[1]

1. a form of energy that gets rid of darkness, and makes it possible for us to see. Light comes from the sun, lamps, candles, and the like. **2.** anything that gives light in order that we can see. The sun, a lamp, or a candle are lights. **3.** to set fire to: *Dad lighted two candles.* **4.** pale in color; not bright: *She has light brown hair.* **lights** (for **2.**)**; lighted** or **lit, lighting; lighter, lightest.**

lighthouse

light²

not weighing very much; easy to lift or carry; not heavy: *A rabbit is light, but an elephant is heavy.* **lighter, lightest.**

lighthouse

a tall building like a tower that has a strong, bright light which shines far out over the water. The bright light keeps ships from coming too close to the shore. **lighthouses.**

lightning

a flash of electricity in the sky. The sound that lightning makes is thunder.

like¹

She looks like her mom. It looks like rain. He had a dollar, and I had a like amount. At the zoo he saw elephants, lions, tigers, and the like.

like²

to be pleased with something or someone: *Most people like apple pie. I like all my friends.* **liked, liking.**

lily

a plant with tall, thin stems and large flowers that are shaped like bells. Lilies grow from bulbs. **lilies.**

limb

a large branch: *They sawed the dead limb off the tree.* **limbs.**

lime

a sour fruit that looks like a green lemon. Limes grow on trees. **limes.**

limp¹

1. a painful step or walk because of an injury: *I walked with a limp after I hurt my knee.* **2.** to walk with a painful step: *I limped for days after my fall.* **limps; limped, limping.**

limp¹ (definition 1)
*The football player **limped** off the field.*

limp²

easy to bend; not stiff: *Spaghetti gets limp when it's cooked.* **limper, limpest.**

line¹

1. a piece of string, rope, or wire: *The gardener cut the telephone line while he was trimming the tree.* **2.** a long, thin mark. Some lines are straight and some are curved. **3.** a row of people or things: *We stood in a line to wait for the bus.* **4.** to arrange or form something in a line: *The teacher asked room 6 to line up against the wall.* **lines; lined, lining.**

line¹ (definition 3)
*They stood in **line** for tickets.*

line²

to put a layer of paper, cloth, or the like on the inside surface of something: *Her boots are lined with fur.* **lined, lining.**

lining

a layer of paper, cloth, or the like that covers the inside surface of something: *The lining of my coat is made of wool.* **linings.**

lion

a large animal like a cat that has yellow fur. Lions can grow to be up to nine feet long. Male lions have long hair, called a mane, around their heads and necks. **lions.**

lion

lip

either of the two front edges of your mouth. You blow through your lips when you whistle. **lips.**

liquid

something that flows like water. A liquid is not a solid or a gas. Juice and milk are liquids. **liquids.**

liquid

list

1. words, names, numbers, and like things that are written one below the other: *Don't forget your grocery list.* **2.** to make a list of something: *A dictionary lists words in alphabetical order.* **lists; listed, listing.**

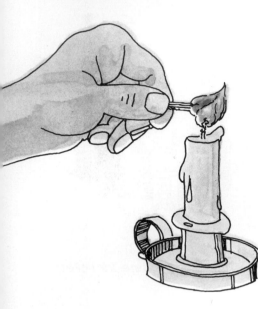

lit—He **lit** a candle.

live²

listen

to try to hear something or someone: *We listened to her story.* **listened, listening.**

lit

He lit a candle. The room was lit with many lamps.

liter

an amount of liquid. A liter is a little more than a quart. **liters.**

literature

something that has been written in a beautiful and thoughtful way. Stories, poems, and plays are kinds of literature. Literature is written at different times and in different places.

litter

1. little bits of things scattered around: *The Boy Scout troop picked up the litter along the road.* **2.** to scatter things around; make untidy: *You have littered the room with your papers.* **littered, littering.**

little

1. small; not big or large: *His pet is a little kitten.* **2.** not long in time or in distance: *It will be dark in a little while.* **3.** not much: *A sick child eats only a little food.* **littler, littlest.**

live¹

1. to be alive; to breathe and grow. Animals live, but rocks do not. **2.** to make your home in a place: *We live in a big city.* **lived, living.** (Live¹ rhymes with give.)

live²

having life; alive: *She brought in a live snake to show the class.* (Live² rhymes with dive.)

lives

more than one life: *Lives are saved when smoke alarms are used.* (Lives rhymes with dives.)

lizard

a long, thin animal with dry, rough skin. Lizards look something like snakes, but do not have a dangerous bite. Most lizards have four legs and a long tail. **lizards.**

lizard

llama

an animal that looks like a camel, but is smaller. Llamas have no hump. They have thick, woolly hair. Llamas come from South America. **llamas.**

llama

load

1. something that is being carried: *The truck carried a load of bricks.* **2.** to put what is to be carried in or on something: *We loaded our bags in the car trunk.* **loads; loaded, loading.**

loaf¹

1. bread that is baked as one piece: *We cut the loaf of bread into slices.* **2.** anything made into the shape of a loaf and then cooked: *We ate meat loaf for dinner.* **loaves.**

loaf²

to spend time doing nothing important: *After working all week, they loaf around on Saturdays.* **loafed, loafing.**

loaves

more than one loaf: *A bakery bakes many loaves of bread every day.*

lobster

an animal that lives in the ocean. Lobsters have hard shells and two large claws. They are used for food. **lobsters.**

lobster

locket

locate

to find out the position of something: *The boy tried to locate his friend's house. Can you locate Canada on a map?* **located, locating.**

lock

1. something that keeps doors, boxes, windows, or other things closed. Many locks must be opened with keys. **2.** to fasten with a lock: *Lock the door before you leave.* **locks; locked, locking.**

locket

a little metal case for holding a tiny picture of someone. A locket is usually worn around the neck on a chain. **lockets.**

log

log

a long piece of wood cut from a tree trunk or a large branch. Some logs are cut into boards. **logs.**

lonely

feeling sad because you are alone and need company: *He was lonely while his brother was away.* **lonelier, loneliest.**

long

1. a great distance from the beginning to the end of something: *An inch is short; a mile is long.* **2.** lasting for some time: *We went on a long trip last summer.* **longer, longest.**

look

1. to see; turn your eyes toward something: *Look at the elephants.* **2.** to try to find something; search: *Did you look in the closet for your coat? Look that word up in your dictionary.* **3.** to seem; appear to be a certain way: *She looked sick this morning.* **looked, looking.**

look (definition 2)
*He **looked** up the word.*

loop

the part of a curved line, string, ribbon, or wire that crosses itself. When you tie your shoelaces, you make two loops. **loops.**

loose

not tight; not firmly fastened: *The top button on my coat is loose.* **looser, loosest.**

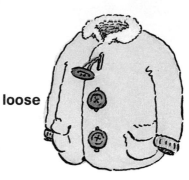

loose

loosen

to make something loose: *Hot water loosened the top to the glue.* **loosened, loosening.**

lose

1. to not have any longer: *I hope we don't lose any pieces to the puzzle.* **2.** to not win: *We may lose the game.* **lost, losing.**

lost

I have lost my new pencil. She lost the race.

lot

a great number of something; a large amount: *There were a lot of birds on the roof.* **lots.**

lot—*There were a **lot** of birds on the roof.*

loud

not quiet; making a great sound: *The door slammed with a loud crash.* **louder, loudest.**

Louisiana

one of the fifty states of the United States.

love

1. a warm, good feeling for someone or something: *She feels love for her puppy.* **2.** to have this warm, good feeling for someone or something: *He loves all of his friends.* **loved, loving.**

lovely

beautiful; good: *She is a lovely girl. We enjoyed the lovely sunset.* **lovelier, loveliest.**

lumber

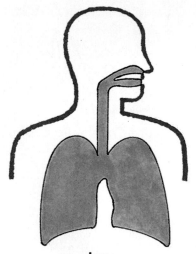

lungs

low

not far above the ground or the floor; not high or tall: *The wall was so low I climbed over it.* **lower, lowest.**

luck

something that just seems to happen to you. A person can have good luck or bad luck.

lucky

having or bringing good luck: *This was my lucky day. I found a dollar bill.* **luckier, luckiest.**

lumber

wood that is cut into boards: *He bought lumber to build a doghouse.*

lump

1. a small, solid chunk of something that has no special shape: *He doesn't like lumps in his oatmeal.*
2. a place that swells up from being hit; a bump: *I have a lump on my head where I ran into the door.* **lumps.**

lunch

a meal eaten in the middle of the day; the meal between breakfast and dinner: *We had tuna sandwiches for lunch.* **lunches.**

lung

the part of your body that holds the air you breathe. People have two lungs. **lungs.**

lying¹

They are not telling the truth; they are lying.

lying²

He is lying on the sleeping bag.

Mm

ma'am

a title used to show respect to a woman: *May I help you, ma'am?*

macaroni

a food made of flour and water, dried in the shape of hollow tubes.

machine

something with moving parts that does work. Machines use power to help people get things done faster and more easily. Cars, washers, and computers are machines. **machines.**

mad

very angry: *He will be mad when he sees me wearing his new sweater.* **madder, maddest.**

made

My sister made the salad. She has made salads before.

magazine

a collection of stories and other things written by different people and printed regularly. Magazines come out usually every week or every month. **magazines.**

magic

the skill of pretending to make things appear, disappear, or change into something else; performing tricks that seem to be impossible: *She made rabbits appear out of the hat by magic.*

machines

magician

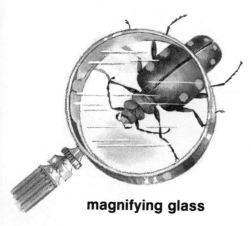

magnifying glass

magician
a person who can use magic or who does magic tricks. **magicians.**

magnet
a piece of metal that pulls bits of iron or steel to it. **magnets.**

magnificent
wonderful to look at; grand: *The king had a magnificent palace.*

magnify
to make something look larger than it really is. A hand lens magnifies the legs of insects so that you can see them better. **magnified, magnifying.**

magnifying glass
a piece of curved glass, called a lens, that makes things look larger than they really are. **magnifying glasses.**

magpie
a noisy, black-and-white bird with a long tail and short wings. **magpies.**

magpie

mail
1. letters and packages sent by one person to another: *Has the mail come yet?* **2.** to send by way of the post office: *Please mail this letter for me.* **mailed, mailing.**

mailbox
a place where you mail letters or cards, or a place where mail is left for you. **mailboxes.**

mail carrier
a person whose job is bringing mail to people. **mail carriers.**

main
most important: *The main road runs through the middle of town.*

Maine

one of the fifty states of the United States.

Majesty

a title used in speaking to or about a king or queen. **Majesties.**

make

1. to put together or build something: *We will make costumes for the party.* **2.** to cause something to happen: *Please don't make any noise. Make her sit down.* **3.** to get money for doing something: *We made money selling lemonade.* **made, making.**

make-believe

not real; pretend: *The story is about a make-believe monster.*

male

the kind of person or animal that can be the father of young. Men and boys are males. A rooster is a male chicken. **males.**

mall

a shopping area with stores built around a wide central walk. **malls.**

mallard

a kind of wild duck. **mallards.**

mama

another word for mother. **mamas.**

mammal

a group of animals usually covered with hair or fur. A female mammal gives milk to her young from her own body. Human beings, dogs, and whales are all mammals. **mammals.**

mammals

man

a grown-up male person. When a boy grows up, he becomes a man. **men.**

mane

manage

to control or guide something: *They hired someone to manage the business.* **managed, managing.**

mane

the long, heavy hair on the back of the neck of a horse. A lion also has a mane around the head and neck. **manes.**

mango

a slightly sour, juicy fruit. Mangoes grow in warm countries. **mangoes.**

Manitoba

one of the ten provinces of Canada.

mangos

manners

polite ways of behaving: *People with manners say "Please" and "Thank you."*

many

a large number of: *Many years ago the house was new. Do you know many of the answers?* **more, most.**

map

a drawing of an area of the earth that shows many places. Maps often show countries, cities, rivers, seas, and lakes. **maps.**

maple

a kind of tree that is grown for shade. One kind of maple has sweet juice that is made into maple syrup. **maples.**

maple

marble

a small glass ball used to play games. **marbles.**

march

to walk in a group in line with everyone taking the same size steps: *The school band marched in the parade.* **marched, marching.**

March

the third month of the year. It has 31 days. It comes after February and before April.

margarine

a soft food like butter. Margarine is made from vegetable oils instead of from cream.

mark

1. a line or dot made on something. **2.** to make a mark on something: *Mark the cities on the map.* **marks; marked, marking.**

—**mark** (definition 1)

marker

a kind of pen used for writing or drawing. **markers.**

marker

market

an outdoor place where people buy and sell food and other things. **markets.**

marry

to take as husband or wife: *They plan to be married in June.* **married, marrying.**

Maryland

one of the fifty states of the United States.

mash

to beat into a soft mass: *I'll mash the potatoes after they have cooked.* **mashed, mashing.**

mask

a covering that hides or protects the face: *The firefighter wore a gas mask.* **masks.**

mask

Massachusetts

one of the fifty states of the United States.

mat

a small rug or a thick pad: *Wipe your feet on the mat. Put a mat under the hot dish.* **mats.**

mat

match²

match¹

a short stick of wood or stiff paper. A match has a tip that catches fire when you rub it against something rough. **matches.**

match²

to go well together; find one exactly like: *His scarf and mittens match. Match the words with the pictures.* **matched, matching.**

mate

one of a pair: *Where is the mate to this mitten?* **mates.**

material

1. what a thing is made from: *Wood is a material for building houses.* **2.** something used in doing an activity. Writing materials include paper, pens, and pencils. **materials.**

math

a short word meaning mathematics.

mathematics

the study of numbers. Addition and subtraction are a part of mathematics.

matter

1. what things are made of. Matter takes up space and has weight. It can be a solid, liquid, or gas. **2.** to be important: *Nothing seems to matter to him.* **3.** trouble: *"What's the matter?" she asked.* **mattered, mattering.**

mattress

a covering of strong cloth stuffed with soft material, and used to sleep on. **mattresses.**

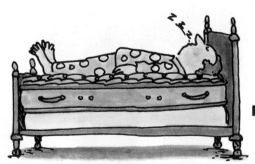

mattress

may

You may have an apple. It may rain tomorrow.

May

the fifth month of the year. It has 31 days. It comes after April and before June.

maybe

Maybe it will rain. Maybe she'll go to the movies.

me

Please give me a piece of paper. Let me go. Come with me.

meadow

a piece of land where grass grows: *Sheep grazed in the meadow.* **meadows.**

meadow

meal[1]

food eaten or served at any one time; breakfast, lunch, or dinner. **meals.**

meal[2]

the seed of wheat, oats, or corn that has been ground up.

mean[1]

1. to have in mind as a goal; want to do: *He didn't mean to break the glass.* **2.** to say the same thing as something else. The word *automobile* means the same thing as *car.* **3.** to be a sign of: *A red light means stop.* **meant, meaning.**

mean[2]

not nice; unkind; cruel: *Don't be mean to the puppy.* **meaner, meanest.**

meaning

something that is meant: *Do you know the meaning of this word?* **meanings.**

mean[1] (definition 1)
*He didn't **mean** to break the glass.*

meant

She meant what she said. He had meant to call.

measles

a disease that causes a bad cold, a high temperature, and small red spots on the skin: *She is sick in bed with the measles.*

measure

to find the size or amount of something: *We measured the room and found that it is 20 feet long.* **measured, measuring.**

meat

a kind of food that comes from animals. Beef and pork are kinds of meat.

mechanic

a person whose job is fixing machines: *A mechanic repaired our car.* **mechanics.**

mechanic

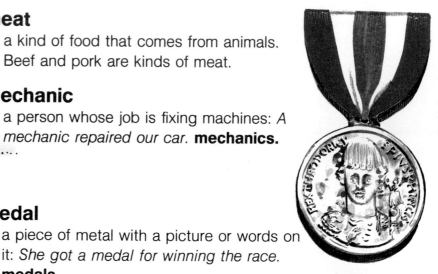

medal

medal

a piece of metal with a picture or words on it: *She got a medal for winning the race.* **medals.**

medicine

something used to make a sick person well: *He took some medicine for his cold.* **medicines.**

meet

1. to get together with someone: *I'll meet my friend at the library.* **2.** to be somewhere and say hello when other people get there: *They met us at the airport.* **3.** to begin to get to know someone: *I met my friend last year when school started.* **met, meeting.**

meeting

the getting together of people: *The meeting of our club is at four o'clock this afternoon.* **meetings.**

meet (definition 2)
*Grandpa **met** us at the airport.*

216

melon
a large, sweet fruit. Melons grow on vines. Cantaloupes and watermelons are melons. **melons.**

melon

melt
to turn from a solid into a liquid. Ice becomes water when it melts. **melted, melting.**

member
someone who belongs to a group: *Our singing group has four members.* **members.**

members

memorize
to learn and remember; learn by heart: *Everyone in the class has memorized the poem.* **memorized, memorizing.**

memory
the power to remember things, or keep things in the mind: *He should know the answer because he has a good memory.* **memories.**

menu

men
more than one man: *Boys grow up to be men.*

mention
to tell or talk about something: *He mentioned the TV show he watched last night.* **mentioned, mentioning.**

menu
a list of the food served at a meal: *We looked at the menu and chose our lunch.* **menus.**

merry
full of fun; happy and cheerful: *She has a merry laugh.* **merrier, merriest.**

merry-go-round
a machine that goes round and round. It usually has statues of horses or other animals that you can ride on. **merry-go-rounds.**

merry-go-round

mesa

mesa

a high, steep hill that has a flat top and stands all by itself. **mesas.**

mess

a place or a group of things that is not clean or neat: *Please clean up the mess in your closet.* **messes.**

message

the words sent by one person to another: *He got your telephone message.* **messages.**

messenger

a person who carries a message to someone. **messengers.**

messy

not neat or clean; in a mess: *The room was so messy that it took two days to clean it.* **messier, messiest.**

messy

met

They met in the park. Have you met my aunt?

metal

a hard material such as iron, gold, silver, or steel. Metals are usually shiny and are found underground. Metals can be melted or hammered into thin sheets. **metals.**

meter

a unit of length equal to 100 centimeters. A guitar is about one meter long. **meters.**

Mexican

1. a person born or living in Mexico. **2.** of Mexico: *The Mexican capital is Mexico City.* **Mexicans.**

Mexico

the country south of the United States.

Mexico

caption: mice

mice

more than one mouse: *We saw several mice in the basement.*

Michigan

one of the fifty states of the United States.

microscope

something that makes small things look larger. A microscope helps you see things that are too small to see with your eyes. **microscopes.**

caption: microscope

microwave

a special kind of oven that cooks food very quickly. **microwaves.**

middle

the center: *My cap was in the middle of the street. The middle house is ours.*

caption: middle

midnight

twelve o'clock at night; the middle of the night.

might[1]

Mother said we might play after dinner. He might have called yesterday while we were out.

might[2]

great power: *We had to pull with all our might to move the bookcase.*

mile

a unit of length. Distances between American cities are measured in miles. **miles.**

milk

the white liquid from cows, which we drink and use in cooking. Milk helps us grow.

mill

mill

a building where machines are used to make things. Cloth is made at a cotton mill. **mills.**

million

one thousand thousand; 1,000,000. **millions.**

mind

1. the part of a person that knows, thinks, feels, and remembers. You use your mind to learn and to imagine. *She has a good mind.* **2.** to look after; take care of: *Please mind your own business.* **3.** to feel bad about: *I don't mind cold weather.* **minds; minded, minding.**

mine¹

This scarf is mine.

mineral—*Quartz is a mineral.*

mine²

a large hole dug in the earth to get out coal, salt, or anything of value: *We saw a gold mine in California.* **mines.**

mineral

something dug from the earth. Anything that is not a plant, animal, or other living thing is a mineral. Coal and gold are minerals. **minerals.**

Minnesota

one of the fifty states of the United States.

mint

a sweet-smelling plant used for flavoring, or a piece of candy that tastes like mint. **mints.**

mint

minus

1. less: *7 minus 2 leaves 5.* **2.** without; not having: *The book was returned minus its cover.*

minute

1. one of the 60 equal parts of an hour; 60 seconds.
2. a short time: *We will be there in a minute.* **minutes.**

minus—*7 minus 2 leaves 5.*

mirror

a glass in which you can see yourself. **mirrors.**

mischief

a way of acting that causes harm or trouble, often without your meaning it: *Don't get into mischief.*

miss

1. to not find, get, or meet something; fail to do: *He tried to catch the ball, but missed it.* **2.** to feel bad because someone or something is gone: *We miss you. I did not miss my glove until I got home.* **missed, missing.**

Miss

a title used before the name of a young girl or an unmarried woman. **Misses.**

Mississippi

one of the fifty states of the United States.

Missouri

one of the fifty states of the United States.

misspell

to write or say the wrong letters, when you are spelling a word. **misspelled, misspelling.**

mistake

something that is not right or done the way it ought to be: *I made a mistake in adding those numbers.* **mistakes.**

mitten

a kind of glove that covers the four fingers together. A mitten has a special place for the thumb. **mittens.**

mix

1. to put together and stir well: *We mixed butter, sugar, milk, flour, and eggs to make the cake.* **2.** something that is already mixed: *We used a mix to make the pie crust.* **mixed, mixing; mixes.**

misspell—*Someone **misspelled** Mississippi.*

mobile

moccasin

mole

mixture
something that has been mixed or put together. **mixtures.**

mobile
something that hangs from fine wires or threads and that moves when the air around it moves. **mobiles.**

moccasin
a soft shoe without a heel. Moccasins were first made by North American Indians. **moccasins.**

model
1. a small copy of something: *A globe is a model of the earth.* **2.** to make or shape out of something soft: *Let's model an elephant out of clay.* **models; modeled, modeling.**

molasses
a sweet, brown syrup. Molasses is used in cooking.

mole
a small animal that lives underground. Moles have soft, smooth fur and very small eyes that cannot see well. **moles.**

mom
another word for mother. **moms.**

moment
a very short amount or length of time: *In a moment the bell will ring.* **moments.**

Monday
the day after Sunday; the second day of the week. **Mondays.**

money
coins and paper used for buying and selling things. People buy things with money. People who work at jobs are paid money.

monkey

a hairy animal with long arms and a long tail. There are many different kinds of monkeys. Monkeys eat fruits and vegetables and often live in trees. **monkeys.**

monster

a make-believe person or animal that is scary. In stories, some monsters are friendly, and others are not. Dragons are monsters. **monsters.**

monster

Montana

one of the fifty states of the United States.

month

a part of a year. There are twelve months in a year. They are January, February, March, April, May, June, July, August, September, October, November, December. **months.**

moon

the biggest and brightest light seen in the sky at night. The moon is round like a ball and is smaller than the earth. It moves around the earth. Other planets also have moons. **moons.**

moonlight

the light of the moon: *We could almost read by moonlight.*

moose

moose

an animal that looks like a very large deer. It lives in Canada and in parts of the United States. The male moose has a large head and broad antlers. **moose.**

mop

1. a bundle of thick strings or a sponge fastened at the end of a long handle. You use a mop to clean floors. **2.** to wash or wipe up: *We should mop the kitchen floor.* **mops; mopped, mopping.**

more

This soup needs more salt. We need more than three players for the game. This plant needs more sun.

morning

the part of the day between nighttime and noon: *This morning we all ate breakfast together.* **mornings.**

mosquito

a small insect with two wings. The female mosquito bites. **mosquitoes.**

mosquito

moss

tiny, soft, flat, green plants. Moss grows close together on the ground, on rocks, or on trees. Moss looks like a carpet.

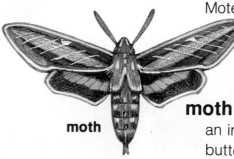

moss

most

Most people like music.

motel

a building where people can rent a room to sleep in. Motels are close to busy roads or highways. **motels.**

moth

moth

an insect with wings, that looks something like a butterfly. Moths fly mostly at night. **moths.**

mother

a woman who has a child or children. **mothers.**

motion

a way of moving. Something is in motion if it is not still. *On a windy day the clouds are always in motion.*

motor

a machine that makes other machines work. Motors run on electricity or gas. Cars have motors that make them run. **motors.**

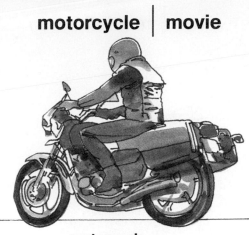

motorcycle

motorcycle
a thing to ride with a motor and two wheels. A motorcycle looks like a bicycle but is heavier and larger. **motorcycles.**

mound
a pile or heap of earth, stones, or other material. **mounds.**

mountain
a very high hill. **mountains.**

mouse
a small animal with soft fur and a long, thin tail. Some mice live in people's houses. Some mice live in fields and meadows. **mice.**

mouth
the part of the body that helps people eat and talk. The mouth is part of the face, and the tongue and teeth are inside the mouth. **mouths.**

move
1. to go from one place to another, or put something in a different place: *She moved from one chair to another. Please move your bicycle out of the driveway.* **2.** to change the place where you live: *We live downtown now, but my parents want to move to the country.* **moved, moving.**

movement
a moving: *The back-and-forth movement of the swing made him a little dizzy.* **movements.**

mover
a person or company whose work is moving furniture from one place to another. **movers.**

movie
a story in pictures. The pictures are taken by a special camera and shown on a screen. **movies.**

movie—*A movie is shot on film.*

225

mower

mow

to cut down grass or grain: *It is time to mow the grass again.* **mowed, mowing.**

mower

a machine that cuts grass: *It was hard to start the lawn mower.* **mowers.**

Mr.

a title used before a man's name.

Mrs.

a title used before a married woman's name.

Ms.

a title used before a woman's name.

much

a great amount: *I don't have much money. I like swimming very much.* **more, most.**

mud

mud

very wet earth that is soft and sticky: *We got some mud on our boots.*

muffler

1. a scarf worn around the neck. **2.** anything used to make a sound quieter or softer: *A car with a muffler that doesn't work is noisy.* **mufflers.**

mug

a heavy cup with a handle. **mugs.**

mule

mule

an animal whose mother is a horse and whose father is a donkey. **mules.**

multiplication

the act of adding one number a number of times; multiplying one number by another: *The multiplication of 3 times 2 gives the product of 6.*

multiply

to add one number a number of times: *To multiply 2 by 5 means to add 2 five times, making 10.* **multiplied, multiplying.**

mumps

a disease that causes your neck and face to swell and makes it hard for you to swallow.

muscle

a part of the body that helps the body move. Without muscles, you could not lift and carry things. Your body has muscles of different sizes and shapes. **muscles.**

museum

a building for keeping and showing interesting things. People visit art museums, science museums, and museums with objects from long ago. **museums.**

mushrooms

mushroom

a small living thing like a plant. A mushroom often has the shape of an umbrella and grows very fast. Some mushrooms are good to eat, but some can poison you. **mushrooms.**

music

the sounds made by a piano, a violin, a guitar, and other musical instruments. The sound of a person singing is also music. *I hear music in the next room.*

musical

sounding beautiful like music: *We heard the musical song from a robin in the tree.*

musical instrument

something that makes beautiful sounds. Guitars, violins, and pianos are musical instruments. **musical Instruments.**

musician

mustard

musician

a person who sings, plays, or writes music. **musicians.**

must

You must eat the right food. I must go now.

mustache

the hair that grows on a man's upper lip. **mustaches.**

mustard

a yellow powder or paste with a sharp, hot taste. Mustard is made from the seeds of a plant. *I like mustard on my hot dog.*

my

I forgot my gloves. My house is around the corner.

myself

I can do it myself. I cut myself.

mysterious

hard to explain or understand: *She heard a mysterious noise.*

mystery

something that you cannot understand nor explain: *It was a mystery why the radio started playing in the middle of the night.* **mysteries.**

Nn

nail

1. a thin piece of metal that has a point at one end. You hammer nails through pieces of wood to hold the wood together. **2.** the hard part at the end of a finger or toe. **nails.**

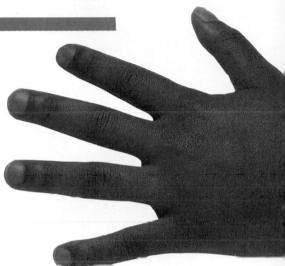

nail (definition 1)

name

1. the word used to speak of a person, animal, place, or thing: *Our dog's name is Lightning.* **2.** to give someone or something a name: *They named the baby after his father.* **names; named, naming.**

nails (definition 2)

nap (definition 1)

nap

1. a short sleep: *Grandma took a nap after lunch.* **2.** to sleep for a short time: *We must be quiet while the baby naps.* **naps; napped, napping.**

napkin

a piece of cloth or paper. Napkins are used at meals to protect your clothes and to wipe your lips and fingers. **napkins.**

narrator

a person who tells a story. **narrators.**

narrow

not wide; not far from one side to the other: *It was hard to drive down the narrow street.* **narrower, narrowest.**

narrow

229

nature

nation

a group of people living in one country with one government. The people of a nation usually speak the same language. **nations.**

nature

everything in the world not made by people. Plants, animals, air, water, and people are parts of nature. The earth and its mountains, oceans, and rivers are parts of nature too.

navy

a large group of sailors and their ships. A navy fights to protect its country in a war. **navies.**

near

close to; not far away from something: *We live near a lake. My birthday is near.* **nearer, nearest.**

nearby

near; not far away: *We visited a park nearby.*

nearly

not quite; almost: *It is nearly time for school to start.*

neat

1. clean and not having things lying around: *She kept her room neat.* **2.** very nice; wonderful: *My uncle gave me a neat gift.* **neater, neatest.**

Nebraska

one of the fifty states of the United States.

necessary

needing to be done: *It is necessary to buy a ticket to get into the show.*

neck

the part of the body between the head and shoulders. **necks.**

necklace

a kind of jewelry worn around the neck. Necklaces may be made of gold, silver, or beads. **necklaces.**

necktie

a narrow strip of cloth worn around the neck. A necktie is worn under the collar of a shirt, tied in front. **neckties.**

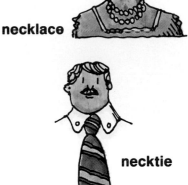

necklace

need

to be unable to do without something: *Plants need water to grow. I need new gloves for the winter.* **needed, needing.**

necktie

needle

1. a very thin, sharp tool used in sewing. A needle has a small hole in one end for thread to pass through. **2.** a thin tube with a sharp point, used by doctors to give shots. **needles.**

needle (definition 1)

neigh

1. a sound that a horse makes: *We heard a soft neigh from the stable.* **2.** to make such a sound: *The horse neighed softly when we entered the barn.* **neighs; neighed, neighing.**

neighbor

someone who lives nearby: *Our neighbors were outside raking leaves in the yard.* **neighbors.**

neighborhood

the streets and houses surrounding the place where you live: *We have a school and a park in our neighborhood.* **neighborhoods.**

neither

Neither child wanted to go to school. Neither you nor I can do that.

nephew

a son of one's brother or sister. **nephews.**

nest

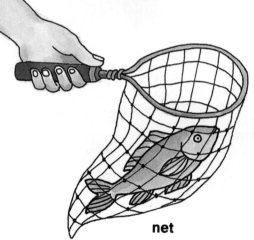

net

nerve

a part of the body that connects the brain with other parts of the body. Nerves carry messages to the brain and from the brain. **nerves.**

nervous

easily excited or upset; uneasy: *He was nervous when he had to speak in front of the class.*

nest

a kind of home that birds build. Nests are made in the shape of a bowl from straw, twigs, and leaves. Birds lay their eggs in nests. **nests.**

net

a kind of cloth with holes in it. A net is made of string tied together. Nets are used in sports like tennis and basketball. They are also used to catch fish. **nets.**

Nevada

one of the fifty states of the United States.

never

He has never flown on an airplane. I will never get all of this work done.

new

1. never made or thought of before; not old: *She had a new idea for an art project.* **2.** not used yet; not worn or used up: *Dad bought a new car.* **newer, newest.**

New Brunswick

one of the ten provinces of Canada.

Newfoundland

one of the ten provinces of Canada.

New Hampshire

one of the fifty states of the United States.

New Jersey

one of the fifty states of the United States.

New Mexico

one of the fifty states of the United States.

news

1. facts about something that has just happened: *Mom told us the good news about her job.* **2.** a report in a newspaper, on TV, or radio about what is happening in the world.

newspaper

sheets of paper printed every day or week telling news and advertising things for sale: *My parents read the newspaper every morning.* **newspapers.**

New York

one of the fifty states of the United States.

next

I borrowed some paper from the girl next to me. I missed school on Monday, but I went back the next day.

nibble

to eat with quick small bites. Mice and rabbits nibble. *I nibbled on some cheese before dinner.* **nibbled, nibbling.**

nibble—*The rabbit is* **nibbling** *some lettuce.*

nice

good; kind: *I had a nice time at the party. They were nice to me.* **nicer, nicest.**

nickel

a coin in the United States and Canada worth five cents. Five nickels make one quarter. **nickels.**

nickels

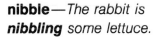

nickname

a name used instead of a person's real name: *Her nickname is "Red" because she has red hair. "Jim" is a nickname for James.* **nicknames.**

nicotine

a drug found in tobacco smoke. Breathing in nicotine makes the heart work harder.

niece

a daughter of one's brother or sister. **nieces.**

night

the time between evening and morning. Another word for night is nighttime. **nights.**

nighttime

the time between evening and morning. Another word for nighttime is night.

nine

one more than eight; 9. **nines.**

nineteen

nine more than ten; 19. **nineteens.**

nineteenth

1. next after 18th; 19th. **2.** one of 19 equal parts. **nineteenths.**

ninety

ten more than eighty; 90. **nineties.**

ninth

1. next after the eighth; 9th. **2.** one of nine equal parts. **ninths.**

nip

to squeeze tight and quickly; pinch; bite: *The kitten nipped at my fingers.* **nipped, nipping.**

no

There are no trees in our front yard. Just say "No, thank you" if you don't want any more to eat.

nobody

Nobody wanted to go home before the game ended.

nip—*The crab **nipped** his toe.*

nod

1. to bow the head a little bit and raise it again quietly: *She nodded at me when we passed.* **2.** to say yes by moving your head in this way: *Dad nodded for us to go on with our play.* **nodded, nodding.**

noise

an unpleasant sound that we do not want to hear: *The noise of the dog barking kept me from sleeping.* **noises.**

noisy

making a lot of noise; full of unpleasant sounds: *The washing machine was noisy. We live on a noisy street.* **noisier, noisiest.**

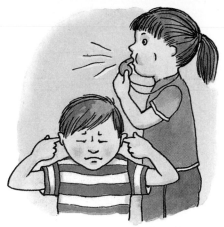

noisy—*It was so noisy he had to cover his ears.*

none

None of the dishes were broken. None of the children wanted to play at the park.

nonsense

words or ideas that don't make sense: *The talk about the haunted house in town was nonsense.*

noodles

a food made of long, flat strips of dried dough. Noodles are often served with a tomato sauce, butter, or in soup.

noodles

noon

the middle of the day; 12 o'clock in the daytime. *Many people eat lunch at noon.*

no one

No one knew the answer.

nor

We had neither food nor water with us on the hike.

north

the direction to the right as you face the setting sun. North is the opposite of south.

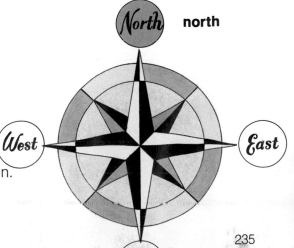

North America

a continent; one of the large masses of land on the earth.

North Carolina

one of the fifty states of the United States.

North Dakota

one of the fifty states of the United States.

northeast

the direction halfway between north and east.

northwest

the direction halfway between north and west.

Northwest Territories

one of the two territories of Canada.

nose

the part of the face that sticks out just above the mouth. The nose is used for smelling and breathing. **noses.**

nose

not

I am not going to school today. Two and two are not five. It is not time to leave.

note

1. a very short letter: *I sent Grandma a note to thank her for the gift.* **2.** a sign in music that shows what sound to make. **notes.**

notes (definition 2)

nothing

There was nothing in the empty closet.

notice

1. to look at; see: *Did you notice the cat's unusual eyes?* **2.** a sign or message that gives facts or directions: *We put up a notice about our lost dog.* **noticed, noticing; notices.**

LOST

GREY DOG NAME FUZZY
2,000 DOLLAR REWARD

notice (definition 2)
*We put up a **notice** about our lost dog.*

noun

a word that names a person, place, animal, or thing. "They get balloons to take home." *Balloons* and *home* are nouns. They name a thing and a place. **nouns.**

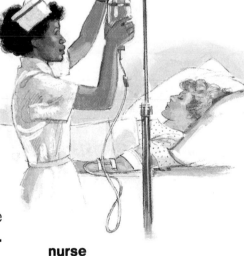

nouns

Nova Scotia

one of the ten provinces of Canada.

November

the eleventh month of the year. It has 30 days. It comes after October and before December.

now

Please take the dog out now. I used to live on Bay Street, but now I live on Lake Avenue.

nowhere

He searched the house, but the book was nowhere to be found. This arguing is getting us nowhere.

number

1. a word that tells how many. Two is a number. Twenty-one is a number. **2.** a figure or group of figures that stands for a number. 9 is a number. 481 is a number. **3.** to give a number to: *We numbered the boxes as we filled them in.* **numbers; numbered, numbering.**

nurse

a person who takes care of sick people. Many nurses work in hospitals. Others visit homes. **nurses.**

nurse

nut

a dry fruit or seed with a hard shell. Nuts hold only one seed. Most nuts grow on trees. A pecan is a nut. **nuts.**

nuts

Oo

oars

oak

a kind of tree. Oaks have hard wood and nuts called acorns. **oaks.**

oak

oar

a long pole with one flat end. You can use two oars to row a boat. **oars.**

oatmeal

a breakfast cereal made of oats: *I cooked my own oatmeal this morning.*

oats

a cereal grain. Oats are eaten by people and farm animals.

obey

to do what the law or a rule tells you to do: *The careful driver obeyed all the traffic laws. You must obey the rules in school.* **obeyed, obeying.**

object

anything solid that you can see or touch. A desk, a pen, and a book are objects. **objects.**

observe

to look at something carefully in order to learn about it: *They observed the birds in the nest to understand how they live.* **observed, observing.**

observe

occasionally

every so often; once in a while: *We get together with our cousins occasionally.*

ocean

a great body of salt water. Oceans cover almost three-fourths of the earth's surface. Fish, dolphins, and whales are some animals that live in the ocean. Another word for ocean is sea. **oceans.**

o'clock

a word we use to say what time it is: *We eat lunch at twelve o'clock.*

October

the tenth month of the year. It has 31 days. October comes after September and before November.

octopus

a sea animal. It has a soft, thick body and eight arms. **octopuses.**

octopus

odd

1. having one left over when divided by two: *Seven, nine, and eleven are odd numbers.* **2.** acting strange or doing something strange: *She has an odd habit of looking over her shoulder at people.* **odder, oddest** (for **2.**).

of

The members of the team went to a party. They built a house of bricks. The state of Alaska is very big.

off

The cat jumped off the bench. The radio is off.

offer

1. to hand something to someone, to see if it will be taken or not: *He offered me his coat.* **2.** to bring a thought to someone's mind; suggest: *He may offer a few ideas to the class.* **offered, offering.**

odd (definition 1)
*These are all **odd** numbers.*

office

a place where some people work: *Mom left the house and went to her office.* **offices.**

often

many times: *It often snows in January. We have been there often.*

oh

a word used to express surprise, joy, pain, and other feelings: *Oh, no! The tiger escaped from the cage!*

Ohio

one of the fifty states of the United States.

oil

1. a thick liquid from animal fat or vegetable fat: *Mother uses olive oil when she cooks.* **2.** a liquid that comes from the earth. Gasoline is made from oil. **3.** to put oil on or in: *Did you oil your bicycle?* **oiled, oiling.**

Oklahoma

one of the fifty states of the United States.

old

1. having lived a long time: *My grandfather is very old.* **2.** not made or thought of just a short time ago; not new: *My cousin has an old bike.* **older, oldest.**

olive

a small, round fruit with a hard stone. Olives grow on trees, and are used to make olive oil. **olives.**

on

The lizard is on the rock. Put your left shoe on your left foot. There is a calendar on the wall. This is a book on dinosaurs.

once

1. one time: *Play that song once more.* **2.** at some time in the past: *The plant was once a sprout.*

olives

one

1. the number 1. **2.** a single thing: *Which one do you want to sit in?* **ones.**

onion

a vegetable with a strong flavor. An onion grows from an underground bulb. **onions.**

onion

only

This is the only road to town. She had three pictures but she sold only two. He is an only child.

Ontario

one of the ten provinces of Canada.

onto

He climbed onto the roof. She drove the car onto the beach.

open

1. so that things or people can get in or out; not shut; not closed: *The window was open so that we could have fresh air.* **2.** to make or become open: *Open the window. The store doesn't open until 9 o'clock. Please open your books to page 30.* **opened, opening.**

operate

1. to run: *You operate this machine by pushing a button.* **2.** to try to cure a sick person by cutting into his or her body: *A doctor will operate on your foot if it is necessary.* **operated, operating.**

operation

cutting into a sick or hurt part of the body by a doctor to help make it better: *Dad had to have an operation after he fell and hurt his knee badly.* **operations.**

opossum

a small animal that often carries its young on its back. When it is caught, it goes limp and appears to be dead. This animal is often called a possum. **opossums.**

opossums

241

oranges (definition 1)

orbit (definition 1)
*This is a diagram of the moon's **orbit** around the earth.*

orchestra

opposite

1. as different from each other as they can be. East and west are opposite directions. Running fast is the opposite of walking slow. **2.** directly across from; face to face: *The post office is opposite the firehouse.*

or

Is that apple sweet or sour? Hurry, or you will be late.

orange

1. a round, yellowish-red fruit that grows on trees. Oranges are full of juice. **2.** the color of an orange or a pumpkin. **oranges.**

orbit

1. the path of the earth or other planet around the sun; the path of the moon around the earth: *The orbit of the earth around the sun takes one year.* **2.** to travel around the earth or around the sun: *The spaceship orbits the earth several times a day.* **orbits; orbited, orbiting.**

orchard

a piece of ground on which fruit trees are grown: *He went to the apple orchard to pick a basket of apples.* **orchards.**

orchestra

a large group of musicians playing music together. An orchestra usually has many violin players. **orchestras.**

order

1. the way one thing comes after another in a special way: *Please line up in order of size to take your class picture. The words in the dictionary are in alphabetical order.* **2.** telling someone what to do, or what you want: *We had orders to come straight home after school. At the restaurant we gave our order to the waitress.* **3.** to tell someone what to do, or what you want: *The police officer ordered the driver to stop. Mom ordered lunch for all of us.* **orders** (for **2.**); **ordered, ordering.**

order (definition 2)
*The soldier is taking **orders** from an officer.*

Oregon
one of the fifty states of the United States.

organ
1. a musical instrument that looks like a piano: *She plays the organ in church.* **2.** a part of your body that does a special job: *The heart is the organ that pumps blood through your body.* **organs.**

oriole
a bird with yellow-and-black or orange-and-black feathers. **orioles.**

oriole

ostrich
a large African bird with long legs. Ostriches can run very fast but they cannot fly. **ostriches.**

other
He is better in math than the others in the class. It's raining, so we'll have to play ball some other day. I can't find my other glove. **others.**

ostrich

Ottawa
the capital of Canada.

otter
an animal with thick brown fur and strong claws. Otters are good swimmers. **otters.**

ought
He ought to take better care of his dog. You ought to be careful when you cross that busy street.

otter

ounce
1. a unit of weight. Sixteen ounces equal one pound.
2. an amount of liquid. Sixteen ounces equal one pint.
ounces.

our
Our team won and his team lost.

ours
This house is ours. Ours is a very large house.

outside—The dog is **outside** trying to get in.

overflow—The bathtub is **overflowing.**

ourselves

We helped ourselves to more cake.

out

The kids ran out of the yard. I called you last night, but you were out. The lights went out.

outdoor

done or used outside of a house or building: *They went swimming at an outdoor pool.*

outdoors

out of or outside a building: *Kids at our school had recess outdoors today.*

outer

on the outside. The outer part of a banana is the peel.

outside

The outside of the house needs painting. Please go outside and get the paper.

oval

shaped like an egg: *A football has nearly an oval shape.*

oven

the part of a stove that you use to bake things in: *He put the turkey in the oven.* **ovens.**

over

I wore a sweater over my shirt. They came over to our house after school. I have over three dollars in my bank.

overflow

to flow over; flood: *The river overflowed its banks after the heavy rains.* **overflowed, overflowing.**

owe

to have to pay: *My neighbor owes me a dollar for washing her car.* **owed, owing.**

owl

owl

a bird with a big head, big eyes, and a short, curved bill. Owls fly around at night. **owls.**

own

1. to have or keep something because you bought it, or because someone gave it to you: *I own a bicycle.*
2. belonging to you: *I make my own bed every morning.* **owned, owning.**

ox

a kind of animal that is used for farm work. Oxen are cattle. **oxen.**

oxen

oxen

more than one ox: *On the farm, oxen pulled heavy wagons.*

oxygen

a gas without color, taste, or odor. Oxygen forms a part of both air and water. Animals and plants need oxygen in order to live.

oyster

a sea animal with a shell. Sometimes the shell of an oyster may contain a pearl. **oysters.**

oyster

Pp

pad (definition 2)

pack

1. a bundle of things that are wrapped up or tied together: *I had a pack of gum.* **2.** to put things into something; fill a space: *We can pack clothes in a suitcase. A crowd of people packed the elevator.* **packs; packed, packing.**

package

a bundle of things tightly packed or wrapped together; a box or bag with things packed in it. **packages.**

pad

1. a tablet of writing paper: *Please hand me that pad and a pencil.* **2.** a large floating leaf: *The pond was covered with lily pads.* **pads.**

paddle

1. a short oar used to move a canoe. **2.** to move a canoe by pulling a paddle through the water: *She paddled up the river.* **paddles; paddled, paddling.**

page

one side of a sheet of paper: *Open your books to page 20.* **pages.**

paid

I paid a dollar for a pair of socks. Dad is happy now that all the bills are paid.

pail

something to carry things in. You can carry water or sand in a pail. Another word for pail is bucket. **pails.**

pain

a feeling that hurts: *After eating too fast, she has a pain in her stomach.* **pains.**

paint

1. a liquid that you spread on a surface to color and protect it. Paint comes in many different colors. **2.** to cover with paint: *We painted the garage.* **3.** to draw a picture with colors: *The artist paints pictures of flowers.* **paints; painted, painting.**

painter

1. a person who paints pictures; artist. **2.** a person who paints rooms, houses, or other buildings. **painters.**

pair

1. a set of two things; two things that go together: *I can't find my brown pair of shoes.* **2.** one thing with two parts that work together: *Please hand me a pair of scissors.* **pairs.**

pajamas

clothes to sleep in. Pajamas have a shirt and loose pants.

pajamas

palace

a very large, grand house. Kings and queens live in palaces. **palaces.**

pale

without much color: *When he is ill, his face is pale.* **paler, palest.**

palm¹

the inside of the hand between the wrist and the fingers. **palms.**

palm²

a tree that grows in warm places. There are many kinds of palm trees. Most palm trees have tall trunks without branches. **palms.**

palms²

pan

pan

something to cook food in. Many pans are made of metal, and some have handles. **pans.**

pancake

a thin, flat cake made of batter. Pancakes are fried in a pan. **pancakes.**

panda

a large black and white animal that looks like a bear. There are very few pandas alive today. **pandas.**

panda

pane

a sheet of glass or plastic in a window: *The hail broke two panes.* **panes.**

pants

clothing worn to cover the legs, from the waist to the ankles. Some pants are short, covering only part of the legs. Another word for pants is trousers.

papa

another word for father. **papas.**

paper

1. what you use to write, print, or draw on. Paper is also used for wrapping packages and covering walls. Many bags are made of paper. Paper is made from wood. **2.** a piece of paper with writing or printing on it: *Our teacher collected the papers we had written.* **3.** a short word meaning newspaper. **papers.** (for **2.** and **3.**).

parachute

a huge piece of cloth like a big umbrella. A parachute brings a person or thing down safely through the air. **parachutes.**

parachute

parade

1. a group of people marching together in rows down a street. Parades often have bands playing music and cars or trucks decorated with paper or flowers. **2.** to walk in a parade or march like people in a parade: *We paraded around the room singing a birthday song.* **parades; paraded, parading.**

parade (definition 1)

paragraph

a group of sentences that are about one main idea. A paragraph begins on a new line and has a space before the first word. **paragraphs.**

parakeet

a bird with brightly colored feathers and a long tail. A parakeet is a kind of small parrot. Parakeets are often kept as pets. **parakeets.**

parakeet

pardon

a word you use if you have bumped into someone, sneezed loudly, or bothered someone: *Oh, I beg your pardon.*

parent

a father or mother: *All parents were invited to the class program.* **parents.**

park

1. an area of land with grass and trees. People use many parks for walking and playing. Some parks are kept as living spaces for wild plants and animals. **2.** to leave a car, truck, or bike someplace for a time: *Dad will park the car at the curb.* **parks; parked, parking.**

parrot

parking lot
a piece of land where drivers park cars, trucks, or buses. Parking lots are often near stores or other buildings. **parking lots.**

parrot
a brightly colored bird with a curved bill. Some parrots can imitate sounds and repeat words. **parrots.**

part
1. something less than the whole; not all: *He ate only part of his dinner.* **2.** something that helps make up a whole thing. A pedal is part of a bicycle. A TV has many parts. One of them is the screen. **parts.**

partner
a person who works or plays with another person: *She was my tennis partner.* **partners.**

partner

party
a group of people having a good time together: *The birthday party starts at noon.* **parties.**

pass
1. to go by; move past: *The truck passed two cars. Months pass slowly.* **2.** to hand something from one person to another: *Please pass the carrots.* **3.** to succeed in a test: *He passed his reading test.* **passed, passing.**

passenger
a person who rides in a bus, car, train, ship, or airplane. Passengers usually pay a fare to ride. **passengers.**

Passover
a holiday that some families enjoy by sharing a special meal. Passover comes every spring.

passenger—*The bus driver is collecting the **passenger's** ticket.*

past

1. gone by; ended: *I grew an inch in the past year. He's glad winter is past.* **2.** by; beyond: *A ball flew past my head. We rode our bikes past the park.*

past (definition 2)
*The ball flew **past** her head.*

pasta

macaroni, noodles, or spaghetti. Pasta is made of flour, water, and sometimes milk or eggs. Dry pasta comes in many different shapes.

paste

1. a mixture you use to stick things together: *I used paste to fasten the paper hearts to the valentines.* **2.** to stick things together: *Can you paste a cloth circle to the picture?* **pasted, pasting.**

pat

to tap or strike gently with the hand: *She patted me on the back in a friendly way.* **patted, patting.**

patch

1. a piece put on something to mend a hole or tear in it. **2.** to put on a patch; mend: *I had to patch my bicycle tire.* **patches; patched, patching.**

patch (definition 1)

path

a place to walk, made when people or animals travel over the same ground a lot: *We hiked along a path through the woods.* **paths.**

patient

1. able to wait quietly for something that you want: *We must be patient while we are standing in line.* **2.** a person who is being treated by a doctor: *The doctor had to see two more patients before going home.* **patients.**

patio

a small yard that is open to the sky. Patios are next to houses, and some have floors of flat stones. **patios.**

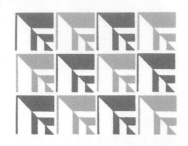

pattern—*This design has a* ***pattern*** *of squares.*

pattern

the way the same colors or shapes appear in order on cloth or printed paper: *The wrapping paper had a pretty pattern of gold circles and silver stripes.* **patterns.**

pave

to cover a street, sidewalk, driveway, or parking lot with concrete or another hard, smooth surface. **paved, paving.**

paw

one of the four feet of an animal that has claws. Dogs and cats have paws. **paws.**

pay

1. to give money to someone for things or for work that has been done: *I can pay for the popcorn. Grandma pays me to mow her lawn.* **2.** to give or offer: *Please pay attention!* **paid, paying.**

peas

pea

a round, green seed that people eat as a vegetable. Peas are small, and they grow in pods on a vine. **peas.**

peace

1. a being free from quarreling; being quiet or calm: *Instead of arguing, let's have some peace in this house.* **2.** a being free from war: *Those two countries have lived in peace for many years.*

peaches

peach

a round fruit that grows on a tree. Peaches have fuzzy yellow and red skin. A peach is juicy and has a big seed inside called a pit. **peaches.**

peacock

a large bird with green, blue, and gold feathers. A male peacock's tail spreads out high and wide. **peacocks.**

peacock

peak

the pointed top of a mountain or hill: *Snow lies on the high peaks all summer.* **peaks.**

peanut

a seed that looks like a nut. Peanuts grow in shells underground and are good to eat when they are roasted. **peanuts.**

peanuts

peanut butter

a food made of ground peanuts. Peanut butter is spread on bread or crackers.

pear

a sweet, juicy fruit that is round at one end. Pears are green or yellow and grow on trees. **pears.**

pearl

a white jewel that has a soft shine. Pearls are sometimes found inside oyster shells. **pearls.**

pecan

a nut that is shaped like an olive and has a smooth shell. Pecans grow on trees in warm places. **pecans.**

pears

peck

to hit at something and pick it up with the beak. A bird pecks the ground to find seeds. **pecked, pecking.**

pedal

1. a part of a bicycle or machine moved by the foot: *Pushing down on the pedals makes a bicycle go.* **2.** to move something by pushing its pedals: *I can pedal my bike up the hill.* **pedals; pedaled, pedaling.**

peek

1. to look quickly at something: *Close your eyes and do not peek at the surprise yet!* **2.** a quick look: *He wanted to take a peek.* **peeked, pecking; peeks.**

253

peel

1. the outside covering of fruit; skin: *She never eats orange peels!* **2.** to strip the skin or covering from: *He peeled the banana before he ate it.* **peels; peeled, peeling.**

peep

to look quickly through a hole or crack; take a quick look: *She peeped through the hole in the fence.* **peeped, peeping.**

pelican

pelican

a large sea bird with a pouch under its huge bill. A pelican scoops up fish into its pouch for food. **pelicans.**

pen¹

a tool you use when you write or draw with ink. **pens.**

pen²

1. a small, closed place to keep animals: *We saw pigs in a pen at the farm.* **2.** to shut in a pen: *Please pen your dog inside the fence.* **pens; penned, penning.**

penguins

pencil

a pointed tool for writing or drawing. The part of a pencil you write with is called lead. **pencils.**

penguin

a sea bird that dives and swims but does not fly. Penguins live in very cold places and walk on land or ice. **penguins.**

peninsula

an area of land with water on all sides except one: *We noticed on our map that Florida is a peninsula.* **peninsulas.**

Pennsylvania

one of the fifty states of the United States.

penny

the smallest amount of money in the United States and Canada. One hundred pennies make one dollar. Another word for penny is cent. **pennies.**

people

1. men, women, and children; persons: *There were only three people at the meeting.* **2.** a person's family or relatives: *His people live in Iowa.*

pepper

1. a powder with a hot taste, used to add flavor to food. Pepper is a spice. **2.** a hollow red or green vegetable. **peppers** (for **2.**).

peppers (definition 2)

perch[1]

1. a branch, bar, rod, or the like on which a bird can come to rest. **2.** to come and rest; sit. Birds perch on fences, telephone wires, and the edges of buildings. **perches; perched, perching.**

perch[2]

a small fish that lives in fresh water or salt water. Perch are used for food. **perch.**

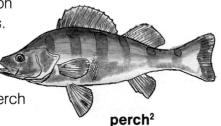

perch[2]

perfect

without any faults or mistakes; not at all spoiled: *I had a perfect spelling paper.*

perform

1. to do: *The doctor performed an operation on Dad's broken shoulder.* **2.** to act, sing, play, or do tricks in public: *Animals performed for the circus crowd.* **performed, performing.**

perhaps

able to happen, but not sure to happen: *Perhaps a card will come in the mail today. My aunt said that perhaps she could visit during the holidays.*

period (definition 2)

pet (definition 1)

pet (definition 2)
*It is fun to **pet** the kitten.*

period

1. a length of time: *Mom asked how long my reading period in school lasts.* **2.** a mark of punctuation. A period is used to mark the end of a sentence or an abbreviation. **periods.**

permanent teeth

the new teeth that grow when a person's first teeth fall out during childhood. Permanent teeth can last the rest of the person's life.

permission

the act of letting someone do something: *Do you have your teacher's permission to leave the room?*

permit

to let someone do something; allow: *Our parents permit us to stay up a bit later on Friday nights.* **permitted, permitting.**

person

a girl, boy, man, or woman; a human being. **persons.**

pet

1. a favorite animal that you take care of and treat with love: *My pet is a hamster.* **2.** to pat gently: *When I pet the kitten, he purrs.* **pets; petted, petting.**

petal

one of the parts of a flower. Many petals are brightly colored. **petals.**

petal

petition

a letter that many people sign to ask for something to be changed. A petition might ask someone in charge to make a new rule or to protect someone in some way. **petitions.**

phone

a short word meaning telephone. **phones; phoned, phoning.**

256

photo

a short word meaning photograph. **photos.**

photograph

a picture you make with a camera. **photographs.**

photographer

a person who takes photographs. **photographers.**

photographer

piano

a large musical instrument that you play with your fingers. **pianos.**

pick

1. to take the one you want from a group; choose; select: *I picked the red bicycle. He always picks her to be on his team.* **2.** to pull away or take with the fingers: *We pick flowers from the garden. We picked up a lot of trash from the side yard.* **picked, picking.**

pickle

1. a cucumber or any vegetable kept in salt water, vinegar, or spicy liquid to keep it from spoiling. Pickles have a spicy taste. **2.** to keep a vegetable or other food in spicy liquid to keep it from spoiling, or to change its taste: *They will pickle some beets from their garden.* **pickles; pickled, pickling.**

picnic

a party with a meal outdoors: *Our class had a picnic at the park.* **picnics.**

pictograph

1. a picture used as a sign or symbol of something: *The puzzle had pictographs in place of some words.* **2.** a diagram, chart, or graph that uses these signs or symbols to show information. **pictographs.**

pictographs (definition 1)

257

pie

picture

1. a drawing, photograph, or painting of someone or something: *We all drew pictures of our school. Dad took a picture of me and my sisters.* **2.** to form a picture of something in your mind; imagine: *Picture yourself on a rocket ship!* **pictures; pictured, picturing.**

pie

a kind of food made of fruit, meat, or some vegetables baked in a crust. There are apple pies, chicken pies, and pumpkin pies. **pies.**

piece

one of the parts into which something is divided or broken: *I lost one piece of the puzzle and couldn't finish it.* **pieces.**

pig

1. an animal with a fat body, short legs, and a curly tail. Ham and pork are kinds of meat that come from pigs. **2.** a person who is greedy or dirty: *He ate all the candy, so his brother called him a pig.* **pigs.**

pig (definition 1)

pigeon

a bird with a plump body and short legs and tail. **pigeons.**

pile

1. a lot of things lying one upon another: *There was a pile of logs near the house.* **2.** a mound or hill of something: *The truck dumped a pile of dirt.* **3.** to make into a pile; stack: *Let's pile all the blankets here.* **piles; piled, piling.**

pigeon

pilgrim

a person who goes on a journey to a holy place. **pilgrims.**

Pilgrim

one of the English settlers who came to Massachusetts in the year 1620. **Pilgrims.**

Pilgrims

pill

medicine that is made into a tiny ball that you can swallow easily. **pills.**

pillow

a soft bag or case to put your head on when you rest or sleep. Pillows are usually filled with feathers or other soft things. **pillows.**

pilot

1. a person who flies an airplane or helicopter, or who steers a ship: *The pilot spoke to the passengers before the plane took off.* **2.** to act as the pilot of; steer: *She piloted the plane safely.* **pilots; piloted, piloting.**

pin

1. a short, thin piece of wire. A pin has one sharp end to stick through things and fasten them together. **2.** a piece of wood shaped something like a bottle, used in the game of bowling. **3.** to fasten with a pin or pins: *Please pin this flower to my coat.* **pins; pinned, pinning.**

pinch

1. to squeeze something between your thumb and finger: *She pinched my arm to get my attention.* **2.** a squeeze with the thumb and finger that can hurt: *The baby gave my cheek a little pinch.* **pinched, pinching; pinches.**

pine

a tree with evergreen leaves shaped like needles. Pine trees have cones. **pines.**

pineapple

a large, juicy fruit that looks like a big pine cone. Pineapples grow in warm countries. **pineapples.**

pink

1. a color that is made by mixing red and white. **2.** having this color: *The clouds at sunset were pink.* **pinks; pinker, pinkest.**

pineapple

pink (definition 1)

pint

an amount of liquid. Two cups are equal to one pint. Two pints are equal to one quart. **pints.**

pioneer

1. a person who settles in a part of a country where very few people have lived before. **2.** a person who goes first or does something first and so prepares a way for others: *He was a pioneer in space.* **pioneers.**

pipe

a tube through which liquid or gas flows. Pipes are made of metal or plastic. **pipes.**

pirates

pirate

long ago, a person who robbed ships at sea. **pirates.**

pit¹

a hole in the ground. **pits.**

pit²

the hard seed in a cherry, peach, plum, or some other fruit. **pits.**

pitch

1. to throw; toss: *She pitched the softball to the catcher.* **2.** a throw; toss: *The game started as she threw the first pitch.* **pitched, pitching; pitches.**

pitcher¹

something that holds liquids. A pitcher has a handle on one side and a place for pouring on the other side. **pitchers.**

pitcher²

a player on a baseball team who throws the ball to the catcher. The batter tries to hit the ball before it gets to the catcher. **pltchers.**

pizza

a kind of food made of flat crust covered with tomatoes, cheese, spices, and other things such as meat or vegetables. A pizza is baked in an oven. Most pizzas are round. **pizzas.**

place

1. the space where a person or thing is: *Our neighborhood is a nice place to live. Do not leave your place in line.* **2.** a city, town, island, building, or other space: *The auditorium is a big place. We went to a place called Johnstown.* **places.**

plaid

any cloth with a pattern of crossed stripes of different colors and widths. **plaids.**

plaid

plain

1. easy to hear, see, or understand; clear: *The meaning of this sentence is plain.* **2.** without any trimming: *He wore a plain shirt.* **3.** a flat area of land: *The pioneers traveled across the plains in wagons.* **plainer, plainest; plains.**

plan

1. something you have thought out and will do: *Does anyone have a plan for earning money?* **2.** to think out how something is to be done: *We are planning a party.* **plans; planned, planning.**

plane

a short word meaning airplane. **planes.**

planet

one of the nine large objects that move around the sun. The earth and Mars are planets. **planets.**

plank

a long, flat piece of wood. Planks are thicker than boards. *Grandpa put several planks across the ditch so that we could walk across it.* **planks.**

plant

1. any living thing that can make its own food from sunlight, air, and water. Unlike animals, plants cannot move about. Trees, bushes, vines, grass, flowers, and vegetables are all plants. **2.** to put in the ground to grow: *Plant these seeds in the spring.* **plants; planted, planting.**

plastic

a kind of material that can be shaped when it is hot. Plastic becomes hard when it cools. Plastic can be very strong. Many dishes, toys, and combs are made of plastic. **plastics.**

plate

a dish that is almost flat and is usually round. We eat food from plates. **plates.**

platform

a raised, level surface for people to stand or sit on: *The parade judges sat on a platform above the curb.* **platforms.**

platter

an almost flat dish that is longer than it is wide: *Grandma used a platter to serve the turkey.* **platters.**

play

1. to have fun; to take part in a game or sport: *Let's play ball. My sister plays with dolls.* **2.** something done to amuse yourself; fun: *Recess is a time for play.* **3.** a story acted out on a stage: *We saw a play about a king and queen.* **4.** to act a part on stage: *You and I will play Jack and Jill in our show.* **5.** to make believe: *Let's play that this room is a store.* **6.** to perform on a musical instrument: *Can you play the piano?* **played, playing; plays** (for **3.**).

platform

player

a person who plays or a machine that plays: *The football player kicked the ball. The teacher turned on the record player.* **players.**

playground

a place to play outdoors: *We enjoy going to the playground on Saturdays.* **playgrounds.**

playmate

a person who plays with you. **playmates.**

pleasant

giving a happy feeling; nice: *We had a pleasant swim on a hot day. Yesterday was pleasant and sunny.* **pleasanter, pleasantest.**

pleasant

please

1. a polite word you use when you ask someone for something: *Please sit down. Please may I go with you? Mom taught us to say please and thank you.* **2.** to give nice feelings to: *Reading stories to children pleases them.* **pleased, pleasing.**

pleasure

a feeling of being happy: *You could see his pleasure as he opened his gift.*

plenty

enough; all that someone needs: *We have plenty of food.*

plow

1. a farm machine that cuts soil and turns it over before planting seeds. **2.** to turn up soil: *Grandpa plows his farm fields every year.* **3.** to move snow: *They plowed the street to clear a path through the snow.* **plows; plowed, plowing.**

plow (definition 3)

pluck

1. to pick or pull off: *The man plucked feathers from the chicken.* **2.** to pull on the strings of a musical instrument: *The woman plucked her guitar.* **plucked, plucking.**

plug

1. a thing at the end of a wire to connect it to an electric socket: *Don't use a lamp if it has a plug that is worn or bent.* **2.** to put a plug into an opening: *Please plug in the lamp.* **plugs; plugged, plugging.**

plug (definition 1)

plum

a round, juicy fruit with smooth skin. Red, green, purple, and yellow plums grow on trees. Plums are larger than grapes, but smaller than peaches. **plums.**

plums

plumber

a person whose work is putting in and repairing water pipes, sinks, tubs, and the like. **plumbers.**

plump

somewhat fat and round, usually in a way that is nice: *The baby was plump, happy, and healthy. We saw several plump pigeons in the park.* **plumper, plumpest.**

plunge

1. to throw something with force into water: *She plunged her hand into cold water to make the burn on her finger stop hurting.* **2.** to throw yourself into water: *He plunged into the lake to cool off.* **plunged, plunging.**

plural

the form of a word that shows it means more than one. *Dogs* is the plural of *dog*, *porches* is the plural of *porch*, and *men* is the plural of *man*. **plurals.**

plural—*Dogs is the **plural** of dog.*

plus

1. added to: *7 plus 2 equals 9.* **2.** with; in addition to: *This costs one dollar plus five cents tax.*

pocket

a small piece of cloth sewed onto clothing for carrying things. Money and other small things are kept in pockets. **pockets.**

pod

a long, narrow part of a plant in which some seeds grow. Peas and beans grow in pods. **pods.**

pods

poem

a kind of writing that is something like a song without any music. Poems often use special words that rhyme and new ways of putting words together to tell about feelings and thoughts. **poems.**

poet

a person who writes poems. **poets.**

poetry

poems: *We enjoy hearing our teacher read poetry.*

point

1. a sharp end. Needles and pins have points. **2.** a place; spot: *That mountain is the highest point in the state.* **3.** to show the position or direction of something with your finger: *She pointed to the north.* **4.** a unit for keeping score in a game: *The first player with ten points wins.* **points; pointed, pointing.**

point (definition 3)

pointer

a person or thing that points; a small thing shaped like an arrow. A pointer points to what the player should do. *Spin the pointer and move three spaces.* **pointers.**

poison

anything that is dangerous to your body if you swallow or breathe it. A poison can make you very sick or even kill you. The lead in some paint is poison. **poisons.**

poke

1. to push with force against a person or thing: *He poked me in the side with his elbow.* **2.** to push out: *The cat poked its head from under the bed.* **poked, poking.**

polar bear

polar bear

a large, white bear that lives in Alaska, Canada, and other cold places. **polar bears.**

pole¹

a long, round piece of wood or metal. *We used a fishing pole to catch fish. The flag in front of our school flies on a pole.* **poles.**

pole²

1. either end of the earth. The North Pole and the South Pole are opposite each other. **2.** either end of a magnet. The poles of a magnet pull pieces of iron and steel toward them. **poles.**

police

a group of people who protect us and our things, and make sure that laws are obeyed. Police also catch people who break the law.

policeman

a member of the police; police officer. **policemen.**

police officer

a member of the police. **police officers.**

policewoman

a member of the police; police officer. **policewomen.**

polio

a disease that once struck many children. Polio hurt their muscles, often making them unable to walk. Today, children can take a special medicine so they won't get polio.

polite

behaving in a nice, friendly way; having good manners: *A polite classmate helped me pick up my books when I dropped them in the hall.* **politer, politest.**

pollute

to make dirty and harmful to people: *Smoke from the factories polluted the air.* **polluted, polluting.**

pollution

dirty and harmful things in our air or water.

pollute

pond

water with land all around it. A pond is smaller than a lake and does not have waves. **ponds.**

pony

a small horse. **ponies.**

pool

a place that holds water to swim in. A pool can be large or small, indoors or outdoors. **pools.**

poor

1. having very little money: *The family was so poor that they did not have enough food.* **2.** not good: *Poor spelling can make a story hard to read.* **poorer, poorest.**

poorly

not well; badly: *The toy was poorly made and broke within an hour. Our team played poorly in the game.*

pop

1. to make a short, quick, bursting sound: *The fire popped when she put more wood in.* **2.** a short, quick, bursting sound: *The bottle opened with a pop.* **3.** a kind of sweet drink: *I like cherry pop.* Another word for pop is soda. **popped, popping; pops** (for **2.**).

pop (definition 2)
The bottle opened with a pop.

267

porcupine

popcorn

a kind of corn that bursts open noisily and puffs out when you heat it. Popcorn is often eaten with butter and salt on it.

porch

a platform with a roof on the outside of a house. A porch may have no walls or walls with many windows. **porches.**

porcupine

a small animal that is covered with stiff, sharp hairs, called quills. **porcupines.**

pork

the meat of a pig used for food.

porpoise

a sea animal very much like a dolphin, but smaller. Porpoises have flatter noses than dolphins. **porpoises.**

porpoise

position

the place where a thing or person is: · *Grandpa sat in his usual position near the fire.* **positions.**

possible

1. able to be done: *Is it possible to get home before dark?* **2.** not true for sure, but perhaps true: *It is possible that he already returned the books to the library.*

possibly

no matter what happens: *I cannot possibly get home before four o'clock.*

possum

a small animal that often carries its young on its back. When it is caught, it goes limp and appears to be dead. The full name of this animal is opossum. **possums.**

post

1. a piece of wood or metal set in the ground to hold something up: *A sign post points the way to the zoo.*
2. to put up a sign or notice where everyone can see it: *She posted the list of winners on the bulletin board.*
posts; posted, posting.

poster

a large printed piece of paper put up on a wall.
posters.

postman

a person whose job is bringing mail to people. Another word for postman is mail carrier. **postmen.**

post office

a place where workers take in and send out mail and sell stamps. **post offices.**

pot

1. a round, deep pan used for cooking. Pots come in different sizes. **2.** a round plant holder, usually made of plastic or clay: *The flower pots were full of daisies.*
pots.

potato

a vegetable with a thin brown or red skin and a white inside. Potatoes grow underground. **potatoes.**

potatoes

pouch

1. a bag or sack: *The mail carrier put the letters in her pouch.* **2.** the part on the stomach of some animals that is like a bag or pocket. Kangaroos and possums have pouches for carrying their young. **pouches.**

poultry

poultry

birds that people raise for their meat or eggs. Chickens, turkeys, geese, and ducks are poultry.

pound²

pound¹

a unit of weight. A pound is equal to sixteen ounces. **pounds.**

pound²

to hit hard again and again; to hit heavily: *I pounded on the door with my fist.* **pounded, pounding.**

pour

1. to cause to flow in a steady stream: *I poured milk on my cereal.* **2.** to rain heavily: *It poured all afternoon.* **poured, pouring.**

powder

very tiny bits of things ground up as fine as dust. Flour is a powder made from grain. Baby powder is used to help keep babies dry. **powders.**

predicate

the word or words in a sentence that tell what is said about the subject. "The birds built a nest." *Built a nest* is the predicate that tells about the subject. **predicates.**

prepare

to get something ready; get yourself ready for doing something: *We all helped prepare a picnic lunch. When recess comes, we all prepare to go outside.* **prepared, preparing.**

present¹

here; not absent: *Every member of the class is present today.*

present²

1. a gift; something that someone gives you, or that you give someone: *His uncle sent him a birthday present.* **2.** to show, tell, read, or act out something: *Our class wrote and presented a play.* **presents; presented, presenting.**

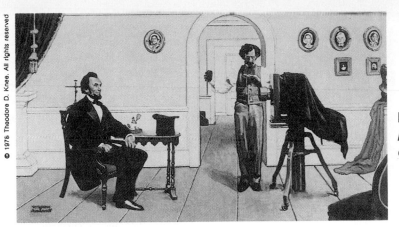

president—*The photographer prepared to take a picture of President Lincoln.*

president

the leader of a country, company, or other group. Not all countries have presidents. **presidents.**

press

1. to push something with steady force: *Press this button to get the elevator to come.* **2.** to make smooth with a hot iron: *I pressed my shirt to get out the wrinkles.* **pressed, pressing.**

pretend

to make believe that something is real when it is not: *Let's pretend we're camping.* **pretended, pretending.**

pretty¹

nice; good to see or hear: *She wore a pretty dress. That is a pretty song.* **prettier, prettiest.**

pretty²

She has a pretty good idea. It is pretty late to play outdoors.

prewriting

things you do before you write a story, poem, or report. You listen to or read a story, poem, or book, or you look at a picture. Perhaps you think about something you have done, or you talk to others about what you want to write about.

price

the amount of money someone must pay to buy something: *The price of this sweater is $10.* **prices.**

pretend—*Let's pretend we're camping.*

princess

prince

primary teeth

the first teeth a person gets as a baby. Between the ages of five and seven, permanent teeth take the place of primary teeth.

prince

a son of a king or queen: *There are many stories about princes in books.* **princes.**

Prince Edward Island

one of the ten provinces of Canada.

princess

a daughter of a king or queen: *There are many stories about princesses in books.* **princesses.**

principal

a person who is the head of a school. **principals.**

print

1. to write words with letters that do not touch each other: *Please print your name on your paper.* **2.** to use a machine to make copies of words and pictures on paper. This book is printed using different colors of ink. **printed, printing.**

print (definition 2)
Here a newspaper is being **printed.**

printer

a machine that prints, run by a computer. **printers.**

private

not for everyone; belonging to just one person: *That road is private; only the people living on it and their visitors may use it. The letters a person receives are private, and others should not read them without permission.*

prize

something you win for doing something well; reward:
The judges liked her story best and gave her the prize.
prizes.

prize

probably

*You probably know my brother. We should probably
wait for them.*

problem

something you have to work out; a difficult question:
*How did you solve that math problem? Making friends
at a new school can be a problem.* **problems.**

process

the doing or making of something by following steps in
order: *They explained the process by which they make
butter.* **processes.**

produce

1. to make or grow: *My cousin's factory produces
cheese. Some farmers produce wheat and corn.* **2.** to
give: *Cows produce milk. Sheep produce wool.*
produced, producing.

producer

a person who makes or grows things or who provides
a service. **producers.**

product

1. something that someone makes or grows. Cloth is a
factory product. Grain and milk are farm products.
2. the number that you get when you multiply two or
more numbers together: *10 is the product of 2 and 5.*
products.

profit

the money someone in business has left after all the bills are paid. **profits.**

program

what you hear on the radio, or see on television: *Mom and Dad watch a news program every evening.* **programs.**

project

a plan for doing something: *My project was making a poster. Our science project won a prize.* **projects.**

promise

1. words that you say or write that tell that you will or will not do something: *He kept his promise to walk the dog.* **2.** to say or write that you will or will not do something: *You promised to help rake the yard.* **promises; promised, promising.**

pronoun

a word that takes the place of a noun or nouns. The words *she, he, it, they, I, me,* and *you* are pronouns. "Mom and Dad stayed home because they were tired." *They* is a pronoun that takes the place of the nouns *Mom* and *Dad.* **pronouns.**

pronouns

proof

a way of showing that something is true: *If what he says is correct, he should have proof.* **proofs.**

proofread

to read something and mark mistakes like spelling mistakes that you need to correct: *She proofread her story before handing it in.* **proofread, proofreading.**

propeller

the blades that turn and make some boats and aircraft move. Engines make the propellers turn. **propellers.**

propeller

proper noun

a word that names a special person, place, or thing. "Jason and Carol left for Florida last Sunday." *Jason, Carol, Florida,* and *Sunday* are proper nouns. Proper nouns begin with capital letters. **proper nouns.**

property

1. something that someone owns: *This bike is my property.* **2.** a piece of land: *My aunt owns property by the lake.* **3.** a special power that something has, or something that it can do. Since wood can float, we say that wood has the property of floating. **properties** (for **2.** and **3.**).

protect

to keep someone or something safe from harm or danger. An umbrella protects you from rain. **protected, protecting.**

protect

protection

keeping someone or something safe from harm: *Some animals live in caves for protection from bad weather.*

protein

a part of some foods that is important for good health. Meat, milk, cheese, eggs, and beans contain protein.

proud

thinking well of yourself or of people or things that have something to do with you: *They were proud of the children.* **prouder, proudest.**

prove

to show that a thing is true: *Can you prove that the dog is really yours?* **proved, proving.**

provide

to give something that is needed or wanted: *Cities and towns provide streets and sidewalks for people to use.* **provided, providing.**

province

one of the main divisions of a country. Canada is divided into provinces instead of states. **provinces.**

public

1. for everyone; belonging to the people: *Anyone can use the services of a public library.* **2.** everyone; all the people: *Television and radio stations warned the public that a tornado might come.*

puck

a hard, black, round piece of rubber that players use in the game of ice hockey. **pucks.**

pudding

a soft, cooked food that is usually sweet. People eat pudding as a dessert or as a snack. **puddings.**

puddle

a small amount of water: *The rain left puddles in the yard.* **puddles.**

pueblo

an Indian village in which homes are grouped together to form a large building. They are several stories high and usually have a flat roof. Pueblos are built of baked clay bricks and stone. **pueblos.**

pueblo

Puerto Rico

an island off the coast of Florida. It is protected by the United States, but it makes its own laws for itself.

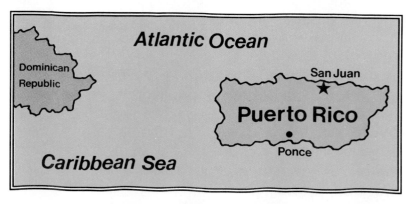

Puerto Rico

puff

1. to breathe fast and hard: *She puffed as she ran up the hill.* **2.** to swell up: *Popcorn puffs up when you heat it.* **puffed, puffing.**

pull

1. to move something toward you: *I pulled the closet door open. We pulled the wagon up the hill.* **2.** to take hold of something with your fingers or a tool and tug it out: *I pulled weeds in the garden for an hour.* **pulled, pulling.**

pump

1. a machine for making liquids or gases go into or out of things: *The pump brought water up from the well.* **2.** to move liquids or gases with a pump; to move like a pump does: *He pumped gasoline into the car. The heart pumps blood to all parts of the body.* **pumps; pumped, pumping.**

pumpkin

a large orange fruit that grows on a vine. Pumpkins are used to make jack-o'-lanterns and pies. **pumpkins.**

pumpkins

punch

1. to hit with your fist: *She punched him on the arm to get his attention.* **2.** to make a hole in: *The bus driver punched our tickets.* **punched, punching.**

punctuation

the use of periods, commas, and other marks in writing. Punctuation helps make the meaning of sentences clear.

punish

to cause pain or unhappiness to someone who did something wrong: *Pupils who don't behave in class may be punished by the teacher.* **punished, punishing.**

pups (definition 2)
fox; wolf; seal

pup
1. a short word meaning puppy. **2.** a young fox, wolf, or seal. **pups.**

pupil¹
a person that is learning in school or that someone is teaching. **pupils.**

pupil²
the center of the eye that looks like a black dot. Light enters your eyes through your pupils. **pupils.**

puppet
a toy that looks like a person or an animal. You put one kind of puppet over your finger to move it. You move another kind of puppet by wires or strings. **puppets.**

puppet

puppy
a young dog; a baby dog. **puppies.**

pure
1. not mixed with anything else: *He has a sweater made of pure wool.* **2.** perfectly clean; not dirty: *We buy pure water in bottles to drink.* **purer, purest.**

purple
a dark color that is a mixture of red and blue. **purples.**

purple

purpose
a reason for something that someone wants to do: *Her purpose in calling was to ask us to lunch.* **purposes.**

purr

1. a sound that a cat makes when it is pleased: *Their cat has a loud purr.* **2.** to make this sound: *The cat rubbed against my leg and purred.* **purrs; purred, purring.**

push

to move something away from you: *She pushed the drawer shut. I pushed the chair out of my way.* **pushed, pushing.**

pussy willow

a small tree with furry gray flowers that look like tiny bits of cat's fur. Pussy willows bloom in early spring. **pussy willows.**

put

1. to place or set something somewhere: *I put the letter in an envelope.* **2.** to cause something to be a certain way: *Put these words in alphabetical order. Please put the light out when you leave.* **put, putting.**

puzzle

1. a game that you work out for fun: *Help me put the pieces of this puzzle together.* **2.** to make it hard for someone to understand something: *Why he left so early puzzled us.* **puzzles; puzzled, puzzling.**

pussy willow

Q q

quack

1. the sound a duck makes: *The duck's loud quacks woke us up.* **2.** to make such a sound: *The ducks are quacking loudly in the yard.* **quacks; quacked, quacking.**

quarrel

1. a fight with words; an angry talk with someone who does not agree with you; argument: *The children had a quarrel over how to divide up the candy.* **2.** to fight with words; speak angrily to each other about something; argue: *The two friends quarreled and now they don't speak to each other.* **quarrels; quarreled, quarreling.**

quart

quart

an amount of liquid. Two pints are equal to one quart. Four quarts are equal to one gallon. **quarts.**

quarter

1. one of four equal parts: *Each of the four girls ate a quarter of the apple.* **2.** a coin in the United States and Canada worth 25 cents. Four quarters make one dollar. **3.** one of four equal periods of play in games such as football, basketball, or soccer. **quarters.**

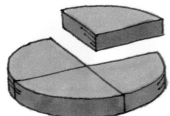

quarter (definition 1)

Quebec

one of the ten provinces of Canada.

queen

the wife of a king; a woman who rules a country and its people. **queens.**

question

a thing asked in order to find out something: *The teacher answered the children's questions about the story.* **questions.**

question mark

a mark of punctuation (?) put after a question. **question marks.**

quick

taking very little time; with great speed; fast: *The cat made a quick jump onto the sofa. We made a quick trip to the store.* **quicker, quickest.**

quiet

1. making no sound; not noisy: *It was a quiet night.*
2. not moving; still; moving very little: *The water hardly moved on the quiet lake.* **quieter, quietest.**

quill

a stiff, sharp hair like the end of a feather. A porcupine has quills on its back. **quills.**

quilt

a soft covering for a bed. A quilt is usually made from two pieces of cloth sewed together with soft material between them. **quilts.**

quilt

quit

1. to stop doing something: *The children quit playing when they saw the rain clouds.* **2.** to leave something: *He is quitting his job tomorrow and going to a new job on Monday.* **quit, quitting.**

quite

There was quite a change in the weather yesterday. It is quite cold today. It is not quite five o'clock.

Rr

rabbit

a small animal with soft fur and long ears. Rabbits have long back legs and can hop very fast. **rabbits.**

raccoon

a small animal with thick fur. Its tail is long and has rings of a different color. Raccoons look for food at night. **raccoons.**

raccoon

rabbit

race

1. a contest to see who can do something the fastest: *Who won the bicycle race?* **2.** to run or go fast: *She raced me to the house.* **races; raced, racing.**

radio

an electric machine that brings voices and music from far away. A radio may be small enough to carry in your pocket. **radios.**

radish

a small red or white vegetable with a strong flavor. Radishes grow underground. **radishes.**

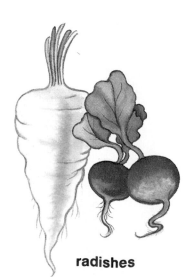

radishes

raft

something made of wood or rubber that can carry people and things on water. A raft is flat and can be moved by a pole or by paddles. **rafts.**

rag

a torn or worn piece of cloth: *I wiped up the spilled paint with an old rag.* **rags.**

rail

a metal bar. Railroad trains run on steel rails. **rails.**

railroad

a road or track of two steel rails on which the wheels of trains run. **railroads.**

railroad

rain

1. the water that falls in drops from the clouds: *The rain got us all wet as we walked home from school.*
2. to fall in drops of water: *It rained all night.* **rains; rained, raining.**

rainbow

a curved band of many colors in the sky. A rainbow sometimes appears when the sun shines right after it rains. **rainbows.**

raincoat

a coat that water will not go through: *I wore a raincoat to stay dry.* **raincoats.**

rainbow

rainy

having a lot of rain: *This was a rainy summer.* **rainier, rainiest.**

raise

1. to lift up: *Raise your hand if you know the answer. We raise the flag every morning at school.* **2.** to look after plants or animals so that they will grow: *My uncle raises wheat and horses on his farm.* **raised, raising.**

raisin

a small, sweet fruit. Raisins are dried grapes. **raisins.**

rake (definition 2)
*She is **raking** the leaves.*

rake

1. a tool with a long handle and a bar with teeth at one end: *She took the rake out of the garage.* **2.** to make clean or smooth with a rake: *Please help me rake the leaves off the lawn.* **rakes; raked, raking.**

ran

I ran all the way home.

ranch

a very large farm and its buildings. Sheep, cattle, or horses are raised on ranches. **ranches.**

rang

When the telephone rang, I answered it.

rap

1. a light, sharp knock: *I heard a rap on the door.* **2.** to knock sharply: *Who rapped on the door?* **raps; rapped, rapping.**

rapid

very quick; fast: *He is a rapid worker.*

rare

not often found; very unusual: *Snow is rare in Louisiana.* **rarer, rarest.**

raspberry

a small black or red berry. Raspberries grow on bushes. **raspberries.**

raspberries

rat

an animal with a long, thin tail. A rat looks like a large mouse. Rats are gray, brown, black, or white. **rats.**

rat

rather

I would rather play soccer than basketball. He was rather annoyed by our noise.

rattle

to make short, sharp sounds: *The wind rattled the loose windows on the front of the house.* **rattled, rattling.**

raw

not cooked: *She will eat raw carrots, but not boiled carrots.* **rawer, rawest.**

raw material

something that comes from nature, such as cotton, trees, and iron. Raw materials are used to make such things as cloth, furniture, and steel. **raw materials.**

ray

a line or beam of light: *The sun's rays shone from behind the cloud.* **rays.**

rays

razor

a very sharp tool used for shaving. **razors.**

reach

1. to stretch out your arm and hand to touch something; try to get: *She reached for the milk carton.* **2.** to get to; come to: *We will reach the camp about eight o'clock.* **reached, reaching.**

read[1]

1. to look at and understand written words: *Have you learned to read?* **2.** to speak out loud the words of writing or print: *Our teacher promised to read a story to us.* **read, reading.** (Read[1] rhymes with <u>seed</u>.)

read[2]

He read that book last week. Have you read it yet? (Read[2] rhymes with <u>head</u>.)

reader

1. a person who reads: *Everyone in our family is a reader.* **2.** a book for learning and practicing reading: *We have a new reader this year, with a lot of good stories in it.* **readers.**

ready

all set to do something: *Lunch is ready. Are they ready to leave for the movie?* **readier, readiest.**

real

not make-believe; true. *Pandas are real, but unicorns are not real. This book is about the real adventures of an Indian girl.*

realize

to understand clearly: *Everyone realizes that she did a good job.* **realized, realizing.**

really

truly; in fact: *Some adventure stories are fun to read, but they could not really happen.*

rear—*The rear of the house has not been painted.*

rear

the side of anything opposite the front side; the back part; back: *The rear of the house has not been painted, but the front is done.*

reason

whatever explains why something happened or why someone did something: *Dad couldn't figure out a reason for the car not starting this morning. He had a good reason for not playing ball yesterday, since his knee was hurting.* **reasons.**

recall

to remember; to call back to mind: *I cannot recall who told me that story.* **recalled, recalling.**

receive

to take or get something that someone gives you or sends you: *She received several gifts at her party.* **received, receiving.**

recess

a short time during which classroom work stops: *We'll finish the game at recess tomorrow.*

recipe

a set of written directions that show how to fix something to eat: *We have a good recipe for cupcakes.* **recipes.**

recognize

to remember from knowing before: *She almost didn't recognize her friend because he had grown a mustache.* **recognized, recognizing.**

recognize

record

something that gives off sounds when it is used on a record player. Records are round and flat, and are made out of plastic. **records.**

record player

a machine that gives off sounds when you play records on it. **record players.**

recover

to get well: *He is recovering from the flu.* **recovered, recovering.**

recreation

play; fun; amusement: *We swim for recreation.*

rectangle

a shape with four sides. **rectangles.**

recycle

to prepare something like paper or glass so that it can be used again. **recycled, recycling.**

red (definition 2)
The band wore **red** uniforms.

redwood

red

1. the color of blood. **2.** having this color: *The band wore red uniforms.* **reds; redder, reddest.**

redwood

a very large evergreen tree. Redwoods are the tallest trees alive today. **redwoods.**

reel

a spool to hold things like thread, fish line, or film. **reels.**

reflect

to give back light, heat, or sound; bounce back. The moon gives off no light of its own, but reflects light from the sun. *A mirror reflects what is in front of it.* **reflected, reflecting.**

refreshment

food and drink: *Fruit juice and cookies were served as refreshments.* **refreshments.**

refrigerator

an electric appliance that keeps food and other things cold. **refrigerators.**

refuse

to say no to: *I refused to let the stranger in the house.* **refused, refusing.**

regular

1. usual: *He bought the regular size box of soap, not the large one.* **2.** coming again and again at the same time: *She makes regular visits to the dentist.*

rehearse

to practice: *We will rehearse the play this afternoon.* **rehearsed, rehearsing.**

refuse—*I* **refused** *to open the door to a stranger.*

reindeer

reindeer

a deer with large antlers. It lives in cold places. People use it to pull sleighs and for milk, meat, and hides. **reindeer.**

relative

a person who belongs to the same family as another, such as a mother, sister, or uncle. **relatives.**

relax

to be free from work, and have a good time: *We relax on vacation.* **relaxed, relaxing.**

release

to let loose; set free: *She released the rabbit from its cage.* **released, releasing.**

remain

1. to stay: *The class should remain in the room until three.* **2.** to be left: *A few leaves remain on the tree. If you take 10 from 20, 10 remains.* **remained, remaining.**

remain (definition 2)
*A few leaves **remain** on the trees.*

remark

1. to say in a few words: *Dad remarked that the grass needed cutting.* **2.** something said: *While we rehearsed, our teacher made few remarks.* **remarked, remarking; remarks.**

remember

1. to call back to your mind: *I can't remember their address.* **2.** to keep in mind; take care not to forget: *Remember to take the books back to the library.* **remembered, remembering.**

remind

to make a person think of something: *This shell reminds me of our days at the beach.* **reminded, reminding.**

rent

1. the money paid for the use of property: *She pays the rent on her apartment every month.* **2.** to pay to use: *We rented a car on our vacation.* **rents; rented, renting.**

repair

to make good again: *Will you repair my torn coat?* **repaired, repairing.**

repeat

1. to do or make again: *Don't repeat your mistakes.* **2.** to say again: *Please repeat that word.* **repeated, repeating.**

reply

1. to answer: *Did you reply to her question?* **2.** something said as an answer: *He did not make a reply to my question.* **replied, replying; replies.**

report

1. words that are said or written to tell about something: *He gives the weather report on the radio.* **2.** to make a report of: *Dad called and reported the fire.* **reports; reported, reporting.**

reporter

a person who gathers and reports news for a newspaper, magazine, or a radio or television station. **reporters.**

reporter

reptile

an animal with dry, rough skin. Snakes, lizards, turtles, alligators, and crocodiles are reptiles. **reptiles.**

reptile

rescue

to save from danger or harm: *The prince rescued the princess from the dragon.* **rescued, rescuing.**

reservoir

a place where water is collected and stored for use. **reservoirs.**

rescue

respect

to feel or show special thought for: *We respect an honest person.* **respected, respecting.**

rest¹

1. to be still or quiet; sleep: *She rests for an hour every afternoon.* **2.** a short stop after working or playing hard: *Take a rest after you finish washing the windows.* **rested, resting; rests.**

rest²

what is left: *He ate most of the apple and threw the rest away.*

restaurant

a place to buy and eat a meal. **restaurants.**

result

what happens because of something: *The result of her fall was a broken arm.* **results.**

return

1. to come back: *He will return soon.* **2.** to give back: *Did you return the library books?* **returned, returning.**

review

1. to look at again: *Let's review yesterday's lesson.* **2.** a looking at again: *Study the review at the end of the chapter.* **reviewed, reviewing; reviews.**

revise

to read carefully in order to correct and improve something you have written: *She revised her story to make the ending more exciting.* **revised, revising.**

revolve

to move in a circle around something: *The earth revolves around the sun. A record revolves on a record player.* **revolved, revolving.**

reward

something you get in return for something you have done: *A trip to the zoo was our reward for raking all the leaves.* **rewards.**

rewrite

to write again: *I rewrote my story to correct the spelling mistakes.* **rewrote, rewritten, rewriting.**

rhinoceros

a large wild animal with thick skin and one or two horns above its nose. **rhinoceroses.**

rhinoceros

Rhode Island

one of the fifty states of the United States.

rhyme

1. to have words or lines that end in the same sound: *"Kitten" rhymes with "mitten." "Go to bed" and "sleepyhead" also rhyme.* **2.** a word or line having the same last sound: *"Blue" is a rhyme for "true." "Five, six" and "Pick up sticks" are rhymes.* **rhymed, rhyming; rhymes.**

rhythm

the natural strong beat that some music or poetry has. The rhythm makes you want to clap your hands to keep time. *We tapped our feet to the rhythm of the music.* **rhythms.**

rib

one of the bones that curve from back to front around your chest. Your ribs protect your heart and lungs. **ribs.**

ribbon

a strip or band of cloth or paper used to tie or trim something. A person who wins a contest sometimes gets a blue ribbon. **ribbons.**

ribbon

rice

a cereal grain. Rice is often white, but may be brown. Rice is grown in warm parts of the world.

rice

rich

having much money or other property: *They can spend a lot because they are rich.* **richer, richest.**

rid

to do away with; cause something to disappear: *We set traps to get rid of the mice.* **rid, ridding.**

riddle

a puzzle that asks a question. Here is a riddle: "What part of a fish weighs the most?" Answer: "The scales." **riddles.**

ride

1. to sit on or in something as you go somewhere: *We will ride our bikes to the park. Sunday we all rode in our new car.* **2.** a trip on or in something: *We took a ride on our bikes.* **rode, ridden, riding; rides.**

right

1. the way it should be; good: *The right thing to do is tell the truth.* **2.** the direction toward the last word on this line; the opposite of left: *When you get to the corner, turn right.*

right (definition 2)

rim

the edge or border around anything: *The rim of the cup is chipped.* **rims.**

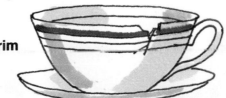

rim

293

ring¹ (definition 2)
The people sat in a ring.

rip (definition 1)
The cloth is ripped in two pieces.

ring¹

1. a thin circle of metal or other material worn on the finger: *She bought a gold ring.* **2.** something in the form of a circle: *The dancers joined hands and formed a ring.* **rings.**

ring²

1. to make a sound like that of a bell: *I heard the phone ring.* **2.** the sound of a bell: *There were three rings and then the person hung up.* **rang, rung, ringing; rings.**

rip

1. to cut or pull off in a rough way; tear off: *They ripped the wrapping off the presents.* **2.** a torn place: *She sewed up the rip in my sleeve.* **ripped, ripping; rips.**

ripe

grown and ready to be picked and eaten: *We bought several bushels of ripe apples at the orchard.* **riper, ripest.**

rise

1. to get up from a lying, sitting, or kneeling position; stand up: *Please rise when your name is called.* **2.** to go up: *What time will the sun rise tomorrow?* **3.** to go higher in cost or value: *The price of fruit rises in winter.* **rose, risen, rising.**

risen

The sun had already risen by the time we woke up.

river

a wide stream of running water. Most rivers flow into a lake or ocean. **rivers.**

road

a way to go between places; way for a car, truck, or bus to go along: *This road goes to the city.* **roads.**

road

roar

1. to make a loud, deep sound: *The crowd roared when he caught the ball.* **2.** a loud, deep sound: *The roar of the lion frightened some people at the zoo.* **roared, roaring; roars.**

roast

1. to cook something by the heat in an oven; bake: *Grandma roasted a chicken and potatoes for dinner.* **2.** a piece of meat cooked by roasting: *Dad cooked a roast.* **roasted, roasting; roasts.**

rob

to take by force something that does not belong to you: *Three men robbed the bank.* **robbed, robbing.**

robber

a person who robs: *The police chased him, but the robber got away.* **robbers.**

robe

a long piece of clothing like a loose coat: *I put a robe on over my pajamas.* **robes.**

robin

a bird with a red or orange front. Robins are found in most places in the United States. **robins.**

robins

robot

a machine that is run by a computer. Robots help people do work. Robots can look like people. **robots.**

rock¹

1. the hard, solid part of the earth that is not soil or metal. You can find rock in small or large pieces. Mountains are formed mostly of rock. **2.** a small piece of this hard material: *She tossed a rock into the pond.* **rocks** (for **2.**).

rock²

to move backward and forward, or from side to side: *We took turns rocking the baby.* **rocked, rocking.**

rocket

rocket

a long metal tube open at one end. When fuel in the rocket is lighted, it burns quickly, and drives the rocket forward, or straight up. Rockets are used to launch spacecraft. **rockets.**

rocky

full of rocks: *The road was very rocky and hard to drive on.* **rockier, rockiest.**

rode

I rode my bicycle to school.

rodeo

a contest or show in which cowboys and cowgirls show their skills. They ride wild horses, steers, and bulls, and rope cattle. **rodeos.**

roll

1. to move along by turning over and over: *The marbles rolled across the floor.* **2.** something rolled up: *I bought a roll of film.* **3.** a kind of bread or cake: *She spread butter on the roll.* **rolled, rolling; rolls.**

roller skate

a roller skate is a shoe, or something you wear on a shoe, that has wheels. Roller skates are used to skate on a floor, a sidewalk, or any other flat, smooth surface. **roller skates.**

roller skates

roof

the top covering of a building: *From our apartment we can see the roofs of many houses.* **roofs.**

room

1. a part of the inside of a building. Each room has walls of its own. *Please clean up your room.* **2.** an amount of space that something takes: *There isn't enough room in the kitchen for everyone to sit down.* **rooms** (for **1.**).

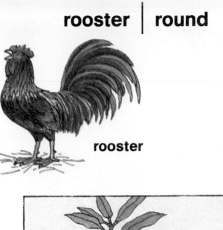

rooster

rooster

a full-grown male chicken. Roosters crow when the sun comes up each morning. **roosters.**

root

1. the part of a plant that grows underground. Plants get food and water through their roots. **2.** a word from which other words are made. The root word *round* can be seen in the words *rounder* and *roundest.* **roots.**

roots (definition 1)

rope

1. a very thick string twisted together: *She tied the boat to the dock with a rope.* **2.** to catch an animal with a rope that has a loop at the end: *At the rodeo we saw my uncle rope a horse.* **ropes; roped, roping.**

rose¹

a flower that grows on a bush. Roses are red, pink, white, or yellow. Some roses have thorns. **roses.**

rose²

The pupils rose from their desks when the principal entered the room.

roses¹

rosy

light red in color; like a rose in color: *Their cheeks are rosy from the cold weather.* **rosier, rosiest.**

rotten

no longer good; spoiled: *The banana is all black outside, and rotten inside.* **rottener, rottenest.**

rough

with an uneven surface; not smooth; not level: *Some trees have very rough bark. His skin became rough from the cold wind.* **rougher, roughest.**

round

shaped like a ball or a circle. The earth is round. A wheel is round. **rounder, roundest.**

route

a way that you choose to get somewhere: *What route do you take to get to the park? We live near the school bus route.* **routes.**

row[1]

a straight line of people or things: *We stood in a row against the wall.* **rows.**

row[2]

to move a boat by using oars. When you row, you sit facing backward, and pull the oars through the water. **rowed, rowing.**

royal

from or about a king or a queen: *The knight received a royal command to go to the queen's castle.*

rub

to move something back and forth against something else: *She rubbed the kitten's back. They rubbed the stain off the floor with a cloth.* **rubbed, rubbing.**

rubber

material made from the juice of certain trees. Rubber can stretch and bounce. Rubber will not let air or water through. Pencil erasers and car tires are made of rubber.

rude

with bad manners; not polite: *My brother was rude and didn't say hello to my best friend.* **ruder, rudest.**

rug

something that covers the floor: *The children wrestled on the rug in the living room.* **rugs.**

rule

1. something that tells what we must do or what we must not do: *You must obey the school rules and not run in the halls.* **2.** to control a country and its people: *The king ruled his kingdom well.* **rules; ruled, ruling.**

rubber

ruler

1. a straight strip of wood, metal, or plastic used to measure how long something is. Rulers also help you to draw straight lines. **2.** anyone who controls a government: *Kings and queens used to be the rulers in France.* **rulers.**

run

1. to move your legs very fast, so that you go faster than walking: *It's hard to run a mile without stopping for breath. My friend's dog ran away.* **2.** to work as it should; go: *The washer doesn't run until it is turned on.* **3.** to be in charge of; manage: *Mom runs a restaurant.* **ran, run, running.**

rung[1]

a round bar used as a step of a ladder. **rungs.**

rung[2]

The church bell has rung several times today.

rungs[1]

runner

a person, animal, or thing that runs: *My sister is a fast runner.* **runners.**

rural

in the country: *Rural life is not like city life.*

rush

1. to move quickly: *They rushed to put out the fire.* **2.** a big hurry: *He was in a rush to get to the bank before it closed.* **rushed, rushing.**

rust

1. the red-brown covering that sometimes forms on iron or steel: *There's some rust on our car.* **2.** to become covered with this: *Don't let your tools rust.* **rusted, rusting.**

Ss

saddle (definition 1)

saddle (definition 2)

sack

a large bag made of paper or rough cloth. Sacks are used to hold grain, flour, potatoes, and other things. **sacks.**

sad

feeling bad about things; not happy; unhappy: *I was sad when my best friend moved away.* **sadder, saddest.**

saddle

1. a seat for a rider to use: *He put a saddle on his horse. I have a saddle on my bike.* **2.** to put such a seat on something: *He saddled up the horses so we could ride.* **saddles; saddled, saddling.**

safe

1. in no danger; free from harm: *We keep our money in a safe place. He looked for a safe place to swim.* **2.** a place for keeping things where they will be in no danger. A safe is a heavy metal box where valuable things are locked away. **safer, safest; safes.**

safety

being in no danger: *The crossing guard watches out for our safety.*

safety belt

a strap or a belt that goes around the shoulders and hips of a rider in a car or an airplane. A safety belt helps you stay in your seat if there is a crash or a sudden stop. **safety belts.**

said

She had said it many times. She said she would help us.

sail

1. a large piece of cloth used on some boats. Sails catch the wind and help boats to move. **2.** to travel on water: *We like to sail on Dad's new boat.* **sails; sailed, sailing.**

sailboat

a boat that is moved by wind that pushes against the sails: *Our sailboat went slowly because there was very little wind.* **sailboats.**

sailboat

sailor

a person who works on a boat or ship. A group of sailors may be called a crew. **sailors.**

salad

vegetables or other food, usually served raw and crisp: *We put lettuce and carrots in the salad.* **salads.**

sale

1. a selling of something: *The library held a book sale last week.* **2.** selling something for less money than usual: *The store was having a sale on winter coats.* **sales.**

salesperson

someone whose job is to sell things: *The salesperson asked the woman whether she needed any help.* **salespersons.**

salmon

salmon

a large fish used for food. **salmon.**

salt

a white material found in the earth or in sea water. Salt makes food taste better and keeps it from spoiling.

salt water

water that is salty. Ocean water is called salt water. Water without any salt is fresh water.

salty

tasting of salt: *This popcorn is too salty to eat.* **saltier, saltiest.**

same

just alike; not different: *We have the same first name. She has the same thing for lunch every day.*

sand

tiny bits of broken rock: *We played in the sand at the beach.*

sandal

a kind of shoe fastened to the foot with straps: *She wears sandals in the summer.* **sandals.**

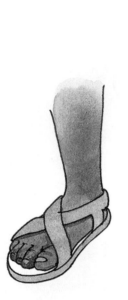

sandals

sandwich

two slices of bread with meat, cheese, or some other food between them: *He brought peanut butter and jelly sandwiches for lunch.* **sandwiches.**

sang

The mother sang to her baby.

sank

The toy boat sank to the bottom of the pond.

Saskatchewan

one of the ten provinces of Canada.

sat

My father sat in his favorite chair. We sat quietly while the teacher read the story.

satisfy

to give enough of something to someone: *She satisfied her hunger with a sandwich and milk.* **satisfied, satisfying.**

Saturday

the day after Friday; the seventh day of the week. **Saturdays.**

sauce

a liquid served with food to make the food taste better: *He likes tomato sauce on spaghetti.* **sauces.**

saucepan

a small pan or pot with a handle. You use a saucepan to heat foods. **saucepans.**

saucer

a small flat dish. You set a cup on a saucer. **saucers.**

sausage

meat that has been chopped, seasoned, and stuffed into a thin tube: *We had sausage for breakfast.* **sausages.**

sausages

save

1. to keep someone from harm or danger: *The fence saved the girl from falling into the hole.* **2.** to keep something that you want to use later on: *He was saving money for a new bike.* **saved, saving.**

saw¹

1. a tool for cutting. A saw has sharp teeth on the edge of a thin blade. *The carpenter used a saw to cut boards for our new porch.* **2.** to cut or be cut with a saw: *He sawed the wood for the house he was building for his dog.* **saws; sawed, sawing.**

saw¹ (definitions 1 and 2)

saxophone

saw²

She saw a robin yesterday.

saxophone

a musical instrument that is played by blowing into it and pressing keys. **saxophones.**

say

to speak out loud; put into words: *He said he couldn't come with us. Please speak up when you say your lines in the play.* **said, saying.**

scale¹

something used to see how much something weighs: *He weighed himself on the scale in the doctor's office.* **scales.**

scale²

one of the thin, hard pieces that form the outer covering of some fish, snakes, and lizards. **scales.**

scale¹

scale²—*The lizard's body is covered with* **scales.**

scamper

to run quickly: *The squirrel scampered up the tree.* **scampered, scampering.**

scare

to frighten; make someone feel that something bad might happen: *The noise scared him. He was scared when he could not see what it was.* **scared, scaring.**

scarecrow

a figure of a person dressed in old clothes. A scarecrow is set in a field to scare birds away from crops that are growing. **scarecrows.**

scarecrow

scarf

a piece of cloth worn on the head or around the neck and shoulders. **scarves.**

scarves

more than one scarf.

scary

making someone fecl afraid: *She saw a scary movie on TV.* **scarier, scariest.**

scatter

to throw a little bit here and a little bit there; sprinkle: *She scattered salt on the driveway to melt the ice.* **scattered, scattering.**

scene

1. the place where something happens in a story or a play: *The first scene is the king's castle.* **2.** a beautiful sight to look at; view: *She looked out her window after the snow and saw a pretty scene.* **scenes.**

scenery

1. what you see when you look around outside; pleasant views of the outdoors. Scenery includes mountains, valleys, forests, and the like. **2.** painted scenes or pictures used on a stage to show where the action of a play is taking place.

scenery (definition 2)

school

1. a place where you learn things: *We learn to read in school.* **2.** all the students and teachers in a school: *My whole school visited the museum.* **schools.**

schoolroom

a room in which students learn. **schoolrooms.**

science

a study of the earth, the sky, animals, and people. Science uses facts that we can observe to tell us why things are the way they are.

scientist

a person who studies a science. A scientist tries to find out why things are the way they are. **scientists.**

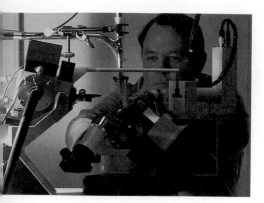

scientist

scissors

a tool for cutting things. A pair of scissors has two sharp edges that work together to cut paper or cloth. **scissors.**

scold

scold

to speak to someone in an angry way: *The mother cat scolded her kittens for losing their mittens.* **scolded, scolding.**

scoop

1. a tool like a small shovel: *She used a scoop to put sugar in the sugar bowl.* **2.** to take up with a scoop, or the way a scoop does: *He scooped up the snow with his hands to make a snowball.* **scoops; scooped, scooping.**

scoop (definition 1)

scooters

scooter

a toy that you can ride, made of a board to stand on, two wheels, and a handle for steering. You move a scooter by pushing one foot against the ground. **scooters.**

score

1. the points made in a game or on a test: *The score of the baseball game was 4 to 2.* **2.** to make points: *Our team scored first.* **scores; scored, scoring.**

scowl

1. to look at in an angry way: *She scowled at the man who tried to take her place in line.* **2.** an angry look: *Her scowl let him know she was unhappy.* **scowled, scowling; scowls.**

scramble

to mix together: *He scrambled eggs for breakfast. We made a code by scrambling the letters of the alphabet.* **scrambled, scrambling.**

scrap

a small piece; a small part left over: *We put the scraps of paper in the wastebasket.* **scraps.**

scrape

1. to rub off with something sharp or rough: *We scraped the peeling paint off the house before we painted it a new color.* **2.** to scratch something by rubbing it against something rough: *I scraped my knee when I fell on the sidewalk.* **scraped, scraping.**

QF LJT QFEHQCHX:
CH UIXYLKGHN
HEEU RFX
KXHYWRYUQ.

								S	A	T	O	P
								U	V	X	Y	Z
W	G	L	A	F	Z	X	U	Q
K	L	M	O	P	Q	R	S	T
Y	K	I	N	H	R	E	C	D
A	B	C	D	E	F	G	H	I	J

scramble—*Match each upside-down red letter with the black letter above it. Write the black letters down, and you will be able to read the* **scrambled** *message.*

scratch (definition 3)
*The cat is **scratching** its chin.*

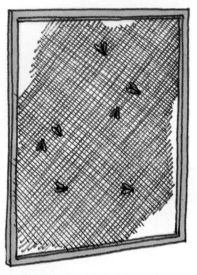

screen (definition 1)

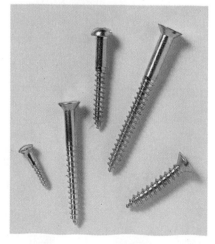

screws

scratch

1. to make a mark on something by using something sharp: *Your buckle scratched the chair. The pin scratched my arm.* **2.** a mark made by using something sharp: *There are deep scratches on our kitchen table.* **3.** to rub something that itches: *It's hard not to scratch mosquito bites.* **scratched, scratching; scratches.**

scream

1. to make a loud, sharp cry. People scream when they are angry, frightened, or excited. **2.** a loud, sharp cry: *We heard screams from the people on the rides at the fair.* **screamed, screaming; screams.**

screen

1. a frame that holds woven wire, which is put in a window or door. The tiny holes in a screen allow air to pass through, but keep out insects. **2.** a glass surface where television pictures, computer information, or video games are seen. **3.** a flat surface for showing movies and slides: *The teacher keeps the screen in the classroom closet.* **screens.**

screw

a piece of metal that is shaped something like a nail. It has a sharp point at one end. A screw is twisted into wood instead of pounded. **screws.**

scrub

to rub something hard in order to get it clean: *The janitors scrub the classroom floors after school.* **scrubbed, scrubbing.**

sculptor

an artist who makes things by cutting or shaping them. Sculptors carve wood and stone statues, and model clay figures. **sculptors.**

sculpture

1. the making of figures out of stone, wood, clay, or other materials: *My aunt has studied sculpture.* **2.** a figure made in this way: *I saw a sculpture of a horse at the museum.* **sculptures** (for **2.**).

sculptor

sculpture
(definition 2)

scurry

to run quickly; hurry: *The mouse scurried past our feet.* **scurried, scurrying.**

sea

a great body of salt water. Seas cover almost three-fourths of the earth's surface. Fish, dolphins, and whales are some animals that live in the sea. Another word for sea is ocean. **seas.**

sea horse

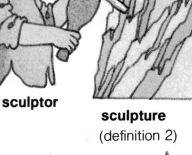

sea horse

a small fish that has a head that looks something like a horse's head. **sea horses.**

seal¹

1. a picture stamped on something. The seal of the United States has an eagle on it. **2.** to close something very tightly: *He sealed the envelope before he mailed it.* **seals; sealed, sealing.**

seal¹ (definition 1)

seal²

a sea animal with thick fur. Seals usually live in cold places. **seals.**

seal²

season (definition 2)
*She **seasoned** the soup with pepper.*

search

to try to find something by looking for it: *We searched the house for Dad's car keys.* **searched, searching.**

season

1. one of the four parts of the year. The seasons are spring, summer, fall, and winter. **2.** to make something taste better: *Mom seasoned the soup with pepper and salt.* **seasons; seasoned, seasoning.**

seat

a place to sit or a thing to sit on: *The woman looked for a seat on the bus. The students took their seats when the teacher walked in.* **seats.**

second[1]

next after the first; 2nd: *B is the second letter of the alphabet. I came in second in the race.*

second[2]

a very short period of time. Sixty seconds equal one minute. **seconds.**

secret

1. not known to everybody; kept hidden from most people: *Our club has a secret code.* **2.** something that you don't tell anyone: *He asked her if she could keep a secret.* **secrets.**

secretary

a person who writes letters, keeps records, answers the telephone, and the like. A secretary can work for another person, a company, or a group of people, like a club. **secretaries.**

section

a part of something: *He cut the pizza into eight equal sections. We are studying the poetry section of our reader today.* **sections.**

see

1. to look at something with your eyes: *We woke up early to see the sunrise.* **2.** to understand something that is said or written: *I see what you mean.* **3.** to visit: *Last summer we went to see our grandparents.* **saw, seen, seeing.**

seeds

seed

the part of a plant that grows into a new plant. A seed has a tiny plant inside it. It also has the food the tiny plant needs to grow. **seeds.**

seek

to try to find something; look for; hunt: *The baseball team is seeking a new place to practice.* **sought, seeking.**

seem

The dog seemed hungry, but it wouldn't eat. Does the music seem too loud to you? I slept well, but I still seem to be tired. **seemed, seeming.**

seen

I have seen that movie already.

seesaw

a long board that balances on something near the middle. Children can sit at opposite ends of a seesaw and move up and down. Playgrounds often have seesaws. **seesaws.**

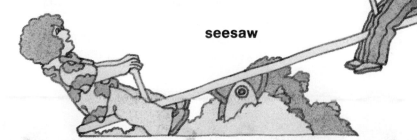

seesaw

select

select

to choose; pick out from a group: *Mother let me select my own clothes for the party.* **selected, selecting.**

selection

a choice; something that is picked out from a group: *This library has a good selection of animal stories. I made my selection at the shoe store.* **selections.**

selfish

caring too much for yourself and not enough for other people: *I think he is selfish because he never shares his things with anyone.*

sell

to trade something for money: *We plan to sell our house.* **sold, selling.**

send

to cause someone or something to go from one place to another: *Mother sent us to the store for bread. I'm sending a package to my friend.* **sent, sending.**

send

sense

1. any of the powers of a living thing to know what is going on around itself. The five senses are sight, smell, taste, hearing, and touch. **2.** the power to think in a clear and wise way: *She had the good sense to wear her boots to school when it snowed.* **3.** what is meant by something; meaning. Some very short words have a number of different senses. *The message was in code, and I couldn't make sense of it.* **senses** (for **1.** and **3.**).

sent

She sent the package last week.

sentence

sentence

a group of words that tells a complete idea. A written sentence begins with a capital letter. It ends with a period, a question mark, or an exclamation mark. Sometimes a single word can be a sentence, like "Listen." The definitions in this dictionary include many sentences. **sentences.**

separate

1. to keep two things apart: *A fence separates our yard from our neighbor's.* **2.** to move some things away from some other things: *He separated his books from mine.* **3.** away from others; apart: *We sat at separate tables in the cafeteria.* **separated, separating.**

September

the ninth month of the year. It has 30 days. September comes after August and before October.

serious

1. not funny; not joking: *Dad had a serious look on his face when he heard about the broken window.* **2.** important because of the harm it may cause: *Pollution is a serious problem for our country.*

serve

1. to put something to eat in front of someone: *The waiter served us our breakfast.* **2.** to work for someone or something: *Police officers and firefighters serve the public.* **served, serving.**

service

a job that a person does to help someone else. Fighting fires, delivering mail, and directing traffic are public services. **services.**

serve (definition 1)
*The waiter **served** us our breakfast.*

313

set (definition 1) below
(definition 2 and 3)
at right

serving

the amount of food served to a person at one time: *She ate two servings of pasta.* Another word for serving is helping. **servings.**

set

1. to put something some place: *Set your suitcase over in that corner.* **2.** to put something in order; arrange: *She set the table for dinner.* **3.** ready: *I was dressed in my winter clothes and all set to play in the snow.* **4.** to go down: *We'll go home when the sun sets.* **5.** a group of things that go together: *We bought a new set of dishes.* **set, setting; sets.**

settle

1. to agree on: *We settled the question of which way to go by looking at the map.* **2.** to go to live in a new place: *Our cousins plan to settle in California.* **settled, settling.**

seven

one more than six; 7. **sevens.**

seventeen

seven more than ten; 17. **seventeens.**

seventeenth

1. next after the sixteenth; 17th. **2.** one of 17 equal parts. **seventeenths.**

seventh

1. next after the sixth; 7th. **2.** one of seven equal parts. **sevenths.**

seventy

ten more than sixty; 70. **seventies.**

several

more than two or three but not many; a few: *He had several questions he wanted to ask the teacher.*

sew

to push a needle and thread through cloth. You can sew by hand or with a machine. **sewed, sewing.**

sewing machine

sewing machine

a machine for sewing. **sewing machines.**

shade

1. a place not in the bright sun, where the light is blocked by something: *We sat in the shade of the tree.*
2. something that shuts out light: *Pull down the window shade if you want to sleep late in the morning.*
3. to make a part of something darker than the rest; to use black in a picture to color in an area: *The teacher shaded part of the circle to explain fractions.* **shades** (for **2.**); **shaded, shading.**

shade (definition 2)

shadow

the shade made by some person, animal, or thing. A shadow is a dark shape made when something blocks the light. **shadows.**

shady

in the shade: *We looked for a shady part of the yard.* **shadier, shadiest.**

shake

to move up and down or from side to side quickly: *Shake your head if the answer is yes. The baby shook his rattle.* **shook, shaken, shaking.**

shake—*He **shook** his head no.*

shaken

The orange juice needs to be shaken up before you pour any.

shall

Shall I call you tomorrow? We shall eat soon.

shame

1. a feeling that you have done something wrong or silly: *He turned red with shame when he dropped his lunch tray.* **2.** something to feel sorry about: *It's a shame that you can't go with us.*

shampoo

1. to wash someone's hair: *I shampooed my hair in the shower.* **2.** something like soap used to wash your hair: *She used the shampoo in the shower.* **shampooed, shampooing; shampoos.**

shampoo (definition 1)
*She is **shampooing** her hair.*

shape

1. the way something looks; the form something takes. Squares, rectangles, triangles, and circles are kinds of shapes. An apple is a different shape from a banana. **2.** to form something into a certain shape: *She shaped the clay into a ball.* **3.** being healthy and fit: *Athletes do exercises to stay in shape.* **shapes; shaped, shaping.**

share

1. the part of something that belongs to one person: *He paid his share of the bill.* **2.** to let someone use something along with you: *The two girls shared a room. Mom shared her sandwich with me.* **shares; shared, sharing.**

shark

a large sea fish. Some sharks are dangerous to people. **sharks.**

shark

sharp

1. with a thin edge or a fine point: *Be careful with that sharp knife. My dog has sharp teeth.* **2.** to notice things quickly; watch carefully: *I needed a sharp eye to watch out for mistakes.* **sharper, sharpest.**

shave

1. to cut hair off the face or chin with a razor: *Dad shaves every morning.* **2.** the cutting off of hair with a razor: *Grandpa always used to get a shave at the barber shop.* **shaved, shaving; shaves.**

shawl

a square or long piece of cloth worn around the shoulders or head. **shawls.**

she

My mother said she would drive me to school. She will not be late.

shed

a building used for shelter or storing things: *The rake is in the tool shed.* **sheds.**

she'd

1. she had: *She'd wanted to go to the store early in the day.* **2.** she would: *She'd like to buy a new dress.*

sheep

an animal with long, thick hair. A sheep is raised for its wool and its meat. **sheep.**

sheet

1. a large piece of cloth used on a bed: *We changed the sheets on the guest bed.* **2.** a piece of paper: *The teacher asked us to write our names on a sheet of paper.* **sheets.**

shawl

sheep

shelf

a flat piece of wood, metal, or some other material that holds things. Books and dishes are often stored on shelves. **shelves.**

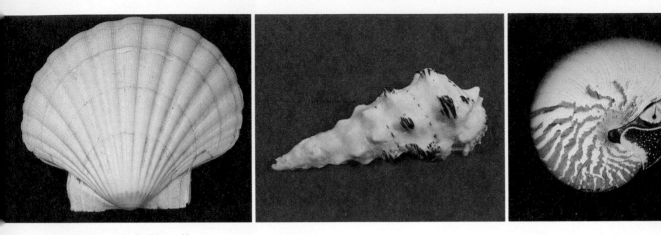

shells (definition 1)

shell

1. the hard outside covering of some animals. Snails, turtles, and oysters have shells. **2.** the hard outside covering of a nut or an egg. **shells.**

she'll

she will: *She'll meet us at five o'clock.*

shelter

1. something that covers or protects something else from the weather or from danger: *We looked for shelter from the freezing wind.* **2.** to protect from harm: *The porch sheltered us from the snow while we waited for our ride.* **shelters; sheltered, sheltering.**

shelves

Dad built new shelves for the garage.

sheriff

the most important police officer in a county. A sheriff has other officers who help keep order. **sheriffs.**

she's

1. she is: *She's happy in her new home.* **2.** she has: *She's gone to visit a friend.*

sheriff

shine

1. to give off a bright light; glow: *The sun is shining.*
2. to make bright: *Shine your shoes with this old rag.*
shone (for **1.**) or **shined** (for **2.**), **shining.**

shiny

bright; giving off a bright light: *Mom gave me a shiny new penny.* **shinier, shiniest.**

ship

1. a very large boat that travels on oceans or large lakes. **2.** to send or carry something from one place to another by boat, plane, truck, or train: *We shipped a package to my cousin.* **ships; shipped, shipping.**

ship (definition 1)

shirt

a kind of clothing for your arms and chest. A shirt can have long or short sleeves. Most shirts have collars and buttons. **shirts.**

shiver

1. to shake with cold or fear: *I shivered in the cold wind.* **2.** a shaking from cold or fear: *A shiver ran down my back after I came out of the swimming pool.*
shivered, shivering; shivers.

shiver (definition 1)
*He **shivered** in the cold.*

shock

1. a sudden hard shake, blow, or crash: *The shock of the explosion broke windows a block away.*
2. something that upsets you suddenly: *The news of their leaving is a shock to us.* **3.** the feeling caused by electricity passing through the body: *He got a shock from touching the toaster.* **shocks.**

shoe

something you wear on your foot. Shoes are often made of leather. **shoes.**

shoelace

a cord or a leather strip used to fasten a shoe.
shoelaces.

shoot (definition 3)

shopping center

shone

The sun shone in the morning before it began raining.

shook

He shook the bottle before he poured the orange juice.

shoot

1. to try to hit something with a bullet or an arrow: *He saw his uncle shoot a rabbit.* **2.** to move very quickly: *Flames were shooting up from the burning building.* **3.** to take a picture with a camera: *She shot several pictures of my dog.* **shot, shooting.**

shop

1. a place where things are sold; store: *We stopped at the candy shop.* **2.** to go to stores to look at or to buy things: *We shopped for clothes this morning.* **3.** a place where things are made or repaired: *I took my broken watch to the repair shop.* **shops; shopped, shopping.**

shopping center

a group of stores built together. Most shopping centers have large parking areas. **shopping centers.**

shore

land at the edge of a sea or a lake: *She likes to spend time at the shore on weekends.* **shores.**

short

1. not a great distance from the beginning to the end of something; not long: *My friend lives on a short street.* **2.** not lasting for very long: *We heard a very short talk by the principal today.* **3.** not tall: *The shortest child went to the front of the line.* **shorter, shortest.**

short (definition 3)

shorts pants that do not reach the knees.

shot[1]
1. the sound a gun makes: *We heard two shots.*
2. putting medicine under the skin by using a needle: *The doctor gave me a shot.* **3.** a kick, a throw, or a hit in some games, in order to score points: *My sister took two shots in the basketball game, but she missed them both.* **shots.**

shorts

shot[2] *He shot a lot of pictures at the picnic.*

should *You should drink milk every day. I should have worn my boots.*

shoulder the part of the body between the neck and the arm. **shoulders.**

shouldn't should not: *You shouldn't be late to school.*

shout to call or yell loudly: *She shouted for help.* **shouted, shouting.**

shove
1. to push something with force: *She shoved the chair across the floor.* **2.** a push: *He gave the door a shove to get it to open.* **shoved, shoving; shoves.**

shovel
1. a tool used to dig a hole or to scoop something up: *I used a snow shovel to clean off the driveway.* **2.** to lift and throw with this tool: *He shoveled the sand into the bucket.* **shovels; shoveled, shoveling.**

shovel (definitions 1 and 2)

321

show

1. to bring or put something so that you can see it: *She took the bicycle out of the garage and showed it to me.* **2.** to explain or to point out something to someone: *He showed us the way to the library. My teacher showed me how to work the problem.* **3.** a place where special things are shown to the public; an exhibit: *We are going to the flower show and the automobile show.* **4.** something that you watch on TV or at the movies: *We watched a good show last night.* **showed, shown, showing; shows.**

shower

1. rain that lasts only a short time: *Spring is the season of many showers.* **2.** a bath in which you stand under running water: *He takes a shower every morning.* **showers.**

shrimp

shrimp

a small sea animal with a long tail. Some shrimp are good to eat. **shrimp.**

shrink

to become smaller; to make something smaller: *My sweater shrank in the hot water. Hot water will also shrink my wool socks.* **shrank, shrunk, shrinking.**

shut

1. to close something or put a cover on something: *He shut the box of toys. Don't shut the window.* **2.** to make or become closed: *Shut your eyes. She shut her book.* **shut, shutting.**

shy

1. not comfortable around people: *Some of the children were too shy to speak to the classroom visitor.* **2.** easy to frighten: *A deer is a shy animal.* **shyer, shyest.**

sick

1. not feeling well; having a disease; feeling bad: *His mother called the school to say he was sick. She felt sick after riding the merry-go-round.* **2.** feeling angry or upset about something: *I'm sick of listening to this loud music.* **sicker, sickest.**

sickness

feeling sick; disease; poor health: *There is more sickness in the winter than in the summer.* **sicknesses.**

side

1. the edge of something: *A square has four sides.* **2.** the part of something that is not the top, bottom, front, or back: *There is a door at the side of his house.* **3.** either the right or the left part of a body or thing: *I felt a pain in my side. Our side of the street gets more sun.* **sides.**

sidewalk

a place to walk on the side of a street. A sidewalk is usually made of concrete. **sidewalks.**

sift

sift

to separate large pieces from small pieces by shaking them through a kind of screen: *I sifted the flour before I baked the cake.* **sifted, sifting.**

sigh

to let out a long, deep breath. People sigh when they are sad, tired, or free from some worry. **sighed, sighing.**

sight

1. the power or sense of seeing. Sight is one of the five senses, along with hearing, smell, taste, and touch. **2.** something worth seeing: *The Grand Canyon is one of the sights we saw on vacation.* **sights** (for **2.**).

sign

1. a mark or words that tell you what to do or what not to do. Cars must stop at stop signs. Some signs tell you facts about something. *The sign on the door said "Open."* **2.** to write your name on something: *She signed the letter and mailed it right away.* **signs; signed, signing.**

signal (definition 1)

signal

1. a sign that warns you about something: *A red light is a signal of danger.* **2.** to make something known by using a signal: *A bell signals the end of the school day.* **signals; signaled, signaling.**

silent

1. without any noise; quiet: *He didn't like to come home to a silent house.* **2.** without speaking: *Please be silent while I give you directions.*

silk

a kind of soft, smooth cloth. Silk is made from threads spun from their own bodies by a certain kind of worm.

silky

like silk; smooth, soft, and shiny: *My kitten's fur is silky.* **silkier, silkiest.**

sill

a piece of wood or stone at the bottom of a door or window: *Your book is on the window sill.* **sills.**

silly

not making sense; not serious: *She told a silly joke that made me laugh.* **sillier, silliest.**

silo

a tall, round building for storing food for farm animals. **silos.**

silo

silver

a shiny white metal of great value. Silver is used to make coins, jewelry, and other things.

simple

1. easy to do or understand: *That was a simple math problem.* **2.** not fancy; plain: *She cooked us a simple lunch of soup and sandwiches.* **simpler, simplest.**

since

I have been up since dawn. He has called only once since last week. Since you are hungry, we can have dinner now.

sincere

meaning what you say or do; honest: *I gave them my sincere thanks for helping me.* **sincerer, sincerest.**

sing

1. to make music with the voice: *He likes to sing happy songs.* **2.** to make pleasing sounds that are like music: *Birds were singing in the trees all morning.* **sang, sung, singing.**

sing (definitions 1 and 2)

325

singer

a person who sings: *The singer had a lovely voice.* **singers.**

single

1. only one: *This button is hanging by a single thread.*
2. not married: *My aunt is single.*

sink

1. to go down or go under: *The ship began to sink when it hit the rock.* **2.** a small tub for holding water: *I washed a few dishes in the kitchen sink.* **sank, sunk, sinking; sinks.**

sip

1. to drink something a little at a time: *Grandpa sipped his tea.* **2.** a small drink of something: *I asked him for a sip.* **sipped, sipping; sips.**

sip (definition 1)
*He **sipped** his tea.*

sir

a title used to show respect to a man: *It's nice to meet you, sir.* **sirs.**

siren

a thing that makes a loud, warning sound: *We could hear the ambulance siren as it came down our street.* **sirens.**

sister

a girl or woman that has the same parents as another person. **sisters.**

sit

1. to rest on the lower part of the body with the knees bent: *We sat together on the sofa.* **2.** to be somewhere: *The cookie jar sits on top of our kitchen counter.* **3.** to take care of a child or children while their parents are away from home: *My mother asked my neighbor to sit for me after school.* **sat, sitting.**

sit (definition 1)
*We **sat** together on the sofa.*

six

one more than five; 6. **sixes.**

sixteen

six more than ten; 16. **sixteens.**

sixteenth

1. next after the fifteenth; 16th. **2.** one of 16 equal parts. **sixteenths.**

sixth

1. next after the fifth; 6th. **2.** one of six equal parts. **sixths.**

sixty

ten more than fifty; 60. **sixties.**

size

how big or how small something is: *What is the size of that picture? The boys are the same size.* **sizes.**

skate

1. something worn on the foot to slide or roll over a smooth surface; ice skate or roller skate. **2.** to move along on ice skates or roller skates: *I skated on the frozen pond.* **skates; skated, skating.**

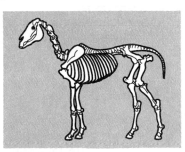

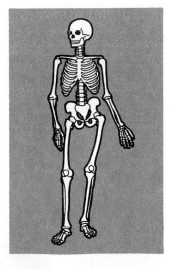

skeleton

the bones of a body that are all put together. It supports the body and gives it shape. **skeletons.**

skeletons—above: *a human skeleton;* at the left: *the skeleton of a horse*

ski

1. a long, narrow board that a person puts on his foot to stand on and slide over snow. Skis usually come in pairs. Some skis can be used on water. **2.** to go over snow or water on skis. **skis; skied, skiing.**

skid

to slip or slide to one side while moving: *His car skidded on the icy road and went into the ditch.* **skidded, skidding.**

skill

the power to do something well. You can develop a skill by practicing often. Reading and writing are important skills. **skills.**

skim

to take something from the top of a liquid: *The cook skims the fat from the soup.* **skimmed, skimming.**

skin

1. the outside covering of human and animal bodies, plants, fruits, and seeds: *Her skin was red from too much sun.* **2.** to hurt yourself by scratching or tearing some of your skin: *I skinned my knee when I fell on the sidewalk.* **skinned.**

skip

1. to hop first on one foot and then the other: *She skipped down the sidewalk.* **2.** to pass over without doing: *Skip the questions you can't answer and come back to them later.* **skipped, skipping.**

skip (definition 1)
*She **skipped** down the hall.*

skirt

a kind of clothing that hangs from the waist. Skirts can be long or short. Women and girls wear skirts. **skirts.**

skunk

a small black animal with a white stripe along its back, and a large, furry tail. When a skunk is scared, it sprays a liquid that smells bad into the air. **skunks.**

skunk

sky

the space high above us that seems to cover the earth; the area where the clouds are: *The sky no longer looks like it will rain.* **skies.**

slacks

long pants worn especially for relaxing.

slam

1. to shut something with a lot of noise: *Don't slam the door!* **2.** to throw something with great force: *She slammed her book down on the desk.* **slammed, slamming.**

slant

to be higher at one end than at the other; lean to one side or the other: *Many roofs slant. The telephone pole slants to the right because a truck ran into it.* **slanted, slanting.**

slant—*This roof **slants**.*

slap

to strike with the open hand or with something flat: *The man slapped his brother on the back.* **slapped, slapping.**

slave

a person who is owned by another person. Slaves are people who are not free. They are made to work for others. **slaves.**

slavery

being a slave; owning slaves. Slavery is against the law in the United States.

sled

1. something used for sliding over ice or snow: *They rode the sled down the snowy hill.* **2.** to ride or coast on a sled: *They sledded down the icy slope.* **sleds; sledded, sledding.**

sled (definitions 1 and 2)

sleep

1. to rest your body and mind: *It's easy to sleep when it's quiet.* **2.** a rest that your body and mind need each night: *I felt better after my long sleep.* **slept, sleeping.**

sleepy

ready to go to sleep: *He is always sleepy because he gets to bed too late.* **sleepier, sleepiest.**

sleeve

the part of a shirt, coat, dress, or sweater that covers your arm. **sleeves.**

sleeve—This is the right *sleeve* of the coat.

sleigh

sleigh

a large cart without wheels for traveling on snow or ice. Sleighs are often pulled by horses. **sleighs.**

slept

I slept in a big bed. I have slept in a tent.

slice

1. a thin, flat piece cut from something: *She cut me a slice of meat.* **2.** to cut into thin, flat pieces: *He sliced the bread.* **slices; sliced, slicing.**

slick

smooth; easy to slide on: *The icy sidewalk was slick.* **slicker, slickest.**

slid

Her sister slid down the hill.

slide

1. to move smoothly: *Let's slide down the hill.* **2.** a smooth metal surface that slants from the top of a ladder to the ground: *We used the slide on the playground.* **slid, sliding; slides.**

slim

thin; not fat: *He's a slim boy.* **slimmer, slimmest.**

sling

a loop of cloth worn around the neck to hold up a hurt arm: *He has his arm in a sling.* **slings.**

sling

slip

1. to slide suddenly and fall: *She will slip on the ice.* **2.** to move smoothly, quietly, or quickly: *She slipped out of the room.* **slipped, slipping.**

slipper

a light, soft shoe for wearing indoors: *Dad usually wears slippers after he comes home from work.* **slippers.**

slippers

slope

1. to lie at an angle rather than flat; slant: *The front yard slopes down toward the road.* **2.** any surface that lies at an angle rather than flat: *We could see the cattle grazing at the bottom of the slope.* **sloped, sloping; slopes.**

slow

1. taking a long time; not fast or quick: *My sister is a slow eater. The slow runners could not keep up.* **2.** to make slow or slower: *The driver slowed down when he came near the corner.* **slower, slowest; slowed, slowing.**

small—A **small** kitten is looking out of the window.

sly

very clever at doing things without people knowing about it; full of mischief: *The sly child threw a snowball while my back was turned.* **slyer, slyest.**

smack

1. to hit with the open hand; slap: *She smacked the mosquito that was on her wrist.* **2.** to make a sound by opening the lips quickly: *He smacked his lips while he was eating the soup.* **smacked, smacking.**

small

not great in size, amount, or number; not large: *We own a small house.* **smaller, smallest.**

smart

having a good mind; clever; bright: *He is very smart and learns quickly.* **smarter, smartest.**

smash

1. to break into pieces: *When he dropped the lamp, it smashed.* **2.** to hit something hard; crash: *The boat smashed into the dock.* **smashed, smashing.**

smell

1. to use your nose to find out about something. Breathing in allows you to smell. *We could smell the flowers in the garden.* **2.** the power of using your nose to find out about something. Smell is one of the five senses, along with hearing, sight, taste, and touch. **3.** something that you breathe in and recognize: *There was a strong smell of smoke just before the fire broke out.* **smelled, smelling; smells** (for **3.**).

smile

1. to look happy by turning up the corners of your mouth: *The baby smiled when she saw her mother.* **2.** curving up the corners of the mouth to show you are pleased: *He has a nice smile.* **smiled, smiling; smiles.**

smog

smoke and fog in the air: *Smog hung over the city.*

smoke

1. gases that rise in a cloud from anything that is hot or burning: *Smoke rose from the burning building.* **2.** to give off smoke: *The fireplace smokes if you try to burn damp wood.* **smoked, smoking.**

smooth

1. with an even surface; not bumpy; level: *The road was very smooth.* **2.** to make even and flat; take out wrinkles and lumps: *She smoothed the towels before she put them away.* **smoother, smoothest; smoothed, smoothing.**

smoke (definition 2)

snack

a small amount of food eaten between meals. **snacks.**

snail

snail

a small animal with a soft body and a shell. Snails crawl very slowly. **snails.**

snake

a long, thin animal with dry, rough skin and no legs. Snakes move by sliding along the ground. Some snakes are small; others are quite large. Some snakes have a very dangerous bite. **snakes.**

snake

333

snap (definition 3)

snap

1. to make a sudden, sharp sound: *The dancer snapped his fingers in time to the music.* **2.** to break suddenly: *The rope snapped when I pulled on it.* **3.** something that fastens two things together: *This jacket fastens with snaps.* **snapped, snapping; snaps.**

sneakers

light cloth shoes with rubber soles.

sneeze

1. to blow air suddenly out through the nose and mouth. A person with a cold often sneezes. *Dust in the air makes her sneeze.* **2.** a sudden blowing out of air through the nose and mouth: *They heard a loud sneeze in the next room.* **sneezed, sneezing; sneezes.**

sniff

to take in air through the nose in short, quick breaths that can be heard: *The dog sniffed at the bone.* **sniffed, sniffing.**

sniff—*The dog* **sniffed** *at the bone.*

snow

1. water that freezes high up in the air. Snow falls as white flakes. **2.** to fall in the form of snow: *It snowed all day.* **snowed, snowing.**

snowball

a ball made of snow pressed together. **snowballs.**

snowflake

a small, very light piece of snow. **snowflakes.**

snowman

snow piled into a shape something like a person. **snowmen.**

snug

1. giving warmth and comfort: *She enjoyed working in the snug corner of the living room.* **2.** fitting one's body closely: *That jacket is a little too snug on him.* **snugger, snuggest.**

so

Don't eat so fast. The fire was so big that the firefighters couldn't put it out. The wind felt cold, so he went inside.

soak

to make or become very wet: *The sudden rain soaked my clothes. I got soaked waiting for the bus.* **soaked, soaking.**

soap

something we use to wash things and get them clean. Soap can be in the form of a bar, powder, or liquid. **soaps.**

sob

1. to cry with short, quick breaths: *The baby sobbed until I picked her up.* **2.** a catching of short breaths when you are crying: *Her sobs could be heard in the next apartment.* **sobbed, sobbing; sobs.**

soccer

a game played on a field by two teams using a round ball. Each team tries to kick or hit the ball into the goal of the other team. Soccer players may not use their hands or arms to hit the ball.

snowman

soccer

335

soda

sock

a short knitted covering for the foot and the lower leg. **socks.**

socket

a hollow part or piece which something fits into. A light bulb is screwed into a socket. **sockets.**

soda

a kind of sweet drink. Another word for soda is pop. **sodas.**

sofa

a long, comfortable seat that has a back and arms. **sofas.**

soft

1. moving when you press against it; not hard: *This pillow feels very soft.* **2.** not loud: *Mother sang to the baby in a soft voice.* **softer, softest.**

softball

1. a game like baseball. Softball is played with a larger, softer ball. **2.** the ball used in this game. **softballs** (for **2.**).

soil[1]

the top layer of the earth; dirt: *Our garden has such rich soil that almost anything will grow in it.* **soils.**

soil[2]

to make or become dirty: *The dust soiled his white gloves.* **soiled, soiling.**

sold

The clerk sold me a green shirt. She could have sold me a red one too.

soldier

someone who is a member of an army. **soldiers.**

soldiers

336

solid

1. something that takes up space and has its own shape. Wood and ice are solids. A solid is not a liquid or a gas. **2.** not hollow: *The steel bar is solid, but the steel pipe is hollow.* **solids.**

solution

the answer to something that puzzles; the solving of a problem: *The police are seeking a solution to the crime.* **solutions.**

solve

to find the answer to something: *The detective solved the mystery by using several good clues.* **solved, solving.**

some

Some people like to swim. Would you like to drink some more water? There must be some treats left over from the party.

somebody

Somebody left the door open.

someday

Someday we will take a trip to Canada.

somehow

Somehow I'll get the work done before Friday.

someone

Someone is knocking at the door. Ask someone to give you a ride.

somersault

a roll or jump, turning your heels over your head: *She turned somersaults on the rug.* **somersaults.**

solve—*Can you **solve** this crossword puzzle?*

Clues across:
1. a covering for the foot.
3. a group of people playing musical instruments.
5. an animal that barks.
6. a large black bird.
8. reports about what is happening.
9. light frames that are flown in the air.
10. She _____ going now.
11. Is that apple sweet _____ sour?
12. a large plant with a trunk.
13. cloth held up by ropes and poles.

Clues down:
1. a hollow piece that something fits into.
2. a small, flat, sweet cake.
3. one of the hard parts of the body.
4. a place without water.
7. knowing a lot.
11. There is a calendar _____ the wall.

somersault

something

Something happened to my bicycle.

sometime

We'll visit you sometime next summer.

sometimes

Sometimes my aunt takes me to the zoo.

somewhat

That hill was somewhat difficult to climb.

somewhere

They are hiding somewhere.

son

a male child. A boy or man is the son of his mother and father. **sons.**

song

music with words; something to sing: *She learned a new song today.* **songs.**

soon

in a short time: *I'll see you soon.* **sooner, soonest.**

sore

1. causing pain; aching: *I have a sore finger.* **2.** a place on the body where the skin is broken: *I have a sore on my leg.* **sorer, sorest; sores.**

sorry

feeling sad about something: *He was sorry that he broke the lamp.* **sorrier, sorriest.**

sort

1. kind; class: *What sort of work do you do? I like this sort of house best.* **2.** to arrange things in some order: *Sort these socks by color.* **sorts; sorted, sorting.**

sought

We sought a new place to go camping.

sort (definition 2)
*He **sorted** the socks by color.*

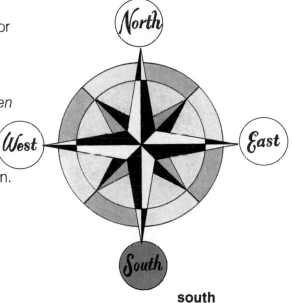

sound (definition 1)
*He heard the **sound** of a dog barking.*

sound

1. something you hear: *He heard the sound of a dog barking. What is the sound of the "a" in "hat"?* **2.** to make a sound or sounds: *The wind sounds like a whistle blowing. The words "ate" and "eight" sound alike.* **sounds; sounded, sounding.**

soup

a liquid food made by cooking meat, fish, grains, or vegetables in water or in milk. **soups.**

sour

tasting like vinegar or lemon juice; not sweet: *Green peaches are too sour to eat.* **sourer, sourest.**

south

the direction to the left as you face the setting sun. South is the opposite of north.

south

South America

South America

a continent; one of the large masses of land on the earth.

South Carolina

one of the fifty states of the United States.

South Dakota

one of the fifty states of the United States.

southeast

the direction halfway between south and east.

southwest

the direction halfway between south and west.

sow

to scatter seed on the ground; plant seed: *Dad sowed some grass seed on some bare spots on the lawn.* **sowed, sowing.**

soybeans

soybean

a kind of bean. Soybeans are used in making food for farm animals, food for humans, and oil. **soybeans.**

space

1. room for something to fit in: *There wasn't space in the closet for everyone's clothes.* **2.** the area around the earth. The sun and stars are in outer space. **spaces** (for **1.**).

spacecraft

something used to travel through space to other planets. Another word for spacecraft is spaceship. **spacecraft.**

spaceship

something used to travel through space to other planets. Another word for spaceship is spacecraft. **spaceships.**

spaghetti

a food made of flour and water. Spaghetti is rolled into long, thin sticks or strings.

Spanish

the language spoken by people in Spain, Cuba, Puerto Rico, Mexico, and other countries.

spare

1. to get along without something: *Father could spare the car, so he let my sister take it.* **2.** extra: *Do you have a spare tire?* **spared, sparing.**

spark

a small bit of something that is on fire: *Sparks flew up from the fire in the fireplace.* **sparks.**

sparkle

1. to send out little sparks; shine brightly: *A diamond sparkles.* **2.** a shine; a flash: *She has a sparkle in her eyes.* **sparkled, sparkling; sparkles.**

sparrow

a small, brown-gray bird. **sparrows.**

sparrow

speak

to say words; talk: *She spoke to her friend in the hall before school started. He spoke to our class about swimming.* **spoke, spoken, speaking.**

special

unusual or different in some way: *Your birthday is a special day.*

sped

She sped down the hill on her sled.

speech

a talk to a group of people: *We heard the governor's speech yesterday on the radio.* **speeches.**

speed

1. how fast something is going: *The speed of the boat made the ride exciting.* **2.** to go fast: *His car was speeding as it went around the corner.* **speeds; sped, speeding.**

speed (definition 2)
*The car was **speeding** as it went around the track.*

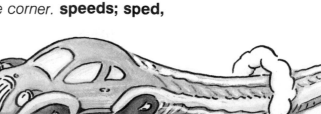

341

spell¹—He **spelled** out the words on the sign.

spell¹

to say or write the letters of a word in order: *I showed my little sister how to spell her name.* **spelled, spelling.**

spell²

a group of words that some people think has magic power: *In the story, the witch's spell turned the girls into frogs.* **spells.**

spelling

writing or saying the letters of a word in order: *She is good at spelling, but she's even better at math.*

spend

1. to use money to buy something: *We will spend a lot of money on our vacation.* **2.** to pass time in some place: *We are going to spend a week at the lake.* **spent, spending.**

spent

She spent quite a bit of money on school clothes.

spice

a seasoning used to make food taste better. Pepper is a spice. **spices.**

spicy

tasting and smelling like spice: *The fish tasted very spicy.* **spicier, spiciest.**

spider

spider

a very small animal with eight legs. Spiders have no wings and are not insects. Many spiders make webs and catch insects in them. **spiders.**

spike (definition 1)

spike

1. a large, thick nail: *Workers used spikes to fasten the rails to the wooden beams.* **2.** a piece of metal or other material with sharp points on it: *Baseball players wear spikes on their shoes. Some dinosaurs had spikes on their backs.* **spikes.**

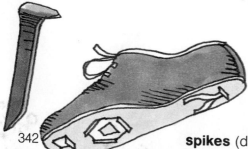

spikes (definition 2)

spill

to let something fall out or run out: *Dad spilled the syrup. All the milk spilled when the glass fell over.* **spilled, spilling.**

spin

1. to turn or make something turn around quickly: *Can you spin a nickel on the table?* **2.** to twist material into thread: *Early Americans had to spin their thread from cotton or wool.* **spun, spinning.**

splash

1. to cause liquid to fly about: *The children splashed in the pool. The car splashed me when it went through a puddle.* **2.** the sound of something dropping into liquid: *We heard a loud splash when the dog leaped into the lake.* **splashed, splashing; splashes.**

split

1. to break or cut trom end to end: *He split the log with an ax.* **2.** to separate into parts; divide: *My friend split the candy bar into two pieces so we could share it.* **split, splitting.**

spoil

1. to become bad, or not good to eat. *The milk spoiled because we didn't put it in the refrigerator.* **2.** to give a child too much of what it asks for: *They tended to spoil the baby to keep it from crying.* **spoiled, spoiling.**

spoke¹

I spoke to him yesterday.

spoke²

one of the bars that runs from the center of a wheel to the outer ring. Bicycle wheels have spokes. **spokes.**

splash (definition 1)

spokes²

sponge (definition 1)

spool

spoken

My dad has already spoken to me about cutting the grass.

sponge

1. a kind of sea animal with many small holes in it. Sponges live on the ocean floor. **2.** a piece of sponge or material like a sponge that is used in bathing or cleaning: *We washed our car with a sponge.* **sponges.**

spool

a round piece of wood or plastic. Thread, tape, fish line, and camera film are wound onto spools. **spools.**

spoon

something to eat with. A spoon has a small, round bowl at the end of a handle. You can eat cereal with a spoon. **spoons.**

sport

a game that needs skill and gives exercise. Baseball, swimming, and tennis are sports. **sports.**

spot (definition 3)
*She **spotted** a rabbit in the grass.*

spot

1. a mark that you can see on the surface of something: *She has a spot of ink on her sleeve.* **2.** a place: *From this spot you can see the whole valley.* **3.** to find by using your eyes; locate: *She spotted a rabbit in the grass.* **spots; spotted, spotting.**

sprang

He sprang out of bed when the phone rang.

spray

1. a liquid that flies through the air in small drops: *When the dog shook herself, we all got damp from the spray.* **2.** a liquid closed up in a can that you can shoot out when you want some: *She bought a can of hair spray from the drugstore.* **3.** to scatter small drops of liquid on something: *He sprayed water on the plants.* **sprays** (for **1.**); **sprayed, spraying.**

spray (definition 3)
*She **sprayed** water on the plant.*

spread

1. to cover with a thin layer of something: *I want to spread peanut butter on a slice of bread.* **2.** to cover a large area with something; open out: *Spread a blanket on the ground.* **3.** to pass on to other people: *Sneezing and coughing can spread germs.* **spread, spreading.**

spring

1. to jump up from the ground suddenly: *I saw the deer spring over the wall.* **2.** the season of the year between winter and summer. Spring is the season when plants begin to grow. **3.** a small stream of water that flows naturally from the ground: *Wild animals drank from the spring.* **sprang, sprung, springing; springs.**

spring (definition 3)

sprinkle

1. to scatter in drops or tiny bits: *He sprinkled salt on the icy walk to make it safer to walk on.* **2.** to rain a little bit: *It's beginning to sprinkle.* **sprinkled, sprinkling.**

sprinkler

something that sprinkles water on the grass. **sprinklers.**

sprout

1. to start growing: *The buds are sprouting on that blackberry bush.* **2.** a young plant or a new part of an old plant: *Sprouts were shooting up from the soil.* **sprouted, sprouting; sprouts.**

sprung

The vegetables have sprung up in the garden.

spun

Her wheels spun on the wet street. Our car has spun completely around.

spy

1. a person who secretly watches what others are doing: *The spy tried to steal some secret papers.* **2.** to watch secretly: *The other team spied on us to see if we had any secret ways to win the game.* **spies; spied, spying.**

square

1. a shape with four sides, all of the same length: *The yard is almost a perfect square.* **2.** having this shape: *I need a square piece of paper.* **3.** having length and width. A square foot is the area of a square whose sides are each one foot long. **squares.**

squash¹

to press against something until it is soft or flat; crush: *Be careful not to squash this package.* **squashed, squashing.**

squash¹

squash²

a vegetable that grows on a vine. Squash have different shapes and colors, and are usually yellow, green, or white. **squash.**

squash²

squeak

1. to make a short, sharp, loud sound: *This chair squeaks when you sit on it.* **2.** this sound: *There was a faint squeak in the corner.* **squeaked, squeaking; squeaks.**

squeeze

to push or press hard against something: *Will you squeeze the oranges to make juice? Squeeze these books onto the shelf.* **squeezed, squeezing.**

squint

to look at something with the eyes partly closed: *I squinted at the bright sun.* **squinted, squinting.**

squirrel

a small animal with a large, furry tail. Squirrels live in trees and eat nuts. **squirrels.**

squirrel

stable

a building where horses or cattle are kept. **stables.**

stack

1. a pile of things lying one upon another: *There is a large stack of papers on the floor.* **2.** to arrange in a pile: *Stack the wood here by the porch.* **stacks; stacked, stacking.**

stage

a raised platform in a theater where plays are given: *Several actors stood on the stage practicing their lines.* **stages.**

stairs

a group of steps for going from one floor to another: *He went up the stairs.*

stake

1. a pointed bar of wood or metal driven into the ground: *He fastened one end of the rope to the stake and the other end to the dog's collar.* **2.** to fasten with or to a stake: *We staked down the tent to keep it from blowing away.* **stakes; staked, staking.**

stalk

the tall stem of a plant. Corn grows on stalks. **stalks.**

stamp

a small piece of paper with glue on the back. You put stamps on letters or packages before mailing them. **stamps.**

stand

1. to be on your feet instead of sitting down: *He hates to stand in line.* **2.** to mean the same thing as: *TV is an abbreviation that stands for television.* **3.** a place where you can have a small business: *The children had a lemonade stand.* **stood, standing; stands.**

star

1. one of the very bright points of light that shines in the sky at night: *On a clear night the stars are very bright.* **2.** a shape that has five or six points: *I drew a star on the paper.* **3.** a very well-known person in movies, sports, and the like: *She is a movie star.* **stars.**

stars (definition 2)

stare

to look at someone with your eyes wide open for a long time: *It's rude to stare at someone.* **stared, staring.**

starfish

a sea animal shaped like a star. **starfish.**

starfish

starling

a plump bird with shiny, dark feathers. Starlings often fly in large flocks. **starlings.**

starling

start

to begin to do something: *I started to read a book. Dad had trouble starting the car.* **started, starting.**

starve

to suffer from or die of hunger: *Birds can starve if we don't feed them in winter.* **starved, starving.**

state

1. one of the parts of the United States. There are fifty states. **2.** to say or write something: *She stated that she was born in California.* **states; stated, stating.**

statement

something said or written. A written statement ends with a period. *The driver made a statement about what had caused the accident.* **statements.**

station

1. a place used for a special reason, or where you can get a special service. You buy gas at a gas station. You catch a bus at a bus station. You telephone the police at a police station. **2.** a place for sending out radio or television programs: *We can receive a lot of TV stations on our set.* **stations.**

stationery

writing paper, cards, and envelopes: *I bought Mom some stationery for her birthday.*

statue

a figure made from stone, wood, or metal to look like a person or animal: *There are several statues in the park.* **statues.**

statue

stay

to be in a place for a while: *We stayed inside yesterday because it rained.* **stayed, staying.**

steady

not changing very much; staying as it is: *Mom drove the car at a steady speed. Hold the rope steady.* **steadier, steadiest.**

steak

a slice of meat, especially beef: *They had steak for dinner.* **steaks.**

steal

to take something that does not belong to you: *Someone stole my bike during the night.* **stole, stolen, stealing.**

steam

1. very hot water in the form of gas or a very fine spray. Boiling water creates steam. **2.** to cook by using steam: *He steamed some vegetables for dinner.* **steamed, steaming.**

steel

a very strong metal that is made up mostly of iron. Steel is used to make buildings, cars, tools, and many other things.

steep

having a sharp slope or slant; almost straight up and down: *This hill is too steep to ride a bicycle down safely.* **steeper, steepest.**

steeple

a high church tower that becomes pointed at the top: *As we came near the town, we could see several steeples.* **steeples.**

steeples

steer¹

to cause to go in a certain direction; guide; control: *She steered her bike around the corner and down the street.* **steered, steering.**

steer²

one of a herd of beef cattle raised for food. **steers.**

stem

the main part of a plant above the ground. The trunk of a tree is a stem. Flowers, fruit, and grain have stems. **stems.**

step

1. a movement you make by lifting your foot and putting it down in a new position: *He took a few steps across the room to the chair and sat down.* **2.** to move the legs as in walking: *Please step to the front of the line.* **3.** a place where you put your foot when you go up or down stairs: *She tripped just before she got to the top step.* **steps; stepped, stepping.**

stew

1. to cook something by boiling it slowly: *Grandma stewed a chicken for dinner.* **2.** food cooked by boiling it slowly: *On Sunday we ate beef stew for lunch.* **stewed, stewing; stews.**

stick¹

1. a long, thin piece of wood: *We collected sticks to build a fire.* **2.** something shaped like a stick: *He ate a stick of candy.* **sticks.**

stick²

1. to push something sharp into or through another thing: *Stick a fork into the potato to see if it is cooked enough.* **2.** to put or place: *Stick this handkerchief in your pocket.* **3.** to make things stay tightly together; fasten: *He stuck the pieces of paper together with glue.* **stuck, sticking.**

stems

stickers

sticker

a label that has glue on the back of it. A sticker can be glued or fastened onto something else. **stickers.**

sticky

sticking very tightly to something. Tape and glue are very sticky. **stickier, stickiest.**

stiff

1. hard to bend: *New boots are always stiff.* **2.** not moving easily: *After being out in the cold all day, his joints were stiff and sore.* **stiffer, stiffest.**

still

1. not moving; without moving; quiet: *Please keep still while I am on the telephone.* **2.** up to now; until now: *Is the library still open?*

stilts

a pair of poles with pieces fastened on to hold the feet. It takes practice to learn to walk on stilts.

stilts

sting

1. a very sore, burning wound. A sting is made by a bee using a sharp part of its body. **2.** to wound painfully. Bees and hornets can sting you. **stings; stung, stinging.**

stir

to mix something by moving it around with a spoon or the like: *He stirred the soup to keep it from burning.* **stirred, stirring.**

stole

Someone stole my bike last week.

stolen

Someone has stolen my bike.

stomach

the part of the body that the food we swallow goes into. **stomachs.**

stone

a small piece of rock: *We threw stones into the lake.* **stones.**

stood

We stood in line for an hour.

stool

a small seat without a back and without arms: *We sat on stools in the kitchen.* **stools.**

stoop

stoop

to bend forward at the waist: *She stooped to pick up the oranges.* **stooped, stooping.**

stop

1. to not do something anymore: *We wished the dog would stop barking.* **2.** to cause something not to move or continue: *You must stop your car if the traffic light is red.* **3.** a place where something stops: *She waited an hour at the bus stop.* **stopped, stopping; stops.**

stop sign

stop sign

a sign for cars and other vehicles to stop before moving ahead. **stop signs.**

store

1. a place to buy things: *They went to the store to buy some food.* **2.** to put something away that you will use later: *They stored a lot of winter clothes in the attic.* **stores; stored, storing.**

storm

a strong wind with rain, snow, or hail. Some storms have lightning and thunder. **storms.**

story[1]

a telling about people and places and what happens to them. Stories can be true or make-believe. *I like adventure stories.* **stories.**

storyteller

story[2]

all the rooms on one floor of a building: *Our school has two stories.* **stories.**

storyteller

a person who tells stories: *The storyteller told us about the old West.* **storytellers.**

stove

something to cook or heat food. There are electric, gas, and wood stoves. **stoves.**

straight

1. without a bend or curve: *She drew a straight line. Try to sit up straight.* **2.** in a direct line: *Go straight to the corner and then turn left.* **straighter, straightest.**

straighten

1. to make straight: *He straightened the bent nail.* **2.** to put in order: *Please straighten up your room.* **straightened, straightening.**

strange

1. hard to explain or understand; unusual: *Last night I thought I heard a strange noise in the other room.* **2.** not known, seen, or heard before: *When I came home, a strange dog was sitting on our porch.* **stranger, strangest.**

stranger

a person you have not known, seen, or heard of before: *After meeting some other kids, she didn't feel so much like a stranger.* **strangers.**

strap

a narrow strip of leather, cloth, or other material: *We used a strap to hold the skis on the roof of the car.* **straps.**

straw

a hollow tube you drink liquids through. Straws are made of paper or plastic. *We drank our milk with straws.* **straws.**

strawberry

a red berry. Strawberries grow near the ground on tiny plants. **strawberries.**

streak

1. a long, thin mark or line: *His boot left a black streak of mud on the floor.* **2.** to make long, thin marks or lines on: *Rain streaked the window.* **streaks; streaked, streaking.**

straw

strawberries

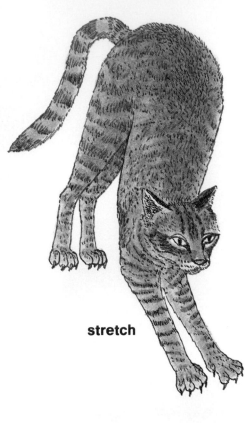

stretch

stream

a narrow flow of water across the land: *We fished in the stream, but didn't catch anything.* **streams.**

street

a road in a city or town. A street usually has homes or buildings along its length. **streets.**

stretch

to make something as long as it can be: *The cat yawned and stretched its legs.* **stretched, stretching.**

strike

to hit: *The captain feared the ship would strike a rock in the storm.* **struck, striking.**

string

1. a very thin cord made of twisted threads: *Please tie the package with string.* **2.** to put on a string: *We decided to string popcorn and put it on the bushes for the birds.* **strings; strung, stringing.**

string (definition 1)

string bean

a kind of bean. A string bean is long, either green or yellow, and has flat seeds. **string beans.**

string bean

strip

a long, narrow, flat piece of cloth or paper: *We tied strips of ribbon to the chairs.* **strips.**

stripe

a long, narrow band of color: *Our flag has seven red stripes and six white stripes. Tigers have black stripes.* **stripes.**

striped

having stripes: *Dad likes striped shirts.*

striped

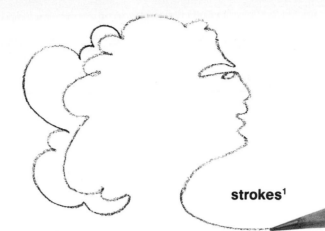

strokes¹

stroke¹

a single movement or mark made by a pen or pencil: *The artist drew a face with a few quick strokes.* **strokes.**

stroke²

to rub something gently with your hand: *I stroked the kitten.* **stroked, stroking.**

strong

not weak; having power and force. A strong person can lift and carry things that are heavy. *A strong wind blew down the tree.* **stronger, strongest.**

struck

The tennis ball struck me on the leg.

struggle

1. to work very hard when you are facing something very difficult: *She struggled with the jammed coat zipper, but could not open it.* **2.** hard work: *It was a struggle to move all the furniture into the other room.* **struggled, struggling; struggles.**

strung

Some people in the class strung berries instead of beads.

stubborn

not giving in to what someone else wants: *The stubborn boy refused to eat.*

stuck

By accident, she stuck her finger with a pin.

stuff (definition 1)

student

someone who studies, or who goes to school: *Many students at our school ride the bus.* **students.**

study

to try to learn by reading and thinking: *She studied math and science all afternoon.* **studied, studying.**

stuff

1. things you need to do something with; things of all kinds that belong to someone: *Please get all your winter clothes and stuff out of the closet.* **2.** to fill something up completely: *She stuffed the sofa pillows with feathers.* **stuffed, stuffing.**

stumble

to almost fall by hitting your foot against something: *The boy stumbled over his toy.* **stumbled, stumbling.**

stump

stump

the lower part of a tree or plant. A stump is what is left after the main part is cut off. **stumps.**

stung

The burn stung for a little while. I have been stung by a bee.

stunt

an unusual, often dangerous act or performance: *The riders at the rodeo did many riding and roping stunts.* **stunts.**

stupid

foolish; not smart; dumb: *He made a stupid mistake, writing a 5 for a 2.* **stupider, stupidest.**

stutter

to say the same sound over and over when you try to speak. People may stutter when they are nervous or uneasy or afraid. **stuttered, stuttering.**

subject

something you think about, talk about, or study: *I study spelling and other subjects.* **subjects.**

subtract

to take a number away from another number: *Subtract 3 from 12 and the answer is 9.* **subtracted, subtracting.**

subtraction

taking a number away from another number. The subtraction of 7 from 10 leaves a difference of 3.

subtraction

suburb

a town or village just outside a city: *He lives in a suburb and takes the train into the city to work.* **suburbs.**

subway

an underground electric railroad. Subways run beneath the surface of the streets in a city. **subways.**

succeed

to do what you planned to do; turn out well: *The class succeeded in putting on two plays last year.* **succeeded, succeeding.**

success

the result that you hoped for; good fortune: *The play was a great success.* **successes.**

such

Mom had such a bad cold that she stayed in bed. The cafeteria has such drinks as milk and orange juice.

sudden

happening very fast; not expected: *The sudden rain at the picnic got us all wet. If you make any sudden moves, the bird will fly away.*

suffer

to feel pain or sad feelings: *They suffered a great deal when they heard about the fire at their neighbor's house.* **suffered, suffering.**

sugar

something sweet to put in food and drinks: *This lemonade needs more sugar.*

sugarless

without any sugar: *If you chew gum, it's better for your teeth to chew sugarless gum.*

suggest

to bring a thought or plan to your mind: *He suggested a hike for this weekend and we agreed.* **suggested, suggesting.**

suit

a set of clothes that goes together. A man's suit has a jacket, pants, and sometimes a vest. A woman's suit has a jacket and pants or a skirt. **suits.**

suits

suitcase

a flat case to carry clothes in when you travel: *We needed three suitcases for our trip last month.* **suitcases.**

sum

1. an amount of money: *She saved the sum of ten dollars out of her allowance last month.* **2.** a number of things added together: *The sum of 7 and 12 and 2 is 21.* **3.** to tell or write something in a few words: *He was able to sum up the long story in just half a page.* **sums; summed, summing.**

summer

the season of the year between spring and fall. Summer is the warmest season of the year. **summers.**

sun

a hot ball of gas in the sky. It is a very great distance from the earth. The sun gives us heat and light. The earth goes around the sun. **suns.**

sundae

a dish of ice cream with fruit, nuts, or some kind of sauce on top. **sundaes.**

Sunday

the day before Monday; the first day of the week. **Sundays.**

sunflower

a large yellow flower. A sunflower grows on a very tall plant. Sunflower seeds are used as food, and to produce cooking oil. **sunflowers.**

sunflowers

sung

She has sung three songs already this morning.

sunglasses

dark glasses used to protect the eyes from the light of the sun. Sunglasses are made of colored glass or plastic.

sunk

Many ships have sunk because of the violent storm.

sunk—*A ship has **sunk** near the beach.*

sunlight

the light from the sun: *Sunlight helps plants to grow.*

sunny

with bright sunshine: *We enjoyed the sunny afternoon.* **sunnier, sunniest.**

sunrise

the coming up of the sun; the time when the sun first appears in the morning. **sunrises.**

sunscreen

a cream rubbed on the skin that helps it to resist the effects of the sun's rays. **sunscreens.**

sunset

the going down of the sun; the time when the sun is last seen in the evening. **sunsets.**

sunshine

the light of the sun: *After the rain he went out into the sunshine.*

super

very, very good; excellent: *It was a super party; we had a lot of fun.*

supermarket

a large grocery store. You pick up what you want and pay the checker on the way out. **supermarkets.**

supper

a meal eaten in the evening: *We had spaghetti last night for supper.* **suppers.**

suppose

1. to imagine that something is true: *Suppose the bus doesn't come. Should we walk to school?* **2.** to have to do something: *I'm supposed to call my parents if I'm going to be late.* **supposed, supposing.**

sunset

sure

feeling no doubt about something; certain: *Are you sure you locked the front door?* **surer, surest.**

surface

the top part, or the outside of something: *The surface of the road was very slippery after the rain. A marble has a smooth, hard surface.* **surfaces.**

surprise

1. something that happens that you did not plan: *The news about Mom's new job was a nice surprise.* **2.** to not tell someone what is going to happen: *My parents surprised me with a bike for my birthday.* **surprises; surprised, surprising.**

surround

to shut something in on all sides: *A fence surrounds our school playground.* **surrounded, surrounding.**

swallow[1]

to make something go from your mouth down your throat to your stomach: *Sometimes it's hard to swallow peanut butter.* **swallowed, swallowing.**

swallow[2]

a small bird with narrow wings. Swallows fly very fast. **swallows.**

swallow[2]

swam

Most of us swam across the pool.

swamp

land that is almost completely covered with water: *In the swamp we saw alligators and snakes.* **swamps.**

swamp

swan

swan

a large white bird with a long, thin neck. Swans live on lakes and rivers. **swans.**

sway

to swing backward and forward or from side to side: *The trees are swaying in the wind.* **swayed, swaying.**

sweat

1. water that comes out through the skin: *His face was covered with sweat from working hard in the sun.* **2.** to give out water through the skin: *Pulling a load made the horse sweat a lot.* **sweated, sweating.**

sweater

a knitted piece of clothing that keeps you warm. A sweater is often worn over a shirt. **sweaters.**

sweater

sweep

to clean a floor with a broom or brush: *I need to sweep my room today.* **swept, sweeping.**

sweet

1. with a taste like sugar or honey: *These ripe grapes are very sweet.* **2.** nice to be around; pleasant: *She's a very sweet, friendly person.* **sweeter, sweetest.**

sweet potato

a sweet, thick, yellow vegetable. Sweet potatoes grow on vines. They are sometimes eaten in pies. **sweet potatoes.**

sweet potato

swell

1. to grow bigger in size: *My finger swelled up from the bee sting.* **2.** excellent; very nice: *That was a swell movie we saw last week.* **swelled, swollen, swelling.**

swept

He swept the dust off the porch.

swift

able to move very fast: *A deer is a swift animal.* **swifter, swiftest.**

swim

1. to move in the water. People use their arms and legs to swim. Fish use their fins to swim. **2.** the act of swimming: *Let's go for a swim this afternoon.* **swam, swum, swimming; swims.**

swimmer

a person or an animal that swims: *The swimmers rested by the side of the pool.* **swimmers.**

swing

1. to move backward and forward: *The kids were swinging from a branch of the tree.* **2.** a seat on which you can move backward and forward: *She pushed me on the swing at the playground.* **swung, swinging; swings.**

swing (definition 2)

swish

to move through the air with a light brushing sound: *She swished the whip up and down.* **swished, swishing.**

switch

1. a button that you can turn electricity on and off with: *The light switch is on the wall.* **2.** to use a switch: *Please switch on the light.* **3.** to change something for something else: *The cowboy switched his tired horse for one that was rested.* **switches; switched, switching.**

switch (definition 1)
*The light **switch** is off.*

swollen

My arm was swollen and sore.

swum

We have swum every day this week.

swung

He swung the bat and hit the ball.

syllables

syllable

a word or part of a word spoken all together. A word is made up of one or more syllables. The word "syllable" has three syllables in it. **syllables.**

symbol

something that stands for something else: *The eagle is a symbol of the United States.* **symbols.**

synagogue

a building where some people worship. **synagogues.**

synonym

a word that means almost the same thing as another word. Car is a synonym of automobile. **synonyms.**

syrup

a sweet, thick liquid. Sugar boiled with fruit juice makes syrup. Maple syrup comes from the juice of the maple tree.

Tt

table (definition 1)

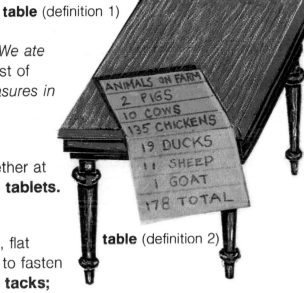

table

1. a piece of furniture with a flat top on legs: *We ate supper sitting around the kitchen table.* **2.** a list of facts or figures: *The table of weights and measures in the back of the book is very helpful.* **tables.**

tablet

a pad made of sheets of paper fastened together at one edge: *I need a tablet of paper for school.* **tablets.**

tack

1. a short nail with a sharp point and a broad, flat head: *I need a tack to hold up the picture.* **2.** to fasten with tacks: *She tacked the carpet to the floor.* **tacks; tacked, tacking.**

table (definition 2)

taco

a thin corn pancake, called a tortilla, filled with chopped meat or chicken, cheese, and other things. **tacos.**

tadpole

a very young frog or toad, when it has a tail and lives in the water. **tadpoles.**

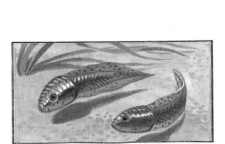

tadpoles

tag¹

a small card that is fastened to something: *There is a price tag on every dress in the store.* **tags.**

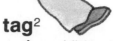

tag² (definition 1)
The children are playing **tag.**

tag²

1. a children's game. One player, who is "it," tries to catch and touch the other players. **2.** to tap with the hand: *When she tagged me, then I was "it."* **tagged, tagging.**

tail

the part of an animal's body farthest from its head: *A lion has a long tail.* **tails.**

take

1. to get hold of something: *Take my hand before we cross the street.* **2.** to get what someone gives you: *I'll take that old baseball glove if you don't want it.* **3.** to carry something to another place: *I think you should take your gloves to school.* **4.** to subtract one number from another number: *If you take 10 from 20, you have 10 left.* **5.** to make use of: *They took a bus to school.* **6.** to study: *She hopes to take piano next year.* **7.** to make by using a camera: *She took a picture of me.* **took, taken, taking.**

taken

He has always taken the bus to school.

tale

a story that is told or read over and over: *Let's read a fairy tale.* **tales.**

talk

1. to use words; speak: *She talked to her friend for a long time. We talked about a lot of things.* **2.** the use of words in speaking; speech: *He gave a short talk about trees.* **talked, talking; talks.**

tall

high; reaching a long way from top to bottom; not short: *That building is very tall.* **taller, tallest.**

tall

tame

1. no longer wild: *My cousin in the country has a tame raccoon.* **2.** without fear: *The deer are so tame that they come into the yard looking for food.* **3.** to make tame: *He tames lions for the circus.* **tamer, tamest; tamed, taming.**

tan

1. a light yellow-brown color: *Tan is my favorite color.* **2.** having this color: *He is wearing a tan jacket.* **3.** to become brown by being in the sun: *She tanned herself at the beach.* **4.** to turn the skin of an animal into leather by taking the hair off and soaking the skin in a special liquid. **tans; tanner, tannest; tanned, tanning.**

tank—*Fish are swimming in the* **tank.**

tank

a large container for liquid or gas: *I need to fill the gas tank in my car. She sprinkled some food into her fish tank, and the fish swam quickly to the surface to feed.* **tanks.**

tap

1. to hit lightly: *He tapped on the table with his fingers.* **2.** a light blow: *We did not hear the tap at the window because of the TV.* **tapped, tapping; taps.**

tape

1. a long strip of cloth, paper, or plastic: *He fixed the torn pages with tape.* **2.** to fasten or wrap with tape: *Some athletes tape their ankles to make them stronger.* **3.** to make a record on a special kind of plastic tape: *The teacher taped our class program.* **4.** a special kind of tape to record sounds or images on: *The class watched tapes of the program.* **tapes** (for **4.**); **taped, taping.**

task

work that needs to be done: *Cleaning up my room is my hardest task.* **tasks.**

taste

1. the flavor something has when you put it in your mouth: *The taste of sugar is sweet.* **2.** to find out whether something is sweet, sour, salty, or bitter, when you put it in your mouth. You taste things with your tongue. **3.** the power to take in the flavor that things have. Taste is one of the five senses, along with hearing, sight, smell, and touch. **tasted, tasting.**

taught

He taught me how to play basketball.

tax

money paid by the people to support a government and pay for public services. Taxes pay for schools, libraries, firefighters, police, and the like. **taxes.**

taxi

a short word meaning taxicab. **taxis.**

taxicab

taxicab

a car with a driver that you pay to take you somewhere. **taxicabs.**

tea

a hot drink made from special leaves. Tea contains caffeine, a drug that can make the heart beat too fast.

teach

to help someone learn: *He teaches people how to play the piano.* **taught, teaching.**

teacher

a person who helps people learn. Most teachers work in schools. **teachers.**

team

a group of people working or playing together: *My sister is on the basketball team.* **teams.**

tear¹

a drop of salty water that comes from the eye. Tears fall when you cry. **tears.** (Tear¹ rhymes with ear.)

tear²

1. to pull something into pieces: *Please don't tear the page out of the book.* **2.** a place that has been pulled apart: *She has a tear in her pants.* **tore, torn, tearing: tears.** (Tear² rhymes with bear.)

teddy bear

a soft toy bear. **teddy bears.**

teenager

someone who is between 13 and 19 years old: *Several teenagers drove past our house.* **teenagers.**

teeth

more than one tooth: *The dentist's helper cleaned my teeth.*

telephone

1. something used to talk to people far away: *Please answer the telephone if it rings.* **2.** to talk to someone by using the telephone: *Let's telephone my cousin today.* **telephones; telephoned, telephoning.**

telescope

something you look through to make things far away seem nearer and larger: *We looked at the moon through a telescope.* **telescopes.**

tear² (definition 2)

telescope

television

an electrical machine that brings sounds and pictures from far away. A television may be small enough to carry in your pocket. Some televisions are as big as large pieces of furniture. **televisions.**

tell

1. to put in words; say: *Please tell us a story.* **2.** to know who someone is; recognize: *It's hard to tell who yelled, because I didn't see him.* **told, telling.**

temperature

how hot or cold something is: *The temperature outside today is nearly ninety degrees. If her temperature is 101, that means she has a fever.* **temperatures.**

temple

a building used by some people for worship. **temples.**

ten

one more than nine; 10. **tens.**

tender

soft; not tough: *Cooking the meat made it tender and easy to chew.* **tenderer, tenderest.**

Tennessee

one of the fifty states of the United States.

tennis

a game played on a special court. Two or four players hit a ball from one side to the other across a net.

tent

a large piece of cloth held up by ropes and poles. A tent covers and protects you when you camp outside. *He slept in a tent under some pine trees.* **tents.**

tenth

1. next after the ninth; 10th. **2.** one of 10 equal parts. **tenths.**

temperature—*She is checking the girl's* **temperature.**

tent

terminal

terminal

an electrical machine by which you communicate with a computer. A terminal usually has a screen like a TV, and letters to press like the ones on a typewriter. **terminals.**

terrible

causing great fear; awful: *The terrible storm destroyed many homes.*

test

1. a way to find out what you know or what you can do. Tests have questions that you answer. *We had a math test today.* **2.** to find out if something is working right: *The mechanic tested our car battery.* **tests; tested, testing.**

Texas

one of the fifty states of the United States.

than

Your house is bigger than ours. My sister sings better than I do.

thank

a polite word you use when you are pleased about something. You thank someone for something they give you or do for you. *We thanked her for the ride.* **thanked, thanking.**

thankful

feeling pleased about something: *She was thankful for his help in changing the tire.*

than—*My sister sings better than I do.*

373

Thanksgiving

a holiday on the fourth Thursday in November. On Thanksgiving we give thanks for the good things we have received. **Thanksgivings.**

that

Shall we take this ball or that one? I know that we can have a picnic today.

that's—*That's the one I'd like to have.*

that's

that is: *That's the one I'd like to have.*

thaw

1. a time of melting: *There was a thaw in January.* **2.** to melt ice, snow, or anything frozen: *Mother thawed the frozen dinners so we could eat.* **thaws; thawed, thawing.**

the

What is the name of your street? The house we live in is white.

theater

a place where people go to see movies or plays: *Mom got us all tickets to see a show at the theater downtown.* **theaters.**

their

They raised their hands in class. They like their new friends.

theirs

Our car is black; theirs is white. Theirs is the red house down the street.

them

Call the kids next door and ask them to play with us. The kittens were very young, so we had to be careful playing with them.

themselves

They recognized themselves in the old photos. The kids themselves knew not to play with matches.

then

The noise stopped and then began again. If he broke the dish, then he should clean it up.

there

There are 12 houses on our block. Is there a park near here?

themselves—*They recognized **themselves** in the old photos.*

there's

there is: *There's room for one more.*

thermometer

something used to measure how hot or cold something or someone is: *Let's check the thermometer to see how hot it is outside. Mom took my temperature with a thermometer.* **thermometers.**

thermometer

these

I've read all these books. These are his books, and those are mine.

they

They are both my friends.

they'd

1. they had: *They'd already gone when we got there.*
2. they would: *They promised that they'd wait.*

these—*I've read all **these** books.*

thick (definition 2)
Thick paint dripped from the tube.

they'll

they will: *They say they'll meet us there.*

they're

they are: *They're going to the circus with us.*

they've

they have: *They've come for a visit.*

thick

1. big from one side to the other of something; not thin: *Dad got thick slices of ham to make sandwiches. This book is about an inch thick.* **2.** like glue; not flowing easily: *It was too cold to pour the thick syrup.* **thicker, thickest.**

thigh

the part of the leg between the hip and the knee. **thighs.**

thin

1. not big from one side to the other of something; not thick: *A sheet of paper is very thin.* **2.** not weighing very much; not fat: *My dad is thin.* **3.** like water; flowing easily: *The cocoa was too thin, and we didn't like it.* **thinner, thinnest.**

thing

Please put these things away. That was a smart thing to do. **things.**

think

1. to use your mind; have ideas: *She will think about it before answering you.* **2.** to believe something without knowing it for sure: *I think it will rain.* **thought, thinking.**

third

1. next after the second; 3rd. **2.** one of 3 equal parts. **thirds.**

thirsty

needing something to drink: *All that playing made me thirsty. Those plants look thirsty.* **thirstier, thirstiest.**

thirteen

three more than ten; 13. **thirteens.**

thirteenth

1. next after the twelfth; 13th. **2.** one of 13 equal parts. **thirteenths.**

thirty

ten more than twenty; 30. **thirties.**

this

This coat is mine, and that one is hers. This year I am seven.

thorns

thorn

a sharp point on a tree or other plant. Roses have thorns. **thorns.**

those

Those are my books. Those books are yours, and these are mine.

though

Though it looked like rain, we went on our hike anyway.

thought

1. something that a person thinks; idea; thinking about something: *She had a sudden thought about what to give her brother.* **2.** *We thought it would snow today. He suddenly thought of the right answer.* **thoughts.**

thought (definition 1)
*She had a sudden **thought** about what to give her brother.*

thousand—*Ten one hun-dreds make a* **thousand.**

```
100
100
100
100
100
100
100
100
100
100
─────
1000
```

thoughtful

1. thinking hard about something: *He was thoughtful for a while and then answered my question.* **2.** careful about the feelings of other people: *Bringing flowers to your mom in the hospital was a thoughtful thing to do.*

thousand

ten times one hundred; 1000. **thousands.**

thread

very thin string that is used for sewing: *He used white thread to sew the button on.* **threads.**

three

one more than two; 3. **threes.**

threw

She threw the ball back to the pitcher.

throat

the part of the body through which air goes to the lungs and food goes to the stomach; the front of the neck. **throats.**

throne

throne

the chair on which a king or queen sits. **thrones.**

through

The kitten ran through the house. We learned a new song all the way through. She won the prize through hard work. Dad is through working every day at three o'clock.

throughout

The Fourth of July is celebrated throughout the United States.

throw (definition 2)

throw

1. to send something through the air by the force of your arm: *Let's throw the ball around for practice.*
2. the act of throwing: *It was a long throw, but he has a strong arm.* **threw, thrown, throwing; throws.**

thrown

She has thrown the ball so much her arm is sore.

thumb

1. the short, thick finger on each of your hands: *He hurt his thumb.* **2.** a part of a glove or mitten that covers the thumb: *There was a hole in the thumb of her mitten.* **thumbs.**

thunder

the loud noise from the sky that comes after a flash of lightning.

Thursday

the day after Wednesday; the fifth day of the week. **Thursdays.**

tick

1. a short, clicking sound made by a clock or watch: *We heard the tick of the clock from the hall.* **2.** to make such a sound: *The clock ticked so loudly it was hard to sleep.* **ticks; ticked, ticking.**

ticket

a card or piece of paper that gives you the right to do something or to go somewhere: *We bought our tickets to the movie.* **tickets.**

thumb (definitions 1 and 2)

tickle (definition 1)
*She **tickled** his nose with a feather.*

tickle

1. to touch someone lightly, causing giggles or little shivers: *Mom tickled my arm.* **2.** to have a feeling something like a small itch: *My nose tickles from the dust.* **tickled, tickling.**

tide

the rise and fall of the ocean about every twelve hours. This rise and fall is caused by the pull of the sun and moon. *We watched the tide come in and go out twice a day.* **tides.**

tidy

neat and in order: *Her room is tidy.* **tidier, tidiest.**

tie

1. to hold something together by putting string or rope around it: *She tied this package tightly.* **2.** to pull the strings into a knot in order to fasten: *He tied his shoes.* **3.** a short word meaning necktie: *Dad likes his new tie.* **4.** having the same number of points in a game: *The game ended in a tie.* **5.** to make the same score: *The two teams tied for first place.* **tied, tying; ties.**

tiger

a large animal like a cat that has dull yellow fur with black stripes. Tigers can grow to be up to nine feet long. **tigers.**

tiger

tight

1. firmly fastened; not loose: *He tied a tight knot in the rope.* **2.** fitting a part of your body closely or too closely: *His jacket is too tight.* **tighter, tightest.**

till

The children played outside till nine o'clock.

time

1. all the days and hours there have been or ever will be. Time is always going by. Seconds, minutes, hours, days, months, and years are ways we measure time. *Look at the clock, and tell me what time it is.* **2.** the right point in time: *It is time to leave now.* **3.** a period of time and how you felt about what was going on: *Everyone had a good time at the picnic.* **times** (for **3.**).

tin

a soft, blue-white metal. Tin is mixed with other metals to make cans and other things.

tiny

very small: *The new kitten was so tiny that he fit in the palm of my hand.* **tinier, tiniest.**

tip¹

the end part of something: *She had a cut on the tip of her finger.* **tips.**

tip²

to turn over: *The boat tipped over, and we all fell out.* **tipped, tipping.**

tip³

a piece of advice that someone gives you; hint: *Dad gave me a tip about how to study better.* **tips.**

tiptoe

1. the tips of the toes: *She stood on tiptoe to watch the parade.* **2.** to walk on the tips of the toes: *She tiptoed quietly along the hall.* **tiptoed, tiptoeing.**

tiptoe (definition 1)
*She stood on **tiptoe** to watch the parade*

tire¹

to make someone worn out and sleepy: *The long hike will probably tire us out.* **tired, tiring.**

tire²

tire²

a band of rubber around a wheel: *Dad had to change a tire on the car.* **tires.**

tired

feeling worn out and ready to rest: *The long hike made me tired.*

title

1. the name of a book, poem, picture, or song: *"The Real Mother Goose" is the title of a book of fairy tales.* **2.** a name showing what a person is or does: *Doctor, King, Mr., and Ms. are titles.* **titles.**

title (definition 1)

to

Are you going to the park after school? You can fasten the poster to the wall. She likes to read. The score of the hockey game was six to five.

toad

a small animal something like a frog. Toads usually live on land. **toads.**

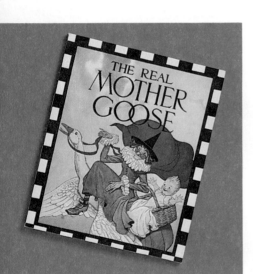

toad

toast

slices of bread made crisp and brown by heat: *Would you like some toast with your eggs?*

toaster

something that toasts bread. Most toasters are electric appliances. **toasters.**

tobacco

the leaves of a plant that are dried and cut up, that some people smoke or chew. Tobacco has in it a dangerous drug called nicotine.

today

this day; now: *Today is my uncle's birthday. Are you going swimming today?*

toe

1. one of the five end parts of the foot: *He hurt his big toe when he hit it on the chair leg.* **2.** the part of a sock or shoe that covers your toes: *There is a hole in the toe of my sock.* **toes.**

together

We all drove together to the lake. Mix the sugar, flour, and chopped nuts together.

told

She told me all about the play. Has she told you about it?

tomatoes

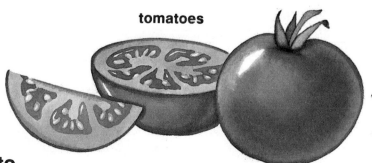

tomato

a round, red fruit. Tomatoes are juicy and grow on vines. They are eaten as vegetables. **tomatoes.**

tomorrow

the day after today: *Tomorrow it is supposed to be rainy. We'll get together tomorrow.*

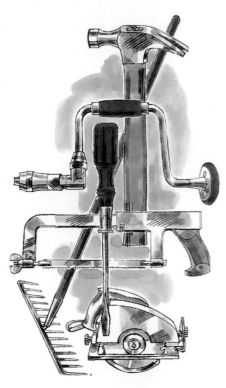

tools

tongue

the part inside your mouth that moves. The tongue moves and bends to help you say different sounds when you talk. Your tongue also helps you taste food. **tongues.**

tonight

this night; the night that follows today: *Tonight I'm getting my homework done early.*

too

After walking all day, the visitors were hungry and tired too. You gave me too much food; save some for yourself.

took

Who took my book? She took the bus to school.

tool

something that helps you do work. Saws, hammers, rakes, and hoes are tools. **tools.**

tooth (definition 2)
*A saw has sharp **teeth.***

tooth (definition 1)
*A crocodile has sharp **teeth.***

tooth

1. one of the hard, white parts in the mouth. You bite and chew food with your teeth. **2.** something like a tooth. Each sharp point on the edge of a saw or on the end of a rake is a tooth. **teeth.**

toothbrush

a small brush used to clean your teeth. **toothbrushes.**

toothpaste

a very thick liquid like paste, used to clean your teeth. Toothpaste usually comes in a tube.

toothpick

a small piece of wood or plastic with a sharp point. A toothpick is used to remove bits of food from between the teeth. **toothpicks.**

top¹ (definition 1)
*She blew out the eight candles on **top** of her birthday cake.*

top¹

1. the highest part of anything: *We climbed to the top of the mountain.* **2.** at the top; highest: *We put the glass jar on the top shelf so that the cat can't knock it off.* **tops.**

top²

a toy that spins: *The kids played with the top.* **tops.**

topic

something that people think, write, or talk about: *Keeping our neighborhood clean was the topic today in health class.* **topics.**

tore

He tore his jeans when he fell off the bicycle.

torn

The high winds have torn part of the garage roof off.

tornado

a very strong whirling wind. A tornado is shaped like a spinning cone and moves across the land in a narrow path. **tornadoes.**

tornado

tortilla

a thin, flat cake, usually made of corn meal and eaten hot. A tortilla is often filled with cheese or meat. **tortillas.**

tortoise

tortoise

a turtle that lives on land. **tortoises.**

toss

to throw something gently or in a careless way: *He tossed his baseball glove into the closet.* **tossed, tossing.**

touch

1. to feel something with your hand: *She touched the kitten's fur.* **2.** to be next to; come up against: *Her sleeve is touching the butter.* **3.** a touching: *Just the touch of my hand woke the baby.* **4.** the power by which a person knows about things by feeling, or handling them. Touch is one of the five senses, along with hearing, sight, smell, and taste. **touched, touching; touches** (for **3.**).

tough

1. hard to cut, tear, or chew; not tender: *The steak was too tough to chew.* **2.** hard to do; not easy; difficult: *Digging a ditch is tough work.* **tougher, toughest.**

toward

He walked toward the door.

towel

a piece of cloth or paper for drying someone or something that is wet: *He dried the dishes with a towel.* **towels.**

tower

a tall building or part of a building: *The castle had towers at two corners.* **towers.**

tower

town

a large group of houses and other buildings. A town is smaller than a city. **towns.**

toy

something for a child to play with. Dolls, balls, tops, blocks, and teddy bears are toys. **toys.**

trace

to copy by following letters or lines with a pen or pencil: *She traced the picture of the clown.* **traced, tracing.**

track

1. a pair of steel rails that the wheels of a train run on: *Be careful crossing the railroad track.* **2.** a mark left by something that passed by: *There were tire tracks in the snow.* **3.** a place where people or animals can run in a race: *We saw a lot of fast runners as they ran around the track.* **tracks.**

track (definition 2)
*There was a tire **track** in the snow.*

tractor

a machine used for farm work. Tractors have big rubber tires and are used to pull things. **tractors.**

tractor

trade

1. getting something in return for giving something; exchange: *An apple for an orange at lunch today was a fair trade.* **2.** to make a trade: *Will you trade your sweater for my jacket?* **trades; traded, trading.**

traffic

the cars, trucks, and buses moving along at the same time: *This road has a lot of traffic in the morning and in the evening.*

traffic light

a signal at a corner where streets cross. A traffic light controls traffic by telling drivers when to stop and when to go. A red light means "stop," a yellow light means "get ready to stop," and a green light means "go." **traffic lights.**

trail

1. a path across a field or through the woods: *We followed the trail until we came to the river.* **2.** to look for by its tracks or its smell: *The hounds trailed a raccoon but lost its scent.* **3.** anything that follows along behind something that is moving: *The airplane left a trail of white in the sky.* **trails; trailed, trailing.**

train

a line of railroad cars hooked together and pulled by an engine along a track: *The freight train blocked traffic at the crossing for twenty minutes.* **2.** to teach: *She trained her dog to sit and to roll over.* **trains; trained, training.**

tramp

1. to walk with firm, heavy steps: *The movers tramped through the kitchen as they carried the furniture into the house.* **2.** a person without a home or a regular job, who wanders around, looking for food and shelter. **tramped, tramping; tramps.**

transportation

carrying something from one place to another; a way of going. Cars, trucks, buses, trains, aircraft, and ships are different forms of transportation.

transportation—*These are several different forms of* **transportation.**

trap

1. a thing for catching an animal: *We set several mouse traps in the closet.* **2.** to catch an animal in a trap: *They trapped two groundhogs in the yard and set them free in the woods.* **traps; trapped, trapping.**

trash

anything of no use or that is worn out; things to be thrown away; garbage.

travel

to go from one place to another: *They want to travel to the mountains this summer. Sound and light travel through the air.* **traveled, traveling.**

tray

a flat piece of metal or plastic. Trays are used in cafeterias to carry your plates and glasses to your table. **trays.**

trap (definition 1)
The squirrel is caught in a **trap.**

treasure

things of great value, such as money and jewels: *The pirates buried the treasure of gold coins under the palm tree.*

treasure

treat

1. to act toward someone or something: *Be sure to treat people the way you would like them to treat you.* **2.** to try to cure: *The doctor is treating my dad's sore shoulder.* **3.** to give something like food, drink, a free ticket, or the like to someone: *He treated each of us to an ice-cream cone.* **4.** a gift of food, drink, a free ticket, or the like: *"This is my treat,"* she said. **treated, treating; treats.**

trees

tree

a large plant with a trunk, branches, and leaves. Oaks, maples, and elms are common trees. **trees.**

tremble

to shake because you are excited, afraid, cold, weak, or the like: *We could see that she was nervous because her hands trembled.* **trembled, trembling.**

triangle

1. a figure having three sides. **2.** a musical instrument shaped like this. To play a triangle, you strike the side of it with a small metal rod. **triangles.**

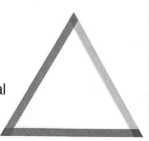

triangle (definition 1)

trick

1. something done to make people laugh or to fool them: *The magician showed us a few tricks with cards that we couldn't figure out. Someone rang the front doorbell as a trick and then hid behind a tree.* **2.** a clever skill that you can teach an animal: *His dog has learned the trick of standing on its hind legs.* **3.** to play a trick on: *He tricked me into telling the answer to the riddle.* **tricks; tricked, tricking.**

tricycle

something for small children to ride. It has one wheel in front and two wheels in back. **tricycles.**

tricycle

tried

He tried to pick up the chair. She has tried on several pairs of shoes.

trim

1. to make neat by cutting away parts that are not wanted: *The barber trimmed Dad's hair.* **2.** to make something beautiful: *She trimmed the tree yesterday with pretty, red velvet ribbons.* **trimmed, trimming.**

trim (definition 1)

trip

1. going from one place to another; journey: *We took a trip to the mountains last fall.* **2.** to hit your foot against something; stumble: *She tripped over a roller skate and almost fell down the stairs.* **trips; tripped, tripping.**

trombone

trombone

a metal musical instrument that you play by blowing into it. You move a long, sliding tube backward and forward to change the notes. **trombones.**

trot

to move at a speed between a walk and a run. Horses and some other animals trot. **trotted, trotting.**

trouble

1. something that upsets, bothers, or disturbs you, or that gives you pain: *Dinner was late tonight because we had trouble with the car and couldn't get home. I had a lot of trouble working those math problems.* **2.** having people angry or upset with you: *You will be in trouble if you knock that can of paint over.* **3.** to cause trouble; disturb: *Her son's poor grades have troubled her for a long time.* **troubles** (for **1.**); **troubled, troubling.**

trousers

clothing worn to cover the legs, from the waist to the ankles. Another word for trousers is pants.

trout

trout

a fish that is used for food. **trout.**

truck

a large machine that can carry heavy loads. A truck has an engine and four or more wheels. **trucks.**

true

right; correct; not false; not made up or make-believe: *This is a true story; everything in it really happened.* **truer, truest.**

trumpet

a metal musical instrument that is played by blowing into it and pressing keys. **trumpets.**

trumpet

trunk

1. the main stem of a tree. Branches and roots grow from the trunk. Bark grows on the trunk. **2.** a part of an elephant's body that looks like a very long nose. Elephants feed themselves with their trunks. **3.** a very large box for carrying clothes. **4.** a place for carrying things in a car, behind the rear seat. Not all cars have trunks. **trunks.**

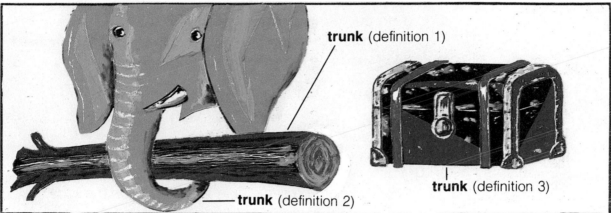

trunk (definition 1)

trunk (definition 3)

trunk (definition 2)

trust

to believe firmly in the honesty, truth, or power of someone or something: *I don't trust him because he cheats.* **trusted, trusting.**

truth

something that is true: *The truth is that she doesn't want to go.*

try

1. to set out to do something if you can: *Let's try to cut the grass before noon. He tried out for the team.* **2.** a chance to try: *In the word game I got only one try to spell the word.* **tried, trying; tries.**

T-shirt

a light, knitted shirt. A T-shirt has short sleeves and no collar. **T-shirts.**

tub

a very large container that holds water. You take a bath in a tub, or wash clothes in it. **tubs.**

tub

tuba
a large, metal musical instrument that is played by blowing into it and pressing keys. **tubas.**

tube
a small container that holds things like toothpaste or paint. **tubes.**

tuck
1. to put into a narrow space: *She tucked the letter in her pocket.* **2.** to put the edge of something into place: *Tuck your shirt in.* **tucked, tucking.**

Tuesday
the day after Monday; the third day of the week. **Tuesdays.**

tug

tug (definition 1)

1. to pull hard on something: *He tugged on the rope, but the donkey would not budge.* **2.** a hard pull on something: *She gave a tug on the rope, and the bell rang loudly.* **tugged, tugging; tugs.**

tulip
a flower shaped like a cup. Tulips come in many different colors and bloom in the spring. Tulips grow from bulbs. **tulips.**

tulips

tumble

1. to fall suddenly: *The child lost her balance and tumbled down the stairs.* **2.** a fall: *She took a bad tumble, but only bruised herself.* **tumbled, tumbling; tumbles.**

tune

1. a piece of music: *He played a tune on the piano, and we hummed along with it.* **2.** to make a musical instrument sound right: *A man came to tune our piano yesterday.* **tunes; tuned, tuning.**

tunnel

a road or path under the ground: *The road went through a tunnel under the mountain.* **tunnels.**

tunnel

turkey

a large bird with brown or white feathers. A turkey has a bare head and a long neck. Turkeys are raised for food. **turkeys.**

turkey

turn

1. to move around a center as a wheel does: *The merry-go-round turned round and round while the music played.* **2.** to go in a new direction: *Turn here at the corner and his house is the third one on the left.* **3.** a chance to do something: *It is my turn to pitch.* **turned, turning; turns.**

turnip

a round, white or yellow vegetable that grows underground. **turnips.**

turnip

turtles

turtle

an animal that has a soft, round body covered by a thick, hard shell. Some turtles live in the water. Others, called tortoises, live on land. **turtles.**

turtleneck

a sweater with a high collar that fits closely. Usually the collar is worn rolled down. **turtlenecks.**

TV

a short word meaning television. **TVs.**

twelfth

1. next after the eleventh; 12th. **2.** one of 12 equal parts. **twelfths.**

twelve

two more than 10; 12. **twelves.**

twentieth

1. next after the nineteenth; 20th. **2.** one of 20 equal parts. **twentieths.**

twenty

ten plus ten; 20. **twenties.**

twice

two times: *She has played ball twice this week already. Their yard is twice as big as ours is.*

twig

a tiny branch that grows out of a tree or other plant. **twigs.**

twin

one of two children born to the same parents at the same time: *There are three sets of twins at our school.* **twins.**

twinkle

to shine with quick little flashes of light; sparkle: *Grandpa's eyes twinkled when he laughed. The stars twinkled in the sky.* **twinkled, twinkling.**

twirl

to turn rapidly; spin: *The dancers twirled around the floor.* **twirled, twirling.**

twist

1. to turn around and around: *She twisted around, trying to get into the tight jacket.* **2.** to curve; turn; bend: *The road twists around the mountain.* **3.** to pull or force out of shape: *He slipped on the ice and twisted his ankle.* **twisted, twisting.**

two

one more than one; 2. **twos.**

typewriter

a writing machine for making letters and numerals on sheets of paper. **typewriters.**

twirl—*Hanging on only by her teeth, the circus acrobat **twirls** in the air.*

Uu

umpire

ugly

not pleasant to look at; not pretty: *The horse had an ugly cut on its leg.* **uglier, ugliest.**

umbrella

something you hold over your head to keep yourself dry when it rains. An umbrella is a folding frame covered with cloth or plastic. **umbrellas.**

umpire

a person who serves as a kind of judge in games such as baseball and tennis. **umpires.**

unable

not able: *A little baby is unable to walk or talk.*

uncertain

not certain; full of doubt: *He was uncertain about going away to camp for two whole weeks.*

uncle

your father's brother or your mother's brother, or your aunt's husband. **uncles.**

uncover

to take the cover from: *Mother uncovered the pot.* **uncovered, uncovering.**

under

They stood under an umbrella in the rain. She had a scratch under her eye. These skates cost under twenty dollars.

underground

beneath the ground: *The mole is an animal that lives underground.*

underline

to draw a line under something: *When you write the title of a book, you need to underline it.* **underlined, underlining.**

underneath

We sat underneath the apple tree.

understand

to know the meaning of something: *I understand what you want me to do.* **understood, understanding.**

understood

She understood the rules of the game after I explained them to her.

underground—*He works **underground** in the mine.*

underwater

beneath the water: *I like to swim underwater.*

uneasy

worried, upset, or anxious; disturbed: *His parents were uneasy when he didn't come right home after school.* **uneasier, uneasiest.**

underwater

unfair

not fair; not going by the rules; not being honest: *It was unfair to let him have an extra turn.*

unfasten

to untie, open, or loosen: *Please unfasten the dog's collar.* **unfastened, unfastening.**

unfold

to spread out: *Unfold your napkin and put it in your lap.* **unfolded, unfolding.**

unfriendly

not friendly: *The unfriendly dog growled at me.* **unfriendlier, unfriendliest.**

unfriendly

unhappy

not happy; sad: *She was very unhappy when her friend moved away.* **unhappier, unhappiest.**

unhealthy

not very healthy: *The child looked pale and unhealthy.* **unhealthier, unhealthiest.**

unicorn

unicorn

a make-believe animal like a horse but with one long horn on its forehead. **unicorns.**

uniform

special clothes worn by people doing a certain kind of work. Police officers, soldiers, and nurses wear uniforms so that you can tell what they do. **uniforms.**

uniform—*Ball players wear uniforms.*

unit

1. a special part of something: *The first unit of our social studies book is about our neighborhood.* **2.** a certain amount used as a way of measuring. A foot is a unit of length. A pound is a unit of weight. **units.**

unite

to join together; make several things into one: *Three small groups were united into one larger group.* **united, uniting.**

United States

the fifty states that make up this country. The United States is part of the continent of North America.

United States of America

the United States.

unkind

not kind; cruel; mean: *Teasing a cat is unkind.*
unkinder, unkindest.

unknown

not known: *An unknown person left these flowers.*

unless

I won't go unless you go.

unload

to take a load of something from what it is in: *Please help dad unload the car.* **unloaded, unloading.**

unlock

to open the lock of: *He unlocked the back door.*
unlocked, unlocking.

unlucky

not lucky; having bad luck: *That unlucky family has had one accident after another.* **unluckier, unluckiest.**

unlock

unpack

to take things out of something: *I unpacked my summer clothes. Please help her unpack the trunk.*
unpacked, unpacking.

unpleasant

not very nice; not pleasant: *What is that unpleasant smell?*

unroll

to open something that was rolled up; spread out: *I unrolled my sleeping bag to dry it out.* **unrolled, unrolling.**

unsafe

not safe; dangerous: *It is unsafe to swim all by yourself.*

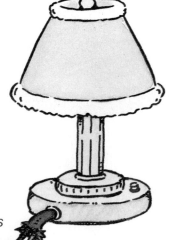

unsafe—*The lamp cord is* **unsafe** *to use.*

unstie—This shoe is **untied.**

unsteady

not steady; shaky: *He was unsteady as he tried to stand.* **unsteadier, unsteadiest.**

untie

to open something that has been tied; unfasten: *She untied the baby's shoes.* **untied, untying.**

until

She did not leave until the following week. We waited until dark before we went in the house.

unusual

not happening very often: *It is unusual for a person to have one blue eye and one brown eye.*

up

The price of a new baseball glove has gone up. The squirrel ran up the tree. We get up for school at seven o'clock. Your time is up now.

upon

He sat upon the bed. Once upon a time there were three elves.

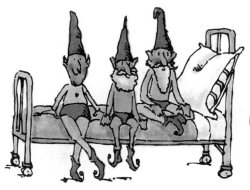

upon—Three elves are sitting **upon** a bed.

upper

higher: *We live on the upper floor of this building. I scratched my upper lip.*

upset

1. very unhappy; greatly disturbed: *She was upset when her dog ran away.* **2.** not feeling well: *My stomach is upset.*

upside down

having the bottom where the top should be: *You are holding the picture upside down.*

upstairs

up the stairs; on the floor or floors above: *He went upstairs to bed.*

upside down

urban

urban

of a city and the towns around it. Many people in the United States live in urban areas.

us

Mom gave us a ride to school. Can you help us with this puzzle?

use

1. to put something into the action that it is meant for. You use a saw to cut wood. You use an umbrella to stay dry with. We can use our new wagon to carry in the wood. **2.** to finish up: *I used up all my money buying lunch.* **used, using.**

used

not new; once owned by someone else: *My parents bought a used car.*

useful

of use; helpful to someone: *A vacuum cleaner is useful in cleaning rugs. Our guest made himself useful after dinner.*

usual

often seen, found, or happening; common: *Our usual dinner time is six o'clock.*

usually

commonly: *We usually eat dinner at six o'clock.*

Utah

one of the fifty states of the United States.

Vv

valentine

vacation

a time of rest when you do not go to school, business, or other work: *Our school has a spring vacation every year.* **vacations.**

vacuum cleaner

a machine you use to clean carpets, curtains, and floors. **vacuum cleaners.**

valentine

a card or a small present that you send or receive on Valentine's Day: *We exchanged valentines today.* **valentines.**

Valentine's Day

February 14th, the day when people send each other valentines.

valley

the low area between mountains or hills. Rivers often run through valleys. **valleys.**

valuable

1. with value; very useful: *His book has valuable information about sea animals.* **2.** worth a lot of money: *She is wearing a valuable ring.*

van

a covered truck used for carrying people or goods. A van has an engine and four wheels. **vans.**

van

vapor

1. steam from boiling water; wetness in the air that you can see; *I could see the vapor from her breath in the cold air.* **2.** a gas formed from something that is usually a liquid or a solid. Water vapor is a gas formed by heating water until it evaporates. **vapors** (for **1.**).

vegetable

a plant whose fruit, seeds, leaves, or roots people use for food. Peas, lettuce, beets, and beans are vegetables. **vegetables.**

vegetables

vehicle

something people ride in or on or carry things in or on. Cars, trucks, buses, wagons, and sleds are vehicles. **vehicles.**

velvet

a very thick, soft cloth. Velvet has a furry surface on one side.

verb

an action word that tells what someone or something does. "The children painted pictures today." *Painted* is the verb. It tells what the children did. **verbs.**

Vermont

one of the fifty states of the United States.

verse

a group of lines of a poem or a song: *Our class sang all three verses of the song we learned yesterday.* **verses.**

very

July was very hot this year. She was very happy today.

verb—*Three **verbs** make up this puzzle.*

veterinarian

a doctor who treats sick or injured animals. **veterinarians.**

405

vibrate

to move forward and backward very quickly. The top of a drum vibrates when you hit it. **vibrated, vibrating.**

video

a tape recording of a movie, concert, TV show, or other program that can be played back on a TV screen: *He saw the video of* The Wizard of Oz *last night.* **videos.**

view

something that you see: *The view of the mountains from his yard was beautiful.* **views.**

village

a small town. There are only a few houses in a village. **villages.**

vine

a plant that grows along the ground. Some vines climb up walls and fences. Pumpkins, melons, and grapes grow on vines. **vines.**

vinegar

a sour liquid. People use vinegar to flavor food or to keep food from spoiling.

violet (definition 1)

violet

1. a small plant with purple, blue, yellow, or white flowers. Violets bloom in early spring. **2.** a light purple color. **3.** having this color: *Her blouse was violet.* **violets.**

violin

a wooden musical instrument with four strings. You push and pull a stick called a bow across the strings to make sounds. **violins.**

violin

Virginia

one of the fifty states of the United States.

virus

a very tiny thing that causes disease. Viruses are too small to be seen even through most microscopes. Viruses cause flu, polio, the common cold, and many other diseases of people, animals, and plants. **viruses.**

visit

1. to go to see places or people: *Next month we are going to visit New York. I visited my aunt for two weeks last summer.* **2.** staying for a while with someone: *We enjoyed our cousins' visit last week.* **visited, visiting; visits.**

visitor

a person who visits; guest: *The two visitors from Canada asked us how to get to the hotel.* **visitors.**

voice

the sound you make with your mouth. You use your voice when you speak or sing or shout. **voices.**

volcano

an opening on the top of a high hill or mountain. Steam, ashes, and hot, melted rock sometimes flow out of a volcano. **volcanoes.**

volcano

vote

1. the choice you make for or against a person or thing: *Whoever gets the most votes will win. We took a vote on where to go for vacation.* **2.** to say or write whether you are for or against a person or thing: *My parents both voted for the mayor.* **votes; voted, voting.**

vowel

the letters a, e, i, o, and u in the alphabet. All the other letters in the alphabet are consonants. **vowels.**

Ww

wade

to walk through water or anything else that is hard to walk through: *We waded around at the beach until we got hungry. He wore high boots to wade through the mud.* **waded, wading.**

wagon (definition 2)

wag

to move from side to side or up and down: *The friendly dog wags its tail at everyone.* **wagged, wagging.**

wagon

1. something used to ride in that has four wheels and usually a handle in front. **2.** something used to carry people or goods. Horses or oxen pulled wagons. **wagons.**

waist

the part of the body between the ribs and the hips: *He wore a belt around his waist.* **waists.**

wait

1. to stay where you are. People wait for something to happen or for someone to come. *We waited at the corner for the bus.* **2.** the time that you stay where you are: *We had a long wait for the bus.* **waited, waiting; waits.**

waiter

a man who brings food to people in a restaurant. **waiters.**

waitress

a woman who brings food to people in a restaurant. **waitresses.**

wake

to stop sleeping or cause someone else to stop sleeping: *I have to wake up early to catch the bus. The noise of the train always wakes the baby.* **woke, woken, waking.**

wake—*He stretched upon waking up.*

walk

1. to move by putting one foot in front of the other: *Let's walk to the park today after school.* **2.** moving along by using the feet: *They took a nice walk around the block with the dog.* **walked, walking; walks.**

wall

1. the side of a building or room: *We need to paint the kitchen wall.* **2.** something built to divide an area, or for protection. A wall may surround a garden, a yard, a castle, or the like. **walls.**

wall (definition 2)
This is a curved brick wall.

wand

a thin stick or rod: *The princess in the story waved a magic wand.* **wands.**

wander

to move here and there without any special goal in mind: *He spent an hour wandering around the park.* **wandered, wandering.**

want

to hope to have something, do something, go somewhere, or the like; to wish: *My sister wants a new winter coat. We want to see the ball game. The baby wants her milk.* **wanted, wanting.**

war

a fight between different countries or groups of people. Soldiers fight in wars. **wars.**

warm

more hot than cold: *The water is warm enough to swim in. He sat in the warm sunshine.* **warmer, warmest.**

warm-up

exercises that you do before a game or contest. A warm-up gets your body warm and ready for making your muscles work hard. **warm-ups.**

warm-up

warn

warn

to tell someone about danger before it happens: *The police officer warned us that the road ahead might be icy.* **warned, warning.**

was

He was a shy boy when he was young. I was late for dinner. The sun was shining. He was going to study.

wash

1. to clean with soap and water: *Be sure to wash your hands before dinner. It is my turn to wash the dishes.*
2. a bundle of dirty clothes that needs to be washed: *Put your jeans and socks in the wash.* **washed, washing.**

washer

a machine that washes clothes. Most washers are electric appliances. **washers.**

Washington

one of the fifty states of the United States.

Washington, D.C.

the capital of the United States.

washroom

a room where people can wash up. A washroom is usually a public bathroom. **washrooms.**

wasn't

was not: *She wasn't home when I called.*

waste

1. to make poor use of something; throw something away without using: *She didn't finish her homework because she wasted time.* **2.** thrown away because it has no use: *Please put all this waste paper with the other trash.* **wasted, wasting.**

wastebasket

something that holds waste paper and other trash that needs to be thrown away. **wastebaskets.**

watch

1. to look at someone or something: *We watched the kittens play. The students watched the teacher do the experiment.* **2.** a small clock that you wear on your wrist. **watched, watching; watches.**

water

1. the liquid that fills oceans, rivers, lakes, and ponds. Water falls from the sky as rain. **2.** to sprinkle something with water: *Mom asked me to water the flowers.* **watered, watering.**

waterfall

water in a stream that falls from a high place: *The log went over the waterfall.* **waterfalls.**

waterfall

watermelons

watermelon

a large, juicy melon that is red or pink on the inside. Watermelons are hard and green on the outside. They grow on vines. **watermelons.**

wave (definition 1)

wave

1. the water in an ocean or lake that rises and moves forward as it comes near the shore. Strong winds cause high waves. **2.** to move your hand up and down, or to one side and then the other: *The children waved good-by to their parents.* **waves; waved, waving.**

wax

something made by bees in which to store honey. Wax is hard when it is cold. It can be shaped easily when it is warm.

way

1. how something is done or can be done: *He showed us the way to work the math problem.* **2.** the direction you follow to get to a place: *Down the hall is the way to the library.* **3.** something that people have learned to do, that they do over and over again: *It's Grandma's way to always leave a light on in the hall.* **ways.**

we

We went riding on our bikes. We are in the same class.

weak

1. not having power; not strong: *He was too weak to lift the chair.* **2.** easily broken; not tough: *As soon as she stepped on the weak branch, it broke.* **weaker, weakest.**

weapon

anything used to fight with. Teeth, claws, hoofs, and fists can be weapons. Clubs, spears, knives, and guns are weapons. **weapons.**

wear

to have something on your body: *She needs to wear a coat today. He wears a beard with his costume.* **wore, worn, wearing.**

weasel

weasel

a small, quick, furry animal with a thin body and short legs. **weasels.**

weather

how it is outside at a certain place and time. The wind, the air temperature, and how wet or dry it is tell us what the weather is.

weather vane

something that shows which way the wind is blowing. A weather vane is a flat piece of metal or wood that turns around on a rod. You may see a weather vane on a roof. **weather vanes.**

weave

to form threads into cloth. You can also weave strips of bark or twigs into a basket. **wove, woven, weaving.**

weather vane

web

web

a woven net of tiny threads made by a spider: *Tiny drops of dew sparkled on the spider web.* **webs.**

we'd

1. we had: *We'd already left before she came in the house.* **2.** we would: *We'd like to play outside later this afternoon.*

wedding

the special happy celebration when a man and woman get married: *He was invited to my cousin's wedding.* **weddings.**

Wednesday

the day after Tuesday; the fourth day of the week. **Wednesdays.**

weed

1. a plant that grows where people do not want it. Dandelions are a common weed in yards. **2.** to take weeds out of: *Dad is outside weeding the garden.* **weeds; weeded, weeding.**

week

a period of time seven days long. There are 52 weeks in a year. The days of the week are Sunday, Monday, Tuesday, Wednesday, Thursday, Friday, and Saturday. **weeks.**

weep

to cry; sob with tears falling: *I began to weep with joy when I won the spelling bee.* **wept, weeping.**

weigh

to find out how heavy something is: *The grocer weighed the bag of oranges. The nurse weighs you when you visit the doctor.* **weighed, weighing.**

weight

how heavy a thing is: *My baby brother's weight is 12 pounds.* **weights.**

welcome

1. a friendly way to greet someone: *Welcome to our house!* **2.** to greet someone kindly: *Grandma welcomed us to her home. They welcomed the visitor with flowers.* **3.** a polite word that we say after someone has said "Thank you": *"You're welcome."* **welcomed, welcoming.**

well[1]

1. all right; in a fine way: *The job of painting the garage was done very well.* **2.** in a thorough way; completely: *Be sure to shake the medicine well before you take it.* **3.** in good health: *She was sick, but now she is well.* **better, best.**

well[2]

a hole dug in the ground to get water, gas, or oil. **wells.**

we'll

we will: *We'll go to the movies tonight.*

went

He went to the library right after school.

wept

I wept with joy when I won the race.

were

We were late and missed the show. The children were picking flowers last time I saw them.

well[2]—*We get water from this **well**.*

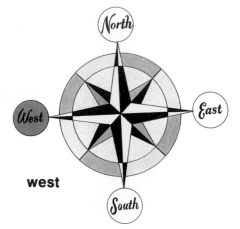

west

we're
we are: *We're going to a picnic today.*

weren't
were not: *They weren't planning on seeing the movie today.*

west
the direction of the sunset. West is the opposite of east.

West Virginia
one of the fifty states of the United States.

wet
covered with water; soaked; not dry: *Her wet shoes made a mess on the kitchen floor.* **wetter, wettest.**

we've
we have: *We've seen this movie before.*

whales

whale
a very large animal that lives in the sea. Whales are not fish. **whales.**

wharf
a platform built along the shore. Ships load and unload at a wharf. **wharves.**

wharves

more than one wharf.

what

What did you say? What time does school start? I don't know what she said. What a great party!

whatever

Do whatever you want to do. Take whatever books you need.

what's

1. what is: *What's that person doing over there?*
2. what has: *What's happened to your foot?*

wheat

wheat

a cereal grain. Wheat is ground up to make flour. It is also used to make breakfast foods.

wheel

something round that turns on its center. Wheels help things move and work. A car has four wheels. A bicycle has two wheels. **wheels.**

when

When does the show begin? He laughed when the clown fell down. We had just started our picnic when it began to rain.

where

Where did you put your coat? Where are you going? Where did you get that pair of jeans?

wherever

Please sit down wherever you like. Wherever you want to go is fine with him.

whether

It doesn't matter whether we go or stay.

which

Which ball is hers? This story, which I have just finished, was a good one.

while

We stayed at my friend's house a little while. The mail came a while ago. While it was raining, he cleaned his room.

whimper

to cry with short, low sounds: *Storms make my dog whimper.* **whimpered, whimpering.**

whine

1. to make a high, unhappy cry or sound: *The dog whined to go out with us.* **2.** to complain about something in a high, unhappy voice: *It's hard to listen to someone who whines a lot.* **whined, whining.**

whip

1. a thing used to hit something with. The rider of a horse sometimes uses a short whip to make the animal go faster. **2.** to hit something with a whip: *He whipped the horse hard, but still lost the race.* **3.** to beat eggs, cream, and the like until it becomes stiff and ready for cooking. **whips; whipped, whipping.**

whip (definition 3)

whirl

to turn round and round very fast; spin: *The blades of a fan whirl when you turn it on. The skater whirled and jumped high in the air off the ice.* **whirled, whirling.**

whisker

1. one of the hairs growing on a man's face. **2.** a long, stiff hair near the mouth of a cat, a rabbit, or other animal. **whiskers.**

whisker (definition 2)
*The cat has long **whiskers**.*

whisper

1. to speak very softly and low: *Please don't whisper to me in class.* **2.** a very soft, low spoken sound: *I couldn't hear her because she spoke in a whisper.* **whispered, whispering; whispers.**

whistle

1. to make a clear, high sound by blowing air through your teeth or lips: *The boy whistled and his dog ran to him.* **2.** the sound made in this way: *She heard a loud whistle at the game.* **3.** a small, hollow metal thing you blow into to make a whistling sound. **whistled, whistling; whistles.**

whistle (definition 3)
*The umpire blew his **whistle**.*

white

1. a very light color; the opposite of black. **2.** having this color: *The pages of this book are white.* **whites; whiter, whitest.**

who

Who is at the door? Tell me who you think the best speller in our class is.

who'd

1. who had: *Who'd seen this movie before?* **2.** who would: *Who'd believe a silly story like that?*

whoever

Whoever reaches the goal first wins. Whoever wants to see the movie, go get in the car.

whole

1. not having any parts missing; having all its parts: *This is not the whole set of books because one book is lost.* **2.** all of something: *Two halves make a whole.* **3.** in one piece: *The dog swallowed the meat whole.*

whole (definition 2) *Two halves make a **whole.***

who'll

who will: *Who'll we invite over for dinner?*

whom

The boy to whom I spoke is new in school.

who's

1. who is: *Who's going to the park with me?* **2.** who has: *Who's already paid for the ticket?*

whose

Whose sweater is this? Whose mittens are these?

why

Why did she bring her cat to class? She doesn't know why the baby is crying. That is the reason why we left early.

wick

wick

a cord of twisted string in a candle. A wick that is lighted soaks up melting wax. **wicks.**

wicked

bad: *In the story, the wicked old witch scared the children.* **wickeder, wickedest.**

wide

big from one side to the other; not narrow: *The road was wide enough for eight lanes of traffic.* **wider, widest.**

width

> how wide something is; the distance from one side to the other side: *The width of that road is ten feet.* **widths.**

wife

> a woman who has a husband; a married woman. **wives.**

wig

> a covering of hair for the head: *The clown wore a bright orange wig.* **wigs.**

wig

wiggle

> to move with short, quick movements from side to side: *The child wiggled in his seat all through the movie.* **wiggled, wiggling.**

wild—*Wild plants grow in the woods.*

wild

> not raised or grown by people. Wild animals live in the forest. **wilder, wildest.**

wilderness

> a wild place; an area where nobody lives: *The Boy Scouts hiked through the wilderness.*

will

> *She will start the job soon. He will go if you go. The boat will hold four people easily.*

willing

> ready to do something; wanting to do something: *She is willing to give us a ride to school.*

willow

willow

a large tree with strong, thin branches and narrow leaves. **willows.**

win

1. to come in first in a race or contest: *I hope our team will win.* **2.** to get something by working hard or by answering questions: *She won a prize for running.* **won, winning.**

wind¹

air that is moving: *The wind blew the leaves off the trees.* **winds.** (Wind¹ rhymes with pinned.)

wind²

1. to roll into a ball or put on a spool: *Did you wind up the loose string?* **2.** to make something go by turning some part of it: *The clock had stopped, so I thought I had better wind it.* **wound, winding.** (Wind² rhymes with find. Wound rhymes with found.)

window

an opening in a wall or roof. Windows are made of glass, and some can be opened. A window lets light or fresh air in. **windows.**

windy

with a lot of wind: *The weather last week was windy.* **windier, windiest.**

wing

1. one of the parts of a bird, insect, or bat. Wings move and are used in flying. **2.** one of the parts of an airplane that help it to fly: *That plane's wing was over sixty feet long.* **wings.**

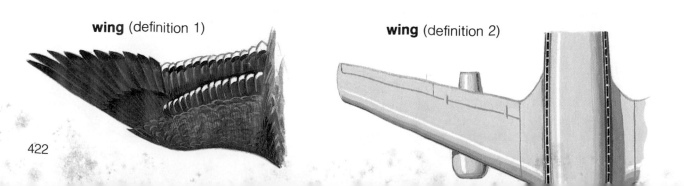

wing (definition 1)

wing (definition 2)

wink

1. to quickly close and open one eye as a hint or signal: *I winked at my sister when it was time to leave.* **2.** the act of winking: *Father's wink told me he knew the answer.* **winked, winking; winks.**

winner

a person or thing that wins: *The winners of the race each got a medal.* **winners.**

winner—*She was a* **winner** *in the race.*

winter

the season of the year between fall and spring. Winter is the coldest season of the year. **winters.**

wipe

to rub something to clean it or dry it off: *Wipe your shoes on the mat. Please wipe up the spilled milk.* **wiped, wiping.**

wire

metal in the form of a long, strong thread. Electricity is carried through wires. Some fences are made out of wire. **wires.**

Wisconsin

one of the fifty states of the United States.

wise

knowing a lot about many different things; not stupid: *My grandfather is very wise.* **wiser, wisest.**

wish

1. to hope to have something, do something, go somewhere, or the like; want: *He wishes he had a new bike. I wish it would stop raining.* **2.** something wished for: *Her wish for a new friend came true.* **wished, wishing; wishes.**

witch

in stories, a woman that has magic powers. **witches.**

with

I cut the meat with a knife. Do you want sugar with your tea?

within

The park is within a mile of our house. Stay within my sight so you won't get lost.

without

A cat walks without making any noise. She left without saying good-by.

wives

more than one wife.

wizard

in stories, a man that has magic powers: *We saw the movie* The Wizard of Oz. **wizards.**

woke

I woke up early today.

woken

He has woken up early every morning to go fishing.

wolf

a wild animal that looks like a large dog. Wolves live together in large groups. **wolves.**

wolves

more than one wolf: *The wolves howled to let us know they were near.*

wizard

wolves

woman

a grown-up female person. When a girl grows up, she becomes a woman. **women.**

won

Their team won the game. They have won three games in a row.

wonder

to wish to know about something: *I wonder what will happen next. He wondered what time it was.* **wondered, wondering.**

wonderful

causing great pleasure to someone; excellent: *The ocean was a wonderful sight. She had a wonderful time at the party.*

won't

will not: *I won't help you clean your room.*

wood

the hard part of a tree's trunk and branches. Wood is used to build houses and make paper.

woodchuck

a small animal with a bushy tail. Another word for woodchuck is groundhog. **woodchucks.**

wooden

made of wood: *There is an old wooden fence around the yard.*

woodpecker

woodpecker

a bird with a hard, pointed bill. The woodpecker uses its bill to make holes in trees to get insects to eat. **woodpeckers.**

woods

land that is covered with trees and bushes all growing together: *We took a long walk through the woods to the shore of the lake.*

wool—*He is cutting* **wool** *from a sheep's body. It is then piled into a bin.*

wool

the soft curly hair or fur that covers the body of a sheep. Wool is made into cloth.

word

1. a sound or group of sounds that means something. We speak words when we talk. **2.** the written or printed letters that stand for a word: *This page is filled with printed words.* **words.**

wore

She wore her old sweater. I wore out my new shoes in one month.

work

1. a job you do for a special purpose. Usually people do work to earn money. *Driving a truck is hard work. Digging in a garden is hard work.* **2.** to do work: *He works at an airplane factory.* **3.** to do the job it is supposed to do; run: *This TV isn't working right.* **worked, working.**

worker

a person who works: *He is a worker in an automobile factory.* **workers.**

workout

exercise; practice: *Before our game we had a good workout running around the gym.* **workouts.**

workshop

1. a shop or building where work is done: *Dad has a workshop in the basement.* **2.** a group of people that are working together on, or studying a special project of some kind: *This week the mayor has planned a workshop for new firefighters.* **workshops.**

world

the earth and everything on it. **worlds.**

worm

a small, thin animal with a soft body. Worms have no legs and move by crawling or creeping. **worms.**

worm

worn

I've worn these jeans all week.

worry

to feel uneasy or upset: *They will worry if we're late. She was worried when her dog didn't come home.* **worried, worrying.**

worse

not as good; not as well: *Yesterday she felt better, but she feels worse today. I played worse in the game today than I did last week.*

worship

to show great honor, respect, and love for something: *Some people go to church or a synagogue to worship.* **worshiped, worshiping.**

worst

least good; least well: *This is the worst I've ever felt with a cold. That's the worst movie I've ever seen.*

worth

1. good or useful or important enough for: *That book is worth reading.* **2.** how much a certain amount of money will buy: *I bought five dollars' worth of stamps.*

would

Would you like an apple? They said they would wait for us at the corner. The kitten would play with the yarn for hours.

wouldn't

would not: *He wouldn't help us. The car wouldn't start.*

wound¹

1. a cut or torn place on your body: *Mom put a large bandage over my wound.* **2.** to hurt by causing a cut or a tear in someone's body: *A hunter wounded the buffalo.* **wounds; wounded, wounding.** (Wound¹ rhymes with tuned.)

wound²

She wound the yarn into a ball. I wound my watch. (Wound² rhymes with sound.)

wove

My sister wove a basket for me. The spider wove a web.

woven

The scarf was woven out of wool. The spider has woven a web.

wrap

to cover something by winding or folding something around it: *We wrapped presents all morning. Wrap up if you're going out.* **wrapped, wrapping.**

wrestle

to try to throw or force someone to the ground: *The boys wrestled on the grass.* **wrestled, wrestling.**

wrestle

wrinkle

1. a fold on the surface of something that is usually flat: *She used the iron to press out the wrinkles in her dress.* **2.** to make folds in: *He wrinkled his jacket when he threw it in a ball on the floor.* **wrinkles; wrinkled, wrinkling.**

wrist

the part of the body between the hand and the arm. **wrists.**

write

to make letters or words with pen, pencil, or chalk: *Write your name at the top of your paper.* **wrote, written, writing.**

writer

a person who writes: *Everyone can be a writer.* **writers.**

written

I have written a letter to my uncle.

wrong

1. not the way it should be; not right; bad: *It was wrong to take her bike without asking her.* **2.** not true; not correct: *He must have written down the wrong number.* **3.** not working right; out of order: *Something is wrong with the brakes on my bicycle.*

wrote

She wrote out a list of things she has to do.

Wyoming

one of the fifty states of the United States.

wrinkle (definition 1)
*She has **wrinkles** in her dress.*

Xx

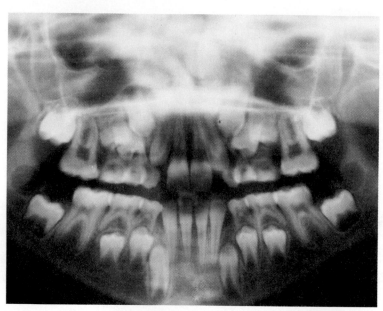

X ray—*In this **X ray** of a young person's face, you can see primary teeth, and permanent teeth beneath them, growing in the gums.*

X ray

a kind of picture that shows what is inside something. An X ray can tell if you have a broken bone. It can tell you if you have any cavities in your teeth. **X rays.**

xylophone

a musical instrument. You play it by striking wooden bars with two small wooden hammers. **xylophones.**

xylophone

Yy

yak
a large animal with long hair. Yaks live in cold places. **yaks.**

yak

yam
a sweet, thick, yellow vegetable. Yams grow on vines. A yam is something like a sweet potato. **yams.**

yams

yard[1]
a piece of ground next to a house or a school. A yard may have a fence around it. *He played in the front yard.* **yards.**

yard[2]
a unit of length equal to 3 feet. Most doors are one yard wide. **yards.**

yarn
a kind of thread, usually used for knitting: *Mother bought four balls of yarn to knit a sweater.*

yawn
to open your mouth wide to get more air. People yawn when they are sleepy, tired, or bored. **yawned, yawning.**

year
a period of time. A year has twelve months. The new year starts on January 1. **years.**

yarn—*She has begun to knit a sweater from* **yarn.**

431

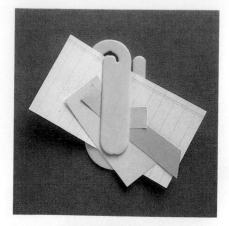

yellow (definition 2)

yell
1. to cry out with a strong, loud sound: *He yelled for help when he saw the fire.* **2.** a strong, loud cry: *We heard excited yells from some of the players.* **yelled, yelling; yells.**

yellow
1. the color of lemons or butter: *Yellow is my favorite color.* **2.** having this color: *She has a yellow sweater.* **yellows; yellower, yellowest.**

yes
Yes, you may go to the park. The answer to your question is yes.

yesterday
the day before today: *Yesterday it rained all day.*

yet
We haven't given up yet. It isn't raining yet.

yogurt
a soft food made from milk. Some yogurt is sweet and has a fruit flavor.

yolk

yolk
the yellow part of an egg. **yolks.**

you
You can use my bike if you need to. You have to be friendly to make friends.

you'd
1. you had: *I think you'd better hurry.* **2.** you would: *You'd like to go with him, wouldn't you?*

you'll
you will: *Hurry, or you'll be late.*

young

in the early part of life; not old. A colt is a young horse. **younger, youngest.**

your

Your shoes are under the chair. Tell me about your dream.

you're

you are: *You're very funny.*

yours

My dog is bigger than yours. Yours is the blue book; mine is the red one. Is this lunch yours?

yourself

You can see yourself in a mirror. Can you carry that heavy box yourself?

yourselves

Can you see yourselves in the mirror? Can you children do this by yourselves?

you've

you have: *You've seen her before.*

yoyo

a toy made of two round pieces joined together. A string is tied to a yoyo. The yoyo goes up and down along the string. **yoyos.**

Yukon Territory

one of the two territories of Canada.

you're—**You're** very funny.

yoyo

Zz

zebras

zipper

zebra

an animal that looks like a horse. Zebras have black and white stripes. **zebras.**

zero

1. the number 0. If you put a zero after the number 2, you get the number 20. **2.** nothing; none at all: *The score was five to zero.* **zeros** (for **1.**).

zigzag

1. with short, sharp turns first to one side, then to the other side: *The path through the woods goes in a zigzag direction.* **2.** to move in a zigzag way: *The mouse zigzagged across the kitchen floor.* **zigzagged, zigzagging.**

zip

to close something with a zipper: *She zipped up her jacket before going outside.* **zipped, zipping.**

zipper

something that fastens two edges together. Zippers are used to fasten clothes and other things. **zippers.**

zoo

a place where wild animals are kept. People visit the zoo to see the animals. **zoos.**

zookeeper

a person who takes care of animals in a zoo. **zookeepers.**

Find Out the Facts!

You can use a computer to do work.
You can use a computer to play games.
A computer can store information.
Do you know the parts of a computer?

printer paper

printer

screen

monitor

keyboard

computer

cable

disk drive

mouse

joystick

disk

instruction book

disk holder

floppy disk

Finding Places

	State	U.S. Post Office Abbreviation	State Capital
■	Alabama	AL	Montgomery
■	Alaska	AK	Juneau
■	Arizona	AZ	Phoenix
■	Arkansas	AR	Little Rock
■	California	CA	Sacramento
■	Colorado	CO	Denver
■	Connecticut	CT	Hartford
■	Delaware	DE	Dover
■	Florida	FL	Tallahassee
■	Georgia	GA	Atlanta
■	Hawaii	HI	Honolulu
■	Idaho	ID	Boise
■	Illinois	IL	Springfield
■	Indiana	IN	Indianapolis
■	Iowa	IA	Des Moines
■	Kansas	KS	Topeka
■	Kentucky	KY	Frankfort
■	Louisiana	LA	Baton Rouge
■	Maine	ME	Augusta
■	Maryland	MD	Annapolis
■	Massachusetts	MA	Boston
■	Michigan	MI	Lansing
■	Minnesota	MN	St. Paul
■	Mississippi	MS	Jackson
■	Missouri	MO	Jefferson City

	State	U.S. Post Office Abbreviation	State Capital
■	Montana	MT	Helena
■	Nebraska	NE	Lincoln
■	Nevada	NV	Carson City
■	New Hampshire	NH	Concord
■	New Jersey	NJ	Trenton
■	New Mexico	NM	Santa Fe
■	New York	NY	Albany
■	North Carolina	NC	Raleigh
■	North Dakota	ND	Bismarck
■	Ohio	OH	Columbus
■	Oklahoma	OK	Oklahoma City
■	Oregon	OR	Salem
■	Pennsylvania	PA	Harrisburg
■	Rhode Island	RI	Providence
■	South Carolina	SC	Columbia
■	South Dakota	SD	Pierre
■	Tennessee	TN	Nashville
■	Texas	TX	Austin
■	Utah	UT	Salt Lake City
■	Vermont	VT	Montpelier
■	Virginia	VA	Richmond
■	Washington	WA	Olympia
■	West Virginia	WV	Charleston
■	Wisconsin	WI	Madison
■	Wyoming	WY	Cheyenne

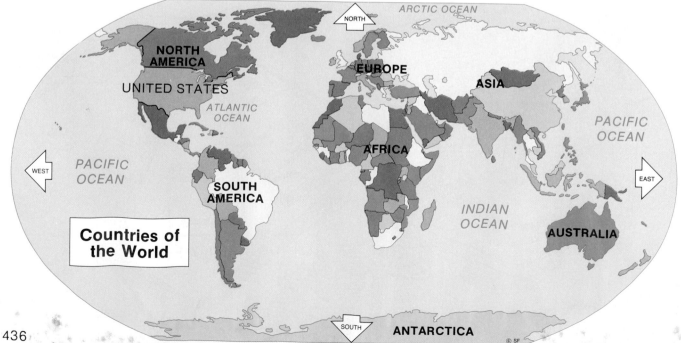

Countries of the World

The United States

(★) National capital

CANADA

MONTANA
NORTH DAKOTA
MINNESOTA
NEW HAMPSHIRE
VERMONT
MAINE

IDAHO
WYOMING
SOUTH DAKOTA
WISCONSIN
NEW YORK
MASSACHUSETTS
RHODE ISLAND
CONNECTICUT

MICHIGAN

NEBRASKA
IOWA
INDIANA
OHIO
PENNSYLVANIA
NEW JERSEY
DELAWARE
MARYLAND

UTAH
COLORADO
ILLINOIS
WEST VIRGINIA
Washington, D.C.

KANSAS
MISSOURI
KENTUCKY
VIRGINIA

ARIZONA
NEW MEXICO
OKLAHOMA
ARKANSAS
TENNESSEE
NORTH CAROLINA

ATLANTIC

OCEAN

TEXAS
MISSISSIPPI
ALABAMA
GEORGIA
SOUTH CAROLINA

LOUISIANA

FLORIDA

ALASKA
CANADA
MEXICO

© SF

The World: Continents and Oceans

ARCTIC OCEAN

NORTH AMERICA
EUROPE
ASIA

ATLANTIC OCEAN

PACIFIC OCEAN

PACIFIC OCEAN

AFRICA

SOUTH AMERICA

INDIAN OCEAN

AUSTRALIA

ANTARCTICA

© SF

437

Landforms

mountain

valley

hill

plain

river

lake

canyon

island

ocean

desert

peninsula

Where would you like to go?

What can you do to help?

1. Ride your bike or walk whenever you can.
2. Turn down your TV and radio to help with noise pollution.
3. Ask people to stop smoking. Stay out of rooms where people are smoking.
4. Use pump cans instead of spray cans.

1. Clean up the banks of rivers and streams. Dump trash in the right place.
2. Help protect open marshes and swamps.
3. Mound the dirt around the plants in your yard. It will help catch and hold water.

1. Put litter where it belongs.
2. Recycle cans, glass, and paper.
3. Plant flowers and trees in your yard.
4. Turn off lights when you don't need them.
5. Take care of the woods and parks. Open space should be saved for everyone to use.

Healthy Foods

Stay healthy by eating right.

- Eat a good breakfast
- Eat three meals a day.
- Choose foods from the four basic food groups.
  (1) vegetable-fruit group
  (2) bread-cereal group
  (3) meat-poultry-fish-bean group
  (4) milk-cheese group
- Eat healthy snacks that are not too salty or too sweet
- Choose snacks from the four basic food groups.

Measurement

Did you know that long ago...

- the king's favorite wine cup was used to measure amounts of milk and water
- an inch was the length of the last bone in a man's thumb
- a yard was the distance from the tip of the King's nose to the tip of his middle finger when his arm was stretched out
- the length of the king's foot was how a foot was measured

1 centimeter

12 inches = 1 foot

3 feet = 1 yard

1 yard = 36 inches

10 millimeters = 1 centimeter

100 centimeters = 1 meter

1 meter = 1000 millimeters

12 inches

1 millimeter

thick

1 yard

1 inch

Measurement

Measures
8 ounces = 1 cup
2 cups = 1 pint
2 pints = 1 quart
4 quarts = 1 gallon
1000 milliliters = 1 liter
16 ounces = 1 pound
1000 grams = 1 kilogram

1 pound

1 ounce

1 gram

2 CUPS

1 pint

MILK

gallon

quart

liter

pint

443

Calendar

Days of the Week

Sunday
Monday
Tuesday
Wednesday
Thursday
Friday
Saturday

Months of the Year

January
February
March
April
May
June
July
August
September
October
November
December

The name of the month is written here.

Month

Sunday	Monday	Tuesday	Wednesday	Thursday	Friday	Saturday
	1	2	3	4	5	6
7	8	9	10	11	12	13
14	15	16	17	18	19	20
21	22	23	24	25	26	27
28	29	30 Holiday				

The days of the week are listed here.

Each day of the week has a number. The numbers are in order.

Holidays happen on different days and in different months throughout the year. On some holidays, people do not go to work.

January 1

New Year's Day is the first day of the new year.

January

Martin Luther King Day is on the third Monday in January.

February 14

On Valentine's Day, we send cards to people we love.

February

Presidents' Day is the third Monday in February. It honors George Washington and Abraham Lincoln.

March or April

At Easter, Christians mark the return to life of Jesus. It is a Sunday in March or April.

March or April

Passover is a Jewish holiday that comes in the spring. It lasts eight days. It marks the escape of the Jews from slavery.

May

Memorial Day honors Americans who died in war. It is the last Monday in May.

July 4

On Independence Day, Americans started a new country.

September

Labor Day honors working people. It is the first Monday in September.

October 12

Columbus Day honors Christopher Columbus. On this day in 1492 he first arrived in America.

October 31

On Halloween, people carve pumpkins and trick or treat.

November

Thanksgiving is the fourth Thursday in November. On this day we give thanks for what we have received.

December

On Hanukkah, the festival of lights, Jewish children give gifts and light candles.

December 25

Christians mark the birth of Jesus at Christmas.

Parts of a Letter

A letter has five points. They are the date, greeting, body, closing, and name. There are commas in the date, greeting, and closing.

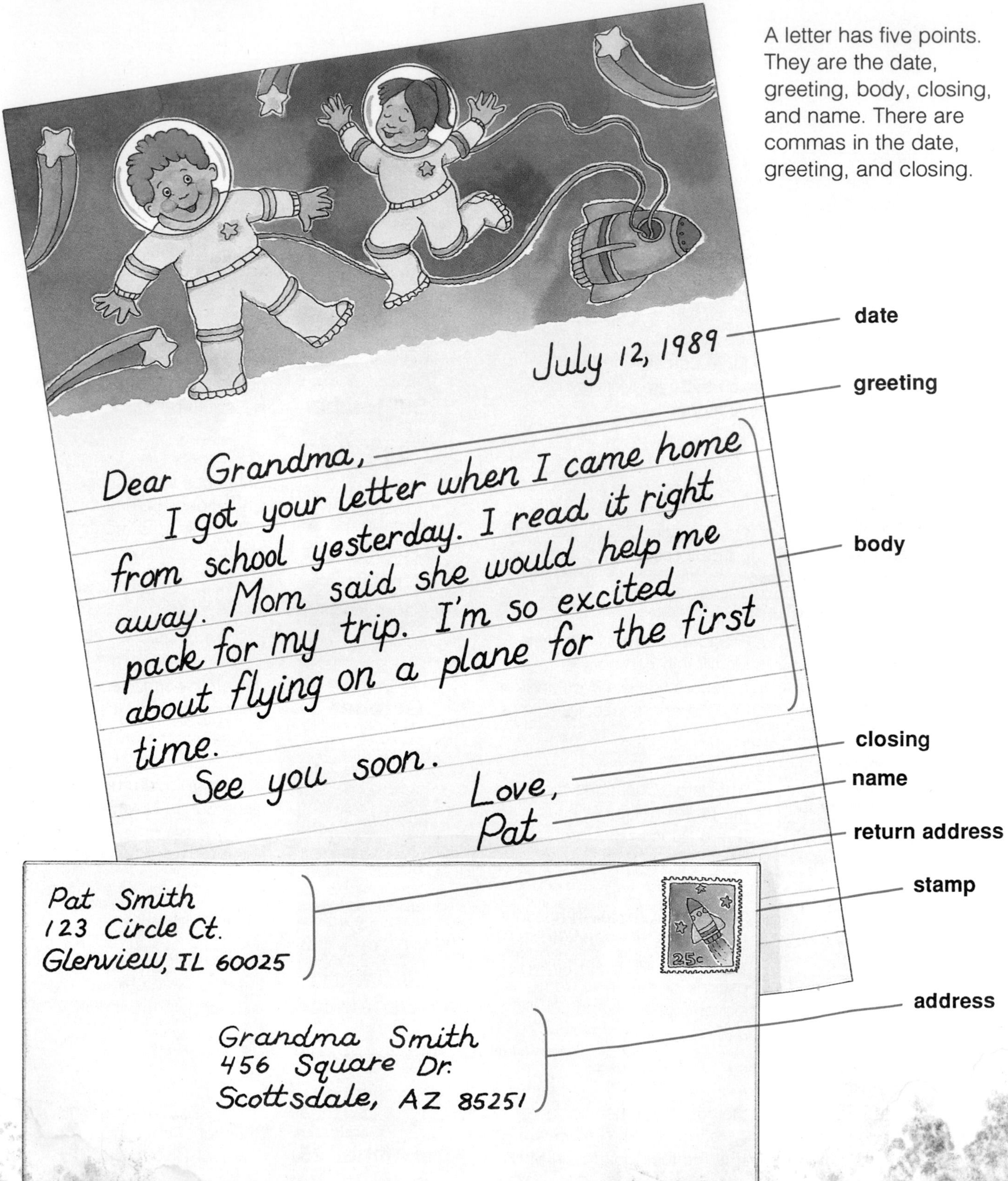

date — July 12, 1989

greeting — Dear Grandma,

body — I got your letter when I came home from school yesterday. I read it right away. Mom said she would help me pack for my trip. I'm so excited about flying on a plane for the first time.

See you soon.

closing — Love,

name — Pat

return address — Pat Smith
123 Circle Ct.
Glenview, IL 60025

stamp — 25¢

address — Grandma Smith
456 Square Dr.
Scottsdale, AZ 85251

Fine Art

audience: "Interior of the Park Theater," (detail) 1822, by John Searle. New York Historical Society, NYC

blacksmith: "Trotting Cracks at the Forge," 1869, lithograph by Currier and Ives. Henry T. Peters Collection, Museum of the City of New York. Photo: The Granger Collection

bridge: "Brooklyn Bridge" by Stephen Hannock. Private Collection

chat: "The Conversation," 1979, by David Hockney. Private Collection. Photo: Art Resource, N.Y.

counter: drugstore scene by Norman Rockwell. © 1953 The Curtis Publishing Company. Printed by permission of the Estate of Norman Rockwell. Copyright 1952 Estate of Norman Rockwell

cowboy: "Bronco Buster," bronze by Frederick Remington. Courtesy the Eiteljorg Museum of American and Western Art

entrance: Carson, Pirie, Scott & Company, Chicago retail store designed 1899 by architect Louis Sullivan.

fife: "The Fifer," 1866, Edouard Manet. Musee d'Orsay, Paris. Photo: Scala/Art Resource, N.Y.

game: "Croquet Scene," 1866, by Winslow Homer. The art Institute of Chicago, Friends of American Art Collection

glow: "The Boyhood of Lincoln," 1868, by Eastman Johnson. The University of Michigan Museum of Art, Bequest of Henry C. Lewis

haystack: "The Yellow Haystacks," 1889, Paul Gauguin. Louvre, Paris. Photo: Giraudon/Art Resource, N.Y.

Independence Day: "The Fourth of July, 1916" by Childe Hassam. Private Collection. Photo: Los Angeles County Museum of Art

jungle: "The Dream" by Henri Rousseau. The Museum of Modern Art, New York, Gift of Nelson A. Rockefeller

kimono: Japanese print. The Art Institute of Chicago, Clarence Buckingham Collection

king: "Royal Dress During the Reign of James I", watercolor from the Folger Shakespeare Library

knight: Heraldic Knight of Prato. Courtesy the Trustees of the British Museum

lighthouse: "The Lighthouse at Two Lights," (detail) 1929, by Edward Hopper. The Metropolitan Museum of Art, Hugo Kastor Fund, 1962

mobile: "Red Petals," by Alexander Calder. The Arts Club of Chicago

oar: "The Fog Warning," by Winslow Homer. The Museum of Fine Arts, Boston, Otis Norcross Fund, 1894

pilgrim: "Pilgrims Going to Church," 1867, by George H. Boughton. The New York Historical Society

pirate: "So the Treasure Was Divided," by Howard Pyle. Delaware Art Museum, Wilmington

president: "President Lincoln Being Photographed by Matthew Brady," by Norman Rockwell. Private Collection

rabbit: "Cottontail Bunny," by Glen Loates. Private Collection

ring: "The Hand Game," by Victor Pepion. The Philbrook Museum of Art

sailboat: "Ground Swell," by Edward Hopper. Courtesy Corcoran Gallery of Art

shawl: "Contessa del Carpio," by Francisco Goya. Louvre, Paris. Photo: Scala/Art Resource N.Y.

sleigh: "The Sleigh Race," 1859, lithograph by Currier & Ives Henry T. Peters Collection, Museum of the City of New York

statue: "The Minuteman," statue in Lexington, Massachusetts. Photo: Eric G. Carle/SuperStock/Shostal

steeple: An East Prospect of the City of Philadelphia by George Heap and Nicholas Scull. Historical Society of Pennsylvania

sunflower: "Sunflowers," by Vincent van Gogh. Neue Pinakothek, Munich. Photo: Giraudon/Art Resource, N.Y.

swing: "Outsider," by Martin Gale. Private Collection

tower: "The Spirit of War," (detail) by Jaspar Cropsey. National Gallery of Art, Washington, D.C.

treasure: pirate scene by Howard Pyle.

vegetable: "Flowers and Vegetables," by James Ensor. Private Collection. Photo: Three Lions/SuperStock

wave: "The Wave," by Hokusai. The Art Institute of Chicago, Clarence Buckingham Collection

Illustration

Cover illustration by Lee Lee Brazeal

Other illustrations by:
Dori Altschuler, Robert Borja, Robin Brickman, Ted Carr, Robert Durham, Julie Durrell, Allan Eitzen, Marlene Ekman, Keith Freeman, Jean Cassells Helmer, Bob Knight, Janet LaSalle, Warren Linn, Diana Magnuson, Dick Martin, Robert Masheris, Betty Maxey, Cathy Pavia, David Povilaitis, Phill Renaud, Slug Signorino, George Suyeoka, Ed Taber, Justin Wager, Robert Wahlgren, Jan Wills, Ann Wilson

Photographs

Any photograph not credited is from Scott, Foresman and Company.

alligator: Arnold Ryan Chalfant
astronaut: NASA
autumn: Franz Altschuler
baby: M. Austerman/ANIMALS ANIMALS
bacteria: Dr. Leon LeBeau, Department of Microbiology, University of Illinois Medical Center, Chicago
ball: SuperStock/Shostal
barge: D.C. Lowe/Shostal
blackberries: Walter Chandoha
blizzard: E. Manewal/Shostal
bone: Shostal
brick: Robert Llewellyn
broadcast: Robert Amft
caboose: Art Pahlke
canyon: Jerry Jacka
cave: David Muench
cloud: Dr. E. R. Degginger
cocoon: Dr. E. R. Degginger
coral: C. C. Lockwood/ANIMALS ANIMALS
court: Focus on Sports
dam: Manley/Shostal
destroy: Pascal Parrot/Sygma
dive: Focus on Sports
dock: Shostal
doll: Franz Altschuler
dragonfly: Dr. E. R. Degginger
drum: Index of American Design, National Gallery of Art, Washington, DC
dust: AP/Wide World Photos
eagle: Index of American Design, National Gallery of Art, Washington, DC
earth: NASA
elevator: Franz Altschuler
entrance: Hedrich-Blessing
evergreen: Grant Heilman Photography
fall: Robert Amft
fellow: Franz Altschuler
flag: Robert Amft
flock: James P. Rowan
fountain: Brent Jones
freeze: Franz Altschuler
gate: Franz Altschuler
gush: Texas Mid-Continental Oil and Gas Association
hatch: Runk/Schoenberger from Grant Heilman
hill: Franz Altschuler
hummingbird: Jack Wilburn/ANIMALS ANIMALS
Indian: United States Postal Service
island: Shostal
jack-o'-lanterns: Art Pahlke
jeep: AP/Wide World Photos
launch: NASA
llama: P. Raota/Shostal
members: Dawn Murray
merry-go-round: J. Barnell/SuperStock/Shostal
microscope: Jean-Claude Lejeune
mill: Cameramann International/Milton and Joan Mann
moss: Dr. E. R. Degginger
orchestra: Michael John Burlingham
pad: Franz Altschuler
palms: Dr. E. R. Degginger
peacock: Dr. E. R. Degginger
point: Franz Altschuler
pollute: Franz Altschuler
printer: SuperStock
pueblo: Franz Altschuler
rainbow: Dr. E. R. Degginger
ray: Robert Amft
red: Franz Altschuler
reindeer: SuperStock/Shostal
scenery: SuperStock/Shostal
scientist: SuperStock
scratch: Walter Chandoha
shell: Dr. E. R. Degginger
shopping center: SuperStock
small: Franz Altschuler
soldiers: AP/Wide World Photos
spider: Walter Chandoha
sponge: Dr. E. R. Degginger
sunk: E. F. Davenport
sunset: Franz Altschuler
swamp: Dr. E. R. Degginger
swan: Dr. E. R. Degginger
telescope: Shostal
tent: Courtesy L. L. Bean
tornado: Dr. E. R. Degginger
trombone: Courtesy Chicago Youth Symphony Orchestra/Photo: Loren Santow
tulip: Robert Amft
tunnel: Dr. E. R. Degginger
twirl: SuperStock/Shostal
umpire: AP/Wide World Photos
uniform: Mickey Pfleger
urban: Cameramann International/Milton and Joan Mann
volcano: Dr. E. R. Degginger
wall: Robert Llewellyn
waterfall: Dr. E. R. Degginger
web: Dr. E. R. Degginger
wild: Torkel Korling
winner: Courtesy Special Olympics
wolves: Alan and Sandy Carey
wool: Dr. E. R. Degginger
X ray: Courtesy Dr. Lawrence H. Zager, D.D.S.
yak: Dr. E. R. Degginger
zebra: Dr. E. R. Degginger

a b c d e f g h i j k l m
n o p q r s t u v w x y z

A B C D E F G
H I J K L M N O P Q
R S T U V W X Y Z

a b c d e f g h i j k
l m n o p q r s t
u v w x y z . ' . ?

A B C D E F G H I
J K L M N O P 2 R
S T U V W X Y Z

1 2 3 4 5 6 7 8 9 10

The **activities** on these two pages encourage children to categorize, to compare and contrast, and to draw conclusions. They also foster creative thinking and independent learning. Not meant to be completed in one sitting, these activities can be done by one or two children alone, or with adult involvement. You might want to have on hand white glue, old magazines, paper, blunt scissors, paper plates, and markers or crayons. Then, step back and let the activities spark an interest in words.

A B C D E F G H I
J K L M N O P Q
R S T U V W X Y Z

☐ Five words are listed below. Put them in the order of the alphabet. If you are right, you'll make a sentence. Use this dictionary if you have to.

broccoli bakers bring brownies bad

☐ Look in this dictionary for words that begin with **hu**. Which word is the brightly colored bird with a long bill?

☐ Look in this dictionary for words that begin with **fe**. Which word is something put around a yard, garden, or field?

☐ Look in this dictionary for words that begin with **gl**. Which word is a list of hard words with their meanings?

☐ Look in this dictionary for words that begin with **ac**. Which word is a person trained to swing in the air?

☐ Look through this dictionary for the names of six jobs you might like to do when you grow up. Write the words you find on a piece of paper. Then look through old magazines for pictures of people doing these jobs. Cut out the pictures and glue them next to the words you have written.

☐ Look through this dictionary for the name of a sport that you like to play. Write it down on a piece of paper. Then draw a picture of yourself playing that sport.

☐ Pictures can tell you a lot. Can you match the words listed below with the correct pictures? Use your dictionary to check your answers.

alley antler balcony cactus engine

☐ Look up the word **bare** in this dictionary. The words in **dark** type at the end show you how the word is written when it means more bare (**barer**) or most bare (**barest**). Make a list of the ways the words below are written when they mean more and when they mean most.

blue angry clean greedy empty